ON DIFFERENT PLANES

Cornell Studies in Industrial and Labor Relations
Number 30

ON
DIFFERENT
PLANES

AN ORGANIZATIONAL ANALYSIS OF
COOPERATION AND CONFLICT
AMONG AIRLINE UNIONS

DAVID J. WALSH

ILR Press
Ithaca, New York

Library of Congress Cataloging-in-Publication Data

Walsh, David J., 1956–
On different planes : an organizational analysis of cooperation
and conflict among airline unions / David J. Walsh.
p.   cm.—(Cornell studies in industrial and labor relations;
no. 30)
Includes bibliographical references and index.
ISBN 0-87546-323-1 (alk. paper).—ISBN 0-87546-329-0 (pbk.: alk. paper)
1. Trade-unions—Airline employees—United States. 2. Strikes and
lockouts—Airlines—United States. I. Title. II. Series.
HD6515.A427W35   1994
331.88'113877'0973—dc20   93-48443

Copies may be ordered through bookstores or directly from

ILR Press
School of Industrial and Labor Relations
Cornell University
Ithaca, NY 14853-3901

Printed on recycled, acid-free paper in the United States of America
5   4   3   2   1

To my wife, Susan

Contents

Tables and Figures

Tables

Figures

Abbreviations

AALS	Association of Air Line Stewardesses
ACCEA	Air Carriers Communication Employees Association
ACFEA	Air Carriers Flight Engineers Association
ACMA	Air Carriers Mechanics Association
AFA	Association of Flight Attendants
AIRCON	Airline Industrial Relations Conference
ALAA	Air Line Agents Association
ALDA	Air Line Dispatchers Association
ALEA	Air Line Employees Association
ALPA	Air Line Pilots Association
ALSA	Air Line Stewardesses Association
ALSSA	Air Line Stewards and Stewardesses Association
APA	Allied Pilots Association
APFA	Association of Professional Flight Attendants
BRAC	Brotherhood of Railway and Airline Clerks
CAB	Civil Aeronautics Board
DOT	Department of Transportation
FAA	Federal Aviation Administration
FEIA	Flight Engineers International Association
IAM	International Association of Machinists
IBT	International Brotherhood of Teamsters
IFALDA	International Federation of Airline Dispatcher Associations
IFALPA	International Federation of Airline Pilot Associations
IFFA	Independent Federation of Flight Attendants
ITF	International Transport Workers Federation
IUD	Industrial Union Department (of the AFL-CIO)
IUFA	Independent Union of Flight Attendants
LECs	Local Executive Councils
LPPs	Labor Protective Provisions
MAP	Mutual Aid Pact
MECs	Master Executive Councils
NMB	National Mediation Board
NTSB	National Transportation Safety Board
PAFCA	Professional Air Flight Control Association
TCU	Transportation Communications International Union
TWU	Transport Workers Union, International
UAL	United Airlines
UFA	Union of Flight Attendants

Acknowledgments

This is a welcome opportunity to express my gratitude to a number of persons who aided the researching and writing of this book. Bob Stern, Clete Daniel, Beth Rubin, and Ron Breiger skillfully and sensibly guided the dissertation research that is this book's basis. Clete Daniel, in particular, was instrumental in encouraging me to present this work in book form. David Krackhardt, Martha Czerwinsky, and Steve Moore provided invaluable programming and computing assistance. Peter Cappelli, Harry Katz, and Mark Kahn offered comments too insightful to ignore on drafts of the book. Other friends and colleagues providing help and support at various points in the process include Ron Seeber, Kate Bronfenbrenner, Jim Rundle, Steve Barley, and Josh Schwarz.

This book would not have been possible without the union officers who graciously consented to be interviewed and gave me the benefit of their considerable experience. While this book is not primarily addressed to them, it proceeds from a premise that I think they would share; that the strength of the labor movement is of great concern to all who care about a more just and humane society. This book, while sometimes critical of the actions of airline unions, unabashedly shares in the commitment to a stronger labor movement and is deeply sympathetic to those who face the difficult task of practicing, rather than merely writing about, labor solidarity.

On the domestic front, my wife, Susan Hurst, unfailingly provided the encouragement and support essential to completing a project of this sort. My parents, Martin and Mary Walsh, consistently expressed their interest in the progress of this work and convincingly suppressed what could only have been their amazement at how anything could take so long to complete.

Director Fran Benson, managing editor Patty Peltekos, and other staff of the ILR Press were consistently helpful, reasonable, and flexible. They made the difficult process of getting a book into print pleasant enough that I might actually consider doing it again.

ON DIFFERENT PLANES

Chapter 1

Introduction

In June 1960, with the sun setting on the Eisenhower administration, pilots went on strike at Southern Airways, a small regional airline. The president of Southern Airways, Frank W. Hulse, had provoked the strike as a means of replacing the carrier's unionized pilots (Hopkins 1982). The struggle at Southern dragged on for almost two years. Using a variety of measures, not the least of which was obtaining a favorable ruling from a Civil Aeronautics Board (CAB) newly stocked with Kennedy appointees, the pilots were ultimately victorious.

The Southern strike was notable for more than its favorable outcome for labor. The extent of support garnered within the labor movement for the striking pilots was unusual and would not be seen again in the airline industry for some time. Charles Overholt, an editor of the *Memphis Union News*, focused on the relationship of the pilots to the larger labor movement in his assessment of the strike's meaning: "Perhaps, after the strike is won, there will be returned to these pilots their highly developed sense of exclusivity. But now, how well the organizational being within the pilot can adopt the cloth of bread-and-butter trade unionism, is the real story of the Southern strike" (quoted in *Air Line Pilot*, May–June 1962: 9).

Overholt's characterization continues to provide insight into the fabric of airline labor. Pilots, and indeed the entire unionized work force of Eastern Airlines, would confront another "Frank" in 1989—and with far more at stake. As in 1960, the response would evidence the potential potency of labor unity, but also underscore its scarcity and limits.

The character of the labor movement derives in large part from the relations between labor unions. The extent to which values are shared and formal structures are inclusive matter too, of course, but it is the way unions

3

deal with one another that largely determines whether labor solidarity is meaningful or a hollow pretense. Unions engage in a wide variety of relations: from mere acquaintance and communication to coalition formation and sympathy strikes; from exchanges of information and ideas to formal pacts; and from support and cooperation to competition and conflict. Yet how much do we really know about how and why unions deal with one another?

To gain a better understanding of inter-union relations, and thus the labor movement, this book examines the interesting case of airline unions, focusing on the latter part of the 1980s. What accounts for the presence or absence, and the quality, of the relations between unions? What are some of the major obstacles unions encounter in trying to work together? How do the many ties between unions combine to form a coherent system of relations or network? What are some of the ways inter-union activity affects labor relations outcomes? These are basic questions this book addresses. It does so with the guidance of organizational theory and by analyzing extensive data on pairs of unions, coalitions, and the airline union network as a whole.

An excursion into the realm of inter-union relations does not lead one very far from the more familiar terrain of labor-management relations. There is a close nexus between the two. Inter-union relations both reflect and shape labor relations. When there is intense labor-management conflict, for example, unions are more likely to look to one another for support. At the same time, the extent of support received can affect the outcome of a struggle. When bargaining outcomes for unions representing employees of the same firm are perceived to be inequitable, inter-union relations may suffer. The representational structure of an industry defines the boundaries across which inter-union relations occur. Yet the nature of inter-union relations helps determine whether that structure results in fragmentation or cohesion. Numerous other examples could be cited. The point is that inter-union relations and labor relations are closely intertwined. In focusing on the often neglected topic of inter-union relations, this book makes the important connections between the two more salient.

A study of inter-union relations begins to fill a large void in the industrial relations literature. Writings directly pertaining to inter-union relations (e.g., Estey 1955; Chernish 1969; Chaison 1986) are few, fragmented, and often dated. In taking a subject that has been treated as background by industrial relations scholars and placing it in the foreground, this book follows a suggestion offered by George Strauss (1977: 238): "Sociologists may find rich pickings, analyzing the various forms of inter-union cooperation, conflict, and exchange, looking at these from the viewpoints both of individual union strategic choice and of system-wide dynamics."

Conceptual work in the area of inter-union relations is perhaps even more limited than empirical offerings. References to the labor movement, labor solidarity, and inter-union relations tend to be as casual as they are common. Most often, the labor movement is implicitly regarded as a simple aggregate of individuals and unions or as a formally structured entity represented by the AFL-CIO. In conceptualizing the labor movement as a differentiated and structured (both formally and informally) inter-union network, this book offers a different view, one with both theoretical and practical significance.

But why airline unions? At first blush, the airline industry does not seem like a promising locus for a study of this kind. Its reputation—in no small part deserved—has long been for its lack of solidarity and its parochialism, rooted in its craft-based bargaining structure. Yet that same craft-based structure implies that there are numerous unions representing different groups of airline workers and having opportunities to establish inter-union ties. Before we conclude anything about the "fragmentation" of airline labor, we need to know whether there are links across the boundaries of these craft-based bargaining units that promote a broader outlook and increase the likelihood of solidaristic action.

There are additional reasons to focus on airline unions. The high rate of unionization in the airline industry, its importance to the U.S. economy, and its extreme volatility have made the fortunes of airline labor a barometer for the entire labor movement in recent years. Airline unions have been confronted with many of the most serious threats faced by U.S. labor. Permanent replacement, bankruptcy, and numerous rounds of concession bargaining are only a few manifestations of the industry's drastically altered competitive environment and labor relations strategies. In the industry, then, we find a setting in which tradition and formal structure tend to weigh against the establishment of close inter-union ties but in which changed and threatening circumstances have heightened the need for cooperation among unions.

To be sure, this book is not filled with tales of inter-union solidarity of heroic proportions. Conflict and cooperation receive roughly equal billing. The "good guys" do not always win, even when they pull together. Ultimately, however, we learn more about the possibilities and limits of labor solidarity by examining an industry in which a tradition of inter-union cooperation has not yet been established, than by looking elsewhere for shining success stories.

The time is certainly ripe for a closer examination of inter-union relations. As James Wallihan has suggested:

> Questions crucial to labor's future revolve around multi-union organizations. The interlocking of the elements of the environment increases the need for inter-union cooperation, which is the strong point of these bodies. They play a key role in keeping the structure of the labor movement relevant to a rapidly changing corporate and technological environment (1985: 174).

Wallihan's argument applies to inter-union relations generally, not just to the activities of formal, multi-union bodies. Unions in the United States are operating in an environment that is more hostile to their cause and institutional survival than at any time since the early 1930s. Fostering more cooperative and supportive inter-union relations is an essential element in any serious effort to revitalize the U.S. labor movement. Building genuine solidarity among unions is critical to the future of the labor movement, along with internal organizing aimed at increasing democracy and participation within unions; intensive efforts to organize and advocate for the interests of women, minorities, low-wage, and temporary workers; and efforts to forge closer ties with community organizations and other social movements.

Cooperation among unions does not ensure that desired outcomes will be realized, but fuller information, support during strikes, unity in dealing with employers, an active and consistent political voice, and other potential benefits of cooperation certainly enhance labor's prospects. Solidarity, however imperfectly enacted, is integral to the practice of unionism and not merely a bag of tricks pulled out to deal with some particular problem and subsequently laid aside. Further, solidarity must not be confined within national boundaries. Unions in North America, dealing with the North American Free Trade Agreement (NAFTA), and in Europe, contending with the challenges of economic integration, find themselves with both antagonistic and shared interests but needing to locate common ground and influence the workings of these new arrangements.

There are signs that an increased "solidarity consciousness" (Moody 1988: 309) has, in fact, taken shape within the labor movement in recent years. The importance of having union members who are truly organized, and not merely part of a head count, has become more widely recognized. While discussions of "internal organizing" (AFL-CIO 1988; Muehlenkamp 1991) focus on intra-union relations, efforts to promote more supportive inter-union relations can be viewed as internal organizing at the level of the labor movement.

As an academic work aimed primarily at the concerns of industrial relations and organizational scholars, this book does not provide detailed practical guidance for those who wish to undertake the difficult but necessary work of solidifying inter-union relations. The concepts developed and the concrete cases considered may prove helpful, however, particularly in identifying potential obstacles to that end.

Plan of this Book

I begin by developing a conceptual framework for understanding inter-union relations (chapter 2). Proceeding from the premise that the labor movement can usefully be viewed as a network of inter-union relations, forms of interdependence between unions are identified and their theoretical implications for the existence and quality of inter-union relations are discussed.

Seeking a relatively fine-grained analysis, this study focuses on a specific context, the U.S. airline industry in the late 1980s. Chapter 3 explores the implications of this setting for inter-union relations, taking account of the formal structure of union representation in the airline industry, the character of airline unionism, and developments that have increased the interdependence of airline unions.

Historical perspective is lent to this inquiry by an examination of airline union relations before 1987 (chapter 4). This discussion provides a baseline for assessing more recent developments and an initial qualitative test of the proposition that increasing interdependence has fostered closer ties among airline unions.

Chapters 5 and 6 contain the results of several quantitative analyses of inter-union relations based on data specifically collected for this study. These data provide a more complete picture of inter-union relations than any other source available to date. The first of these two chapters reports on a regression analysis of relations among pairs of unions and offers answers to the question of why unions establish ties with one another. The second chapter uses network analytic techniques to identify a coherent pattern in the system of relations among airline unions and to infer the consequences of that structure.

Joint efforts by unions often involve coalitions. Chapter 7 examines several case studies of airline union coalitions, focusing on the dynamics of those coalitions and the extent to which they have been able to influence labor relations outcomes.

By far, the single most important locus of inter-union activity in the airline industry during the late 1980s was Eastern Airlines. Chapter 8 analyzes events at Eastern and shows how they embodied both the potential and limitations of solidarity among airline unions.

Chapter 9 states the conclusions of this study and some broader implications.

Moving beyond simplistic formulations such as "airline unions don't want anything to do with one another" to examine actual relations between unions, one finds a complex and not so easily explicated web of connections. Relations between airline unions, like other unions, are shaped by a confluence of factors, but especially formal organizational affiliations, craft, resource inequalities, and environmental threat. Relations between unions reflect the contexts in which they operate, particularly in terms of work organization, representational structures, labor relations practices, economics, and politics. Even when the need to cooperate is acknowledged, working together successfully requires that unions overcome a number of basic impediments.

To a very considerable extent, the diverse set of unions that represent airline workers operate "on different planes." Airline unions have distinct (and sometimes contradictory) interests, widely varying resources at their disposal, and differing capacities to shape events on behalf of their members. Yet, in a turbulent airline industry where unions are regularly confronted with threats to their existence and where it has become far more difficult to autonomously advance members' interests, these different planes increasingly intersect. The ability of airline unions to jointly and proactively shape the future of the airline industry rests heavily upon how they work out the many and thorny interorganizational issues entailed in putting labor solidarity into practice.

Chapter 2

Conceptualizing Inter-Union Relations: Constructing a Theoretical Framework

H aving set out the task of accounting for the nature and effects of relations among unions, a number of questions immediately present themselves: What relations should one look for? What are some possible explanations for why unions establish ties with one another? What common threads weave together the numerous discrete observations of inter-union behavior? A sound theoretical framework is required to answer these questions. Such a framework is absent from the industrial relations literature but can be derived by drawing upon organizational theory. In this chapter, I develop a model of inter-union relations based primarily on organizational theory, particularly the literature on interorganizational relations, but that also takes into account distinctive features of unions as organizations. The core insights expressed in this model are that unions establish relations primarily as a result of their being interdependent and that these relations vary qualitatively depending on the nature of the interdependence.

The Labor Movement as an Inter-Union Network

How can the labor movement best be conceptualized? At one level, it can be viewed as a collection of individuals sharing values and acting (to varying degrees) in concert to realize those values. Yet the fact that many of these individuals are located within formal organizations—labor unions—is of decisive importance. The labor movement, no less (and perhaps more) than other social movements (Zald and McCarthy 1987), depends on formal organizations to remain viable. Thus, an organizational perspective promises to be a fruitful vantage point from which to analyze the labor movement.[1]

Focusing on unions as core elements of the labor movement raises the further issue of how they relate to one another. One possibility, analogous to the notion of a competitive market, is that the labor movement is a simple aggregate of unions, each in the same "line of business" but operating in an atomistic fashion. The activities of unions, particularly insofar as they compete for members or engage in self-interested exchanges, might affect one another from time to time, but there would be little reason or opportunity to establish ongoing relationships. At another extreme, the labor movement might be regarded as a formal hierarchy. Here, the labor movement would be seen as a unified entity capable of authoritatively ensuring coordination across unions, presumably through the auspices of the AFL-CIO.

Casual observation is sufficient to dispel these caricatures of the labor movement as either a market or a hierarchy. Not all unions are AFL-CIO affiliates. The "rope of sand" that is the federation is premised on national union autonomy (Wallihan 1985) and relies heavily on informal influence to elicit cooperation by affiliates. At the same time, the existence of a major labor federation, coordinated bargaining, sympathy strikes, and norms of solidarity supports a strong prima facie case for not viewing the labor movement as an atomistic market.

Rather than a market or a hierarchy, the labor movement can most usefully be viewed as a network (Powell 1990). A network is constituted by a set of actors and the relations between those actors. An inter-union network consists of unions, a few, some, or many of which are linked by transfers of information and other resources, agreements, provisions of strike support, conflict, and any of a myriad of other possible ties. Conceptualizing the labor movement as a network draws attention to the way in which individual unions are embedded in a larger relational context, engage in patterned and recurrent exchanges, and maintain ties that afford them greater or lesser access to resources, opportunities for exerting influence, and reputation or status within the labor movement. Lines of cohesion and division, which may cut across formal organizational boundaries (e.g., AFL-CIO affiliation) or other a priori groupings (e.g., craft versus industrial union), become more visible and the actual capacity of the labor movement for unified, solidaristic action more apparent.

If relations between unions are central to an understanding of the labor movement, several issues readily come to mind: Why do unions enter into relations with one another? Which unions are most likely to establish ties? What can be expected regarding the quality and dynamics of those relationships? What factors limit or enhance cooperation between unions? These are basic questions that the conceptual framework for a study of inter-union relations should address. Although the industrial relations literature offers scant guidance on these matters, organizational theory, particularly the literature on interorganizational relations, has much to contribute. Labor unions have not been prominent among the organizations contemplated by organizational theorists, however, so care is required to make a conceptual framework rooted in organizational theory sensitive to the distinctive features of unions.

Interdependence among Unions

Perhaps the most basic generalization to be drawn from the literature is that interorganizational relations are generated and shaped by environmental interdependencies. In one form or another, it is the interdependence of organizations that moves them from a position in which they are attempting to maintain complete autonomy toward one in which they are dealing with organizations impinging upon them. Interdependence exists whenever an organization does not entirely control all of the conditions necessary for the achievement of an action or for obtaining the desired outcome from that action (Pfeffer and Salancik (1978: 40). When two organizations are interdependent, the behavior of one organization has clear ramifications for the other (Pennings 1981: 434).[2]

There are many different ways in which organizations impinge upon one another. Forms of interdependence likely to be found among unions include competitive interdependence, resource dependence, common problem interdependence, common organizational affiliation, workflow interdependence, bargaining outcome interdependence, and shared domain.

Competitive Interdependence

Organizational theorists (Hawley 1950: 36–41; Guetzkow 1966: 31; Aldrich 1979) have long discussed the distinction between commensalistic interdependence, in which similar elements making similar demands on the environment are at least potential competitors, and symbiotic relationships, in which there is mutual dependence between unlike elements. Other writers (Pennings 1981; Cook 1977) have used different terms (e.g., "horizontal interdependence," "negatively connected exchange relations") to convey the same reality of competition among organizations. To distinguish it from conflict, competition has sometimes been conceptualized as a pattern of parallel striving for rewards mediated by a third party (Schmidt and Kochan 1972).

Competition necessarily involves an incompatibility of goals, but, as Amos Hawley (1950: 40, 211) was early in recognizing, cooperation, as well as antagonism, can emerge among competitors. After all, organizations that are similar enough to compete are also likely to have a great deal in common. Joint strategies pursued by competitively interdependent firms have, in fact, received increased attention in recent years (Pennings 1981; Astley and Fombrun 1987). Similarly, Mayer N. Zald and John D. McCarthy (1980: 18) have noted the frequent confluence of competition and cooperation among social movement organizations. External threats or opportunities have generally been proposed as the basis for collaboration among competitors (Carney 1987: 343; Pennings 1981: 441).

Unions compete in a number of ways, including over status, the size of settlements, and members. The latter form of competition is likely to be the most consequential, since a union's ability to operate (via dues and the voluntary efforts of members), and ultimately its reason for existing, depend upon maintaining an adequate membership. John Dunlop's (1972: 162–63) interpretation of a spate of inter-union agreements that appeared during the 1950s as devices intended primarily to limit competition illustrates one way in which competition among unions can lead to the establishment of ties. Similarly, curtailing rampant and costly raiding was a prominent motive for the merger of the AFL and CIO (Dulles and Dubofsky 1984: 359). The historical trend toward broader union jurisdictions (Chaison and Dhavale 1990) suggests the existence of increased competitive interdependence, as more unions seek available members regardless of industry or craft.

Yet competition among unions for members is also constrained by four factors: norms, the workings of the AFL-CIO, jurisdictions, and the sporadic nature of competitive opportunities. First, competition is most often viewed by unionists as contrary to labor unity and the goals of the labor movement as a whole. Second, the AFL-CIO plays an important role in managing competitive disputes, at least between its member unions. Third, the expansion of union jurisdictions over time has not rendered jurisdictional boundaries irrelevant, particularly in industries with craft organization. Fourth, and finally, highly "organizable" new bargaining units, enticing several unions to invest resources in organizing the same group of workers, and events such as corporate mergers, forcing unions into competition over newly consolidated work groups, are sporadic occurrences.

For several reasons, then, competition among unions, although very much a reality, is less severe than it might otherwise be. Under these circumstances, the common concerns of unions that represent similar groups of workers and the likelihood that these unions have similar characteristics (e.g., size, bargaining power) as a result of similarities in the organization of production across employers provide the bases for collaboration. Even when competition erupts, communication between unions to keep tabs on one another, to lodge complaints, or to negotiate jurisdictional agreements is likely.

Resource Dependence

The resource needs of organizations and the flow of resources among them are central to the literature on interorganizational relations (Pfeffer and Salancik 1978; Cook and Emerson 1984). Organizations require many inputs (e.g., capital, raw materials, members and workers, information) that must be obtained from the environment, usually other organizations. Exchanging resources, and maintaining or acquiring access to them, thus become fundamental to the development of ties between organizations, even as efforts are made to limit dependence and susceptibility to influence.

Unions require resources and some of these resources are best obtained from other unions. The ability to meet basic operating expenses with dues or per capita payments during "normal times" may yield to requests for financial support or the sharing of costs in the face of strikes, protracted litigation, buyout attempts, and other exceptional circumstances. The resource needs of unions are by no means limited to financial resources, however. Perhaps the most important resource that can be rendered is support from other unions for a striking union's picket lines. More generally, the reliance of unions on broad-based collective action makes the support of other unions in undertakings such as lobbying efforts, demonstrations, and boycotts highly meaningful. A more continuous resource requirement of unions is their need for reliable and timely information regarding such matters as negotiation outcomes for related bargaining units, arbitration decisions, the finances and operations of employers, and issues being contested in political, legal, and regulatory forums. Finally, if legitimacy can reasonably be viewed as a resource, it is obtained, in part, through association with other unions. Affiliation with the AFL-CIO, as the major labor federation in the United States and an acknowledged voice of labor, is an important means by which unions gain legitimacy.

Unions, then, sometimes draw upon one another for financial resources in crises and, more regularly, for information, aid in carrying out collective actions, and legitimacy. The level of resources a union requires depends significantly on circumstances, especially whether or not the union is engaged in serious conflict with employers. This somewhat episodic need for resources contrasts with the more routine, ongoing exchange relations between other organizations (e.g., supplier and producer firms), as does the greater significance for unions of nonmonetary resources (e.g., picket line support).

Differences across unions in the need for resources are not entirely a matter of circumstances. Unions vary considerably in their bargaining power, political capacity (i.e., lobbying staff, political action committees [PACs], and entrée to important officials), and access to information. Those unions with more of these resources and capacities have less need to draw on other unions and, instead, are sought out for support and assistance. The unequal distribution of resources and capacities among unions opens up the possibility that relations between unions will be characterized by varying degrees of dependence and power dynamics.

This inequality among unions and its effect on inter-union relations has been referred to by industrial relations scholars, if only obliquely. Gary N. Chaison (1986) has observed that most union mergers are absorptions rather than amalgamations, and that the parties involved have very different motives for merging. Several analyses of coalition bargaining point to the desire of some larger unions for the power gained from leading a coalition as a prime reason for them to participate (Chernish 1969: 258; Hildebrand 1972: 304). Most directly, Marten S. Estey's (1955) early discussion of "strategic alliances" among unions anticipated some of the insights of the resource dependence perspective. Estey (1955: 42, 47) noted that some unions with minimal bargaining power and financial resources were able to draw upon more powerful unions, benefiting from the latter's respect for their picket lines and initial organization of work sites. As with other resource dependence relations, however, these arrangements were fraught with difficulty. The less powerful union was left uncertain regarding the continued availability of support and faced the prospect of infringement upon its autonomy, including demands for formal affiliation with the more powerful union.

Common Problem Interdependence

Organizations may also become intertwined as a result of being confronted with common environmental threats. Organizations faced with a common problem are interdependent in that they are concerned about the same situation, joint effort may be necessary to produce a successful resolution, the ability or inability of one organization to deal successfully with the situation is likely to establish a precedent for other organizations facing the same threat, and unilateral actions by one party may exacerbate the shared problem. In short, organizations sometimes find themselves "in the same boat," and this constitutes a form of interdependence distinct from those discussed thus far (Van de Ven 1976; Staggenborg 1986; Gricar 1981).

The distinctiveness of common problem interdependence is that it is both more collective and less stable than either competitive interdependence or resource dependence. Although organizations facing common problems retain their individual interests, serious shared concerns are more conducive to a collective orientation than are attempts to obtain needed resources or to deal with competitors. It is "our problem" that is at hand, rather than the question of whether to help another union with "its problem." Moreover, problems often emerge suddenly and produce great uncertainty. Yet the fact that problems arise and dissipate, while new threats affecting different sets of unions come along, makes common problem interdependence less stable over time and place than other forms of interdependence.

Recent years have brought many serious shared problems to the doorsteps of unions. The permanent replacement of strikers, plant closings, outsourcing, concession demands, and hostile political administrations are only some of the more obvious examples. That common problems might, in fact, prompt inter-union activity is suggested in analyses of coalition bargaining and bargaining with multinational firms (Chernish 1969: 6, 17; Weber 1974: 237). The coordination of bargaining and other activities is seen as a response to the problems posed by the conglomerate or multinational structures of employers, which allow them to play unions and workers off against one another. Likewise, the hostile political climate in the early post–World War II period is regarded as another major factor prompting the merger of the AFL and CIO (Raybeck 1966: 422).

Although caution is required in extrapolating from labor-management relations to inter-union relations, much work on labor-management cooperation (Schuster 1984; Jacoby 1983) emphasizes the emergence of serious threats in prompting a more integrative, problem-solving approach to labor relations. The prevalent view of unions as reactive organizations (Craft 1991; Cutcher-Gershenfeld, McKersie, and Wever 1987) also fits with the notion that inter-union activity may be heavily shaped by responses to common problems.

Interdependence through Organizational Affiliations

Inclusion within a variety of multi-organization bodies constitutes yet another important form of interdependence. The distinction between formal and informal structure has long been of interest to organizational theorists (e.g., Roethlisberger and Dickson 1943; Blau and Scott 1962). To the extent that relations are formally structured, they are likely to be subject to greater constraint, to evidence continuity, and to have lines of inclusion and exclusion clearly defined by organizational boundaries (Weber 1947; Blau and Scott 1962). A common identity, established communication channels, joint decision-making processes, and some degree of authority are likely to be present when organizations are affiliated with the same larger organizations.

A prime instance of overlapping organizational affiliation in the union context is the affiliation of most local unions with national unions.[3] Local unions are subject (to varying degrees, depending on the politics and structure of the national union) to directives and/or pressure to coordinate with other locals in the same national union or different unions. Locals usually share resources and information to some extent, have forums for periodic contact (e.g., conventions, officer meetings) with other locals, and participate in making decisions affecting one another.

Labor federations, such as the AFL-CIO, are other formal structures that contain multiple unions. Although there is typically less constraint operating within these bodies than is found in national unions, labor federations also provide forums and occasions for inter-union contact, regulate member unions' actions toward one another (particularly competition and jurisdictional disputes), and undertake joint decision making.

The significance of formal affiliations is compounded by the relative insularity of unions and their concern with maintaining autonomy. In contrast to many other organizations, unions do not include individuals from other organizations on their major decision-making bodies, they recruit their leaders primarily from within their own ranks (Clark and Gray 1991: 186), and they usually do not share members. The absence of interpenetration by individuals with concurrent or successive roles within two or more unions renders the formal boundaries of national unions all the more imposing. Likewise, national union autonomy is a basic principle ordering relations among unions in the United States, reflected in the AFL-CIO's mode of operating.

Organizational theorists generally maintain that organizations strive to be as autonomous as possible (Aldrich 1979: 292; Galaskiewicz 1985: 282). Besides the costs in funds and staff, establishing interorganizational ties is constraining; the interests and concerns of other organizations must be more fully taken into account, and it is less possible to act unilaterally. Struggles over autonomy among national unions and between them and their affiliates have a long history in the U.S. labor movement, again suggesting that the organizational boundaries between unions may be especially salient.

Workflow Interdependence

The important insight that organizational structure must be responsive to task-related interdependencies among organizational members and units (Thompson 1967) has implications for interorganizational relations as well. The interconnection of employee groups in the work process creates workflow interdependence between unions, particularly when workers are organized on the basis of craft. Although it is the relations among workers, rather than unions, that are most directly affected by workflow interdependence, unions representing workers closely connected in the work process also tend to be affected by one another's actions. This impact is manifested in jurisdictional conflicts, grievances affecting both work groups, the negotiation of work rules that alter the manner in which work is done, job actions by one group affecting the availability of work for the other, and, in general, greater opportunities for observation and/or contact. Unions that are interdependent in this manner most often are a subset of all the unions that represent workers at a firm or establishment, although workflow interdependence can sometimes extend to all the unions at a firm (if the work process is highly integrated) or to unions representing workers at different firms (if components are produced, delivered, and assembled by different firms).

Interdependence of Bargaining Outcomes

Industrial relations scholars (Ross 1956; Ready 1990) have long discussed (and debated) the manner in which the collective bargaining outcomes of one union influence the bargaining outcomes of other unions. Arnold Weber's (1961) term "unit of direct impact," designating the group of bargaining units directly affected by a particular bargaining agreement, captures the theme of interdependence nicely. This intertwining of negotiations ranges from explicit "patterns," to efforts by unions and companies to maintain labor costs comparable to those of their competitors, to looser comparisons invoked by negotiators and intended to provide a benchmark for identifying a "fair" settlement. Even if pattern bargaining is now in serious decline (Freedman and Fulmer 1982), the centrality of collective bargaining to unions and of comparisons to the bargaining process renders bargaining outcomes a matter of continuing and mutual concern for unions. The extent and direction of bargaining outcome interdependence differ across industries. As a broad generalization, outcomes within the same industry, at competing employers, or for the same categories of workers are most likely to be interdependent.

Shared Domain

At the outer bounds of the concept of interdependence is the notion of shared or overlapping domains (Warren, Rose, and Bergunder 1974; Van de Ven 1976). Domains are those industries, sectors, and problem areas in which organizations are situated and which tend to delimit the concerns and sets of relevant actors for those organizations. The concept of domain can be defined more or less expansively, and, indeed, all unions might be seen as sharing a common "labor" domain. A more useful conception is to identify the domains of unions by the basic categories that bound their jurisdictions: industry, craft, employer, and geographic locale. The interdependence created as a result of a union's location within a domain is more inclusive and diffuse than that implied by the other forms of interdependence discussed thus far. Specific forms of interdependence often occur within domains, such as the competitive interdependence among unions representing the same craft. Unions that operate in the same industry, represent workers employed by the same firm, represent the same category of workers, and/or are located in the same geographic area are more likely to impinge upon one another and to establish relations than are unions in separate domains.

Beyond Interdependence

Although the concept of interdependence subsumes many of the organizational factors that influence the establishment and maintenance of interunion ties, it is necessary to look beyond interdependence. Relations between unions can also be shaped by organizational characteristics that affect their ability or opportunity to interact and by norms or ideology.[4]

Organizational Characteristics

The capacity of and opportunities for organizations to act on their interdependence and form ties with other organizations varies. Several studies (Whetten and Leong 1979; Whetten and Aldrich 1979) have found that such organizational characteristics as budget, staff size, scope of services, and number of organizations in the community are among the best predictors of the number and instrumental value of the interorganizational ties maintained. Budget and staff size can reasonably be viewed as means, while the scope of services and number of organizations in the community suggest variability in the opportunity for interaction. The general argument, then, is that several organizational characteristics related to whether organizations have the means and opportunity to interact may also account for whether interorganizational ties are established.

The number of officers and staff available to unions to engage in boundary-spanning activities is an important and quite variable aspect of the means for maintaining inter-union ties. The range of activities in which a union engages (e.g., grievance handling, bargaining, political action), analogous to a social service agency's scope of services, is an important indicator of its opportunities for contact. The organizational level (e.g., local, intermediate, national) at which a union resides is also likely to be relevant, with contact being more likely between unions with similar authority and standing.

Domain Consensus, Ideology, and Norms

Relations between organizations are shaped not only by interdependence and underlying instrumental concerns but also by the extent to which they share beliefs, values, and norms. The concept of domain consensus is relevant here. Domain consensus has been defined in various ways but generally refers to agreement among organizations regarding their respective jurisdictional claims, purposes, and activities (Levine and White 1961; Thompson 1967). In brief, domain consensus speaks to the issue of whether other organizations are viewed as "legitimate." When there are shared understandings about "turf" issues and a sense of mutual legitimacy, cooperative interaction is facilitated. That a measure of domain consensus and legitimacy may be required for "normal" relations between unions is suggested by the long-standing usage of such terms as "company union" and "dual union" to designate organizations whose legitimacy as the representative of a group of workers or as part of the labor movement is questioned. Legitimacy is conferred on unions through affiliation with the AFL-CIO and by the length of time a union has represented a particular group of workers. The longer that time span, the more likely the union is viewed as established and its role taken for granted.

Ideological compatibility and agreement on strategy and tactics are also important influences on interorganizational relations, especially between social movement organizations (Zald and McCarthy 1980: 9; Staggenborg 1986: 382). Industrial relations commentators have long characterized unions in the United States as "pragmatic" and nonideological (Perlman 1928; Kochan 1979: 23). At times, however, such as during the 1940s and 1950s when conflict between Communist and non-Communist factions in the labor movement was rife (Zald and McCarthy 1980: 9), the ideological persuasions of union leaders and members have mattered a great deal. Even if political ideologies are of limited relevance to the activities of most unions, having a loose body of shared values and beliefs (e.g., gains through collective action, fairness, dignity for workers) and a common identity as participants in the labor movement may help bind unions together. Closer still to the everyday reality of union leaders, beliefs regarding such union goals as employee ownership and labor-management cooperation are rooted in broader values and may prompt either agreement or disagreement among unions.

Some norms, such as the proscription against crossing a picket line, apply directly to inter-union relations. The slogan "An injury to one is an injury to all," however imperfectly practiced, richly conveys the sentiment that solidarity and mutuality are central values within the labor movement. Rick Fantasia (1988) suggests that "cultures of solidarity" emerging among workers in conflict situations are more common and significant than is often supposed. Although actual contact between unions is neither the equivalent of solidarity nor a necessary requirement for its existence, any heightened "solidarity consciousness" (Moody 1988: 309) within the labor movement in recent years is likely to have increased the volume and quality of inter-union ties.[5] At the same time, to the extent that American trade unions continue to subscribe to an ideology of "business unionism"—marked by conservatism, legalism, economistic preoccupation with wages, bureaucracy, and the absence of any broad social and political outlook—inter-union relations are apt to languish:

> In a labor movement now devoid of national political tendencies and debates that crossed union lines, the degeneration of pattern bargaining from a method of multiunion solidarity in the 1940's to a looser "demonstration effect" in the 1950's and after, reinforced parochialism and insularity throughout the unions. One no longer belonged to the labor movement, just to a union. Bargaining was the business of one's own union, and that business ended in the councils of that union. If the other guy did all right, well and good, but it wasn't your concern (Moody 1988: 68).

Industry, Political, and Economic Context

The interdependence of unions, the organizational characteristics of unions, and consensus among unions do not develop in a vacuum. Numerous aspects of the industries in which unions are situated and the larger political economy shape these more immediate determinants of inter-union ties. Perhaps the most basic of these contextual factors is the *formal structure of union representation* in an industry.[6] It is because union members are incorporated within separate bargaining units and unions that relations crossing the organizational boundaries of unions become possible and relevant.

In terms of the foregoing discussion, the representational structure largely defines the domains (e.g., which craft is represented) in which unions operate, their organizational affiliations (e.g., with which national union they are affiliated), the prospects for competition (e.g., how many other unions represent the same category of workers), and the distribution of resources and capacities among unions (e.g., which unions represent job groups with the greatest bargaining power).

Likewise, the *manner in which work is organized* in an industry has obvious implications for workflow interdependence (e.g., which unions represent job groups closely linked by the work process), but it also affects the distribution of resources and capacities among unions (e.g., the size of the bargaining unit, which job groups occupy strategic positions in the production process). *Prevailing labor relations practices* in an industry define the parameters of bargaining outcome interdependence (e.g., whether patterns are followed), affect the need of unions for resources (e.g., the likelihood of a strike and whether permanent replacements will be used), and influence the organizational characteristics of unions (e.g., where responsibility for bargaining is lodged). More broadly, the *financial circumstances of employers*, their *business strategies*, and the *state of the political economy* all directly affect the likelihood that unions will face shared problems (e.g., whether the job security of members is threatened by their employers' indebtedness).

That representational structures, work organization, labor relations practices, and other relevant factors differ across industries means that there are likely to be salient inter-industry differences in the character of inter-union relations. Generalizations about the factors affecting inter-union relations are quite possible, but a solid grasp of the industry and societal context is needed to understand how these factors play themselves out in a particular time and place.

Contents and Forms of Inter-Union Relations

The contents of inter-union relations are numerous and varied, but communication, exchanges of information and support, coalition formation and other joint action, and a variety of perceptions, such as expectations of support, are among the ties warranting particular attention. These and other contents express different underlying forms or dimensions of relations (Knoke and Kuklinski 1982: 15; Marret 1971). For example, relations may be *cooperative, conflictful, or both*. Interdependence is apt to be present in any event, but opposing interests and/or resource scarcity tilt the relationship toward one marked by conflict. Ties between unions may occur in a *collective*, rather than a bilateral, context. Collective action, such as coalition formation, is distinctive in the extent to which the identification of common interests and the submergence of individual interests is required. Collective action is also likely to produce relations that are high in *intensity*, demanding substantial involvement, frequent interaction, and a sizable investment of resources.

Relations also differ in their *instrumentality*. Some ties are of particular importance in shaping outcomes and attaining goals, while others are either more routine or viewed as intrinsically meaningful. To the extent that the instrumentality of a relationship differs between partners, the relations will evidence a greater or lesser degree of *reciprocity*. Reciprocity concerns both the extent to which exchanges are balanced and the degree of mutuality in arranging the terms of interaction.

Lastly, relations differ in form according to their degree of *formalization*. In formalized relations, interdependency is officially recognized, there is a long-term commitment, and there is often an established coordinating mechanism in place.

Interdependence and Qualitative Differences in Relations

The discussion to this point has established that there are several types of interdependence and a wide variety of ties that are possible between unions. Moreover, the concept of relational form speaks to the existence of broad, qualitative differences in the character of inter-union ties. It is possible to extend these insights by considering how specific kinds of interdependence give rise to different forms of relations between unions. These differences in relational form are manifested by pairs of unions, coalitions, and at the network level.[7]

The following paragraphs briefly outline the distinctive implications of formal organizational affiliation, resource dependence, competitive interdependence, and common problems for inter-union relations. To do this, four hypothetical inter-union networks, each based primarily in one of the foregoing types of interdependence, are posited.[8]

Organization-Centered Network

A network in which the ties between unions resulted primarily from their affiliations with formal organizations might be termed an organization-centered network. Because of the nature of the interdependence linking the unions, relations among the unions in such a network would exhibit a relatively high degree of formalization. Organizational boundaries, formal affiliations, and autonomy would matter a great deal. Relations would be contained primarily within the boundaries of the larger organizations with which the unions are affiliated. Hence, ties between unions affiliated with the same national union, and to a lesser extent links between unions both of which are AFL-CIO affiliates, would be most prevalent. That affiliation with the same organization provides ready channels for communication and a common organizational identity suggests that exchanges of information and expectations of support are especially likely between pairs of unions linked in this manner.

Coalitions would not be favored within an organization-centered network. Concern over sacrificing organizational autonomy (Guetzkow 1966; Aldrich 1979) and a preference for dealing with problems within national unions would limit coalition formation. Incorporation (e.g., by merger or affiliation) into the same national union or federation, rather than working together in less formal ways, would be consistent with the underlying logic of this network. The largest national-level unions, because of their scope of responsibilities and ability to coordinate locals, would be central actors within the network. Simply put, the primary structural implication of an organization-centered network is that formal and informal structuring largely coincide. Knowledge of formal affiliations is sufficient to grasp the network's structure. This is not the case for the other networks considered.

Resource-Centered Network

Resource-centered networks are based primarily upon the flow of resources and support among unions. To the extent that the distribution of valued resources and capabilities among unions is unequal, resource dependence relations are likely. The essence of resource dependence is this inequality in resources and capabilities and the potential leverage this confers upon more powerful organizations (Pfeffer and Salancik 1978).

Some unions are especially dependent for their effectiveness or survival on the resources and support of other unions. For example, a small union of less skilled workers is unlikely to be able to mount a successful strike absent the support of other unions representing workers of the same employer. The union in question might be able to draw on other sources of power (e.g., bargaining skill, political connections) or employ alternative strategies (e.g., emphasize cooperation with management), but insofar as a union's bargaining power is critical to its strength and its ability to credibly threaten a strike is the primary source of that power, the support of other unions may well determine the effectiveness and/or survival of a union.

Qualitatively, the ties in a resource-centered network reflect considerable instrumentality, focusing on the acquisition of needed resources and the particular interests of the unions involved. The likely disparity in resources and capacities within a resource-centered network would result in substantially nonreciprocal relations because of the different meanings and importance of relationships to the parties (Knoke and Rogers 1979: 35). Resource dependence relations are both strategically important and problematic, especially for the less powerful actors. Differing interests and the possibility that needed support may not be forthcoming at all, or only on terms that compromise organizational autonomy, set the stage for conflict. Resource dependence between unions thus tends to lead to conflict.

Disparity in the need for and ability to contribute resources also diminishes the incentive to form coalitions, at least on the part of the more powerful unions (i.e., those possessing the greatest resources and capacities and on which other unions depend) (Bacharach and Lawler 1980: 83). Why compromise the freedom to act unilaterally by joining with other unions that have relatively little to offer and with which common interests may be difficult to identify? One answer might be that a problem may emerge of sufficient magnitude to require joint effort. Alternatively, advantages may be perceived to result from the appearance of unity and the ability to control coalition activities. In either case, the logic of a resource-centered network suggests that more powerful unions would be likely to dominate coalition activities and to take unilateral actions without consulting other coalition members.

The basic insight, then, is that the structure of a resource-centered network will mirror the distribution of scarce, valued resources, as well as the distribution of goals or interests determining the need for resources (Laumann, Galaskiewicz, and Marsden 1978: 470). Accordingly, the dominant unions would be those with the greatest resources and capabilities (Wellman 1988: 29; Knoke and Rogers 1979: 35), particularly bargaining power, political capacity, and information. Large national unions might well be included among these central actors, but relations would be structured around resource endowments and needs—not organizational boundaries. A pervasive element of nonreciprocity also distinguishes the ties generated by this form of interdependence. Less powerful unions look to more powerful unions for resources and support, while being unable to reciprocate fully (Knoke and Rogers 1979: 35; Laumann and Marsden 1982: 332).[9]

Craft-Centered Network

A network based largely on the ties among unions representing the same categories of workers, flowing from their competitive and bargaining outcome interdependence, can be termed a craft-centered network. Relations within such a network are likely to be both collective and conflictful in form. Because of regularities in the organization of production across major firms in a given industry, the similarity of competitively interdependent unions is likely to extend beyond common jurisdictions to include such characteristics as their size and bargaining power. Sharing many of the same concerns and possessing similar resources and capacities, joint action presents itself as an attractive option, particularly when the unions' goals cannot be accomplished individually (Hawley 1950: 211; Bacharach and Lawler 1980: 82–83). At the same time, raids and other competitive incidents still occur and fuel conflicts.

Political action on behalf of an occupational group or industry constitutes a surer basis for joint action among competitors than issues concerning particular employers, since the latter are more likely to entail separate or divergent interests. The relative equality of coalition members in a craft-centered network makes it less possible for individual unions to dominate the coalitions or to engage in unilateral actions that seriously affect other coalition members. Coalitions of relative equals may prove difficult to sustain over the long run, however, because continual negotiation and compromise are required, in the absence of a dominant party, to maintain consensus (Lawler and Bacharach 1983: 99).

Structurally, then, a craft-centered network features the confluence of competitive and collaborative elements. Union jurisdictions and craft boundaries provide the essential contours, with unions representing the same categories of workers and sharing a common craft identity relating to one another in both competitive and collective ways.

Problem-Centered Network

Relations based primarily on the common problem interdependence of unions constitute a problem-centered network. Relations within a problem-centered network are collective and intensive in form. The high intensity of the relations, including relatively frequent contact and substantial investments of time and resources, stems from the urgent nature of the common problems. Faced with serious and imminent threats, there is too much uncertainty and too much at stake not to reach out in search of information and ways of dealing with problems. Collective forms of interaction are favored because problems tend to produce common interests and require joint efforts if they are to be resolved.[10]

Without underestimating the obstacles to collaboration, coalition formation would be fairly common within a problem-centered network, as a response to the presence of concerns affecting all the parties similarly and not readily addressed in isolation (Cummings 1984; Gricar 1981; Staggenborg 1986). That unions linked in this manner are subject to the same threats tends to limit the effect of differences in the resources and capacities of individual unions and to render coalition members relatively equal. Yet individual unions may hold very different ideas about how to deal with the shared problems or launch independent initiatives, both of which could increase tensions and make collective effort more difficult. Moreover, since joint efforts would be aimed at solving specific problems, the resolution of those problems or their intractability would lead to the dissolution of the coalition.

The shifting, time-limited nature of common problems, whereby different unions are affected at different times, does not lend itself to the formation of a rigidly structured network. Viewing structure as patterned, recurring relations among actors (White, Boorman, and Breiger 1976; Blau and Scott 1962), the more the basis for the ties shifts with circumstances, the less clear structuring will be evident. Put differently, unlike union jurisdictions, organizational affiliations, and resource endowments, which are relatively stable and identifiable, common problems are less stable and it is less certain which unions are interdependent in this manner. The firmest structural inference that can be drawn from the logic of a problem-centered network is that at any given point in time, it will probably feature clusters of unions intensively interacting to deal with threats directly affecting them while other more peripherally involved unions perhaps provide their support.

Obstacles to Inter-Union Cooperation

The impact of inter-union relations on labor relations and other outcomes depends very much on the extent to which unions are successful in cooperating with one another. Unions may establish ties out of their interdependence but not realize the full benefits of doing so because of problems in working together. For the most part, these impediments reflect the flip sides of the same factors that generate relations among unions.

If the domains in which unions operate, such as the craft(s) they represent and their members' place(s) of employment, provide the grounds for ties among unions sharing these commonalities, they also tend to limit broader cooperation across domains. Strong identification with a particular craft, for example, makes it more difficult to appreciate the relevance of other crafts and to discern common interests with them. Aligning union boundaries with craft boundaries also means that differences across crafts in numbers, bargaining power, national union affiliation, the status of members' work, and other factors are likely to have a profound effect on the prospects for inter-union cooperation. Even as lack of parity across unions in resources and capacities provides a basis for some unions to seek the support of others, this asymmetry makes it much more difficult to identify common interests and to cooperate in ways that are mutually beneficial. Although differences in resources and bargaining power are emphasized here, less tangible matters such as invidious distinctions between types of work also place unions on different footing and impede cooperation. The issue of organizational autonomy is intertwined here. Less powerful unions need support but do not want it to come at the cost of their autonomy, while more powerful unions may choose to maximize their autonomy by "going it alone" or insist upon leading collective efforts as the price for their involvement.

Outbreaks of competition over members can also undermine efforts to work together. Underlying the disruptive effects of both competition for members and perceived inequity in bargaining outcomes is scarcity. In the latter case, clear limits on the ability of an employer to fund contract improvements, or the necessity of providing concessions, pit unions against one another and lead to perceptions of inequity when gains or sacrifices across unions are unequal. Employers can cultivate perceptions of inequity, play favorites, provide inducements for individual unions to defect from a unified stance, press for contract provisions not conducive to labor unity (e.g., nonuniform contract expiration dates), and otherwise impede solidarity among the unions they deal with. Another external obstacle to cooperation is legal constraints. In general, the legal framework for labor relations in the United States, by seeking to confine the scope of conflicts (e.g., distinguishing between "primary" and "secondary" employers) and the tactics available to unions, tends to discourage broad inter-union cooperation, especially in strikes and boycotts.

Just as lack of consensus can negate the establishment of relations, cooperative endeavors can be undermined by disagreements over the nature of problems, what to do about them, and how to do it. Lastly, the absence of strong ideological or normative support for solidarity also limits cooperation. Although unions are unlikely to enter into cooperative efforts solely because it is the solidaristic thing to do, a belief in solidarity as an end in itself imbues struggles with larger meaning, makes it easier to recognize interdependence, and tilts a union toward cooperation when the calculation of self-interest leaves room for discretion.

Outcomes of Inter-Union Cooperation and Support

This study focuses more intently on explaining the pattern of relations between unions than on documenting their impact, but the potential for inter-union relations to shape the outcomes of labor-management relations is clearly a major reason for caring about the pattern of relations. Relations between unions may have their most decisive impact in conflict situations, when the ability or inability to draw upon other unions for resources and support could spell the difference between victory and defeat. Union tactics such as strikes, boycotts, rallies, and corporate campaigns all lend themselves to, and usually are more effective, when many unions are involved. Inter-union relations bear more generally on bargaining outcomes by affecting the extent to which there is pressure to match or exceed the contract terms of other unions, the ability of employers to whipsaw individual unions, and the likelihood that unions will learn about and rapidly adopt strategies that have been successfully employed by other unions.

Political initiatives, which can affect labor relations outcomes, usually require the development of broad coalitions, including other unions, to succeed. Similarly, the ability of unions to alter corporate outcomes in fundamental ways, such as by shopping for new owners or executing an employee buyout, generally depends on a number of unions agreeing on the strategy and working jointly to realize it. Thus, although inter-union cooperation does not offer a panacea for the problems of unions and its impact on outcomes is often difficult to disentangle from other factors, there are reasons to believe that the effect may be substantial. After all, if it is fundamentally unity and the ability to engage in collective action that make individual unions credible entities, then these should also be important at the level of the labor movement.

Model of Inter-Union Relations

The model of inter-union relations developed in this chapter is depicted in figure 2-1. Interdependence between unions is at the core of the model. Unions impinge upon each other in a variety of ways—as competitors, as providers and recipients of resources, as affiliates of the same larger organizations, as parties subjected to the same external threats, as representatives of workers who are linked in particular ways by work processes, as negotia-

Figure 2-1. Model of Inter-Union Relations

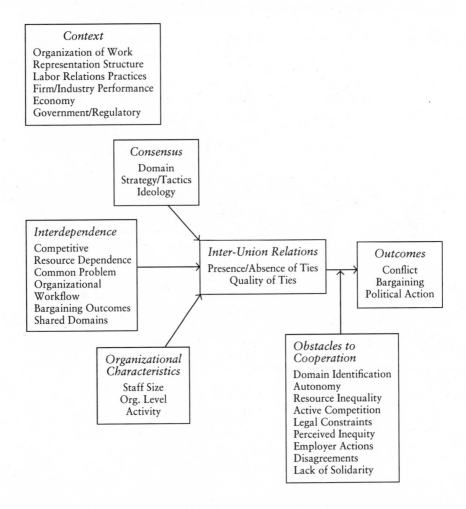

tors of mutually relevant contract terms, and as occupants of the same industry, craft, employer, or geographic domains. Unions that are interdependent in one or more of these ways are likely to be aware of one another, recognize their interdependence,[11] communicate, and establish or maintain ties needed to deal with their interdependence.

It is important to remember, however, that the extent and type(s) of interdependence between unions is determined by a larger context, including the structure of union representation in an industry, the manner in which work is organized, financial conditions, labor relations practices, and the current state of the political economy. The conditions that generate interdependence between unions change over time and vary across industries. Interunion relations are also shaped by the organizational characteristics of unions and the degree to which there is consensus with respect to domain, tactics, and ideology.

Together, all of the aforementioned conditions account for the presence or absence of particular types (contents) of relations between unions. Interunion relations also have underlying forms or qualitative dimensions. Relations can vary in the extent to which they are cooperative or conflictful, intense, instrumental, reciprocal, formalized, or collective. These different relational forms are linked to the different types of interdependence between unions. Relations arising from organizational affiliations tend to be relatively formal; from resource dependence, instrumental, nonreciprocal, and conflictful; from competitive interdependence, collective and conflictful; and from common problem interdependence, intensive and collective.

Several conditions potentially impede the ability of interdependent unions to work together: strong identification with a particular craft or employer; concern with maintaining organizational autonomy; lack of parity in resources and status; outbreaks of competition; perceptions of inequity in bargaining outcomes; divisive employer actions; legal strictures; disagreements over the definitions of problems, strategies, or tactics; and lack of a strong ideological foundation for labor solidarity. To the extent that unions are able to cooperate with one another, they can potentially benefit from participating in coordinated actions, receiving important information, and drawing on the resources and support of other unions. In turn, unions are better able to prevail in conflicts, negotiate more effectively, exert greater influence on employers, and be more effective political actors.

Chapter 3

The U.S. Airline Industry as a
Context for Inter-Union Relations

A irline unions have much in common with labor unions in other industries and, indeed, with organizations in general. Hence, this study draws upon organizational theory for its basic direction and proposes a model of inter-union relations that, at least provisionally, is applicable to all unions. Yet the way in which these general explanatory variables are played out in the contemporary airline industry reflects the unique features of that context. To make sense of the data presented in this book, it is critical that the specific context of the U.S. airline industry in the latter 1980s be taken into account. Essential features of this setting include the structure of union representation in the airline industry, the characteristics of airline unions, and a host of recent developments in the industry that have shaped its labor relations. This contextual information makes clear which union actors are relevant and the nature of their increased interdependence.

Structure of Union Representation

Table 3-1 displays the status of union representation at nine major air carriers. Most crafts at most carriers are, in fact, unionized. Typically, three or four different unions represent workers at a given carrier. Counting national union headquarters and the relevant subunits of national unions separately (e.g., locals, districts), thirty-seven different unions represent the employees at these carriers.[1] These are the unions whose relations are the concern of this study. Some crafts/job groups are basically homogenous with respect to union representation (e.g., pilots, who are heavily repre-sented by ALPA), while representation of other groups (e.g., flight atten-

29

Table 3-1. Union Representation by Craft and Carrier, 1987–89

Carrier	Pilots	Flight engineers and second officers	Dispatchers	Flight attendants	Radio and teletype personnel	Mechanics and related personnel	Office, clerical, fleet, and passenger service workers	Stock and stores personnel	Other[a]
American	APA	FEIA	TWU 540	APFA	TWU 513	TWU 513	N.R.	TWU 513	N.R.
Continental	N.R.[b]	N.R.	TWU 540	UFA	N.R.	N.R.	N.R.	N.R.	N.R.
Delta	ALPA	ALPA	PAFCA	N.R.	N.R.	N.R.	N.R.	N.R.	N.R.
Eastern	ALPA	ALPA	IAM 100	TWU 553	IAM 100	IAM 100	N.R.	IAM 100	N.R.
Northwest	ALPA	ALPA	TWU 540	IBT 2747	TWU 528	IAM 143	ALEA/BRAC/ IAM 143[c]	IAM 143	N.R.
Pan Am	ALPA	FEIA	TWU 540	IUFA	N.R.	TWU 504	IBT 732	IBT 732	N.R.
TWA	ALPA	ALPA	TWU 540	IFFA	N.R.	IAM 142	IAM 142	IAM 142	N.R.
United	ALPA	ALPA	IAM 141	AFA	IAM 141	IAM 141	IAM 141	IAM 141	TWU 540
U.S. Air	ALPA	ALPA	N.R.	AFA	N.R.	IAM 141	IBT 2707	IAM 141	TWU 540

Sources: U.S. National Mediation Board, Annual Report of the U.S. National Mediation Board 1985, 1986; "Airline Labor Contract Status," Air Line Pilot, July 1987, June 1988, June 1989; ALPA, Negotiator's Summary of Pilot Agreements, June 1988.

[a] Includes meteorologists and flight simulator technicians.

[b] The representational status of pilots and mechanics at Continental was murky and contested throughout this period. Since neither group was being actively represented in bargaining, however, these units are listed as "not represented (N.R.)."

[c] Representation rights changed hands during the study period. The union initially representing the unit is listed first.

dants) is more dispersed. The unions of airline workers are varied as well as numerous, including AFL-CIO affiliates (e.g., IAM) and single-carrier independent unions (e.g., IUFA), craft (e.g., ALPA) and industrial (e.g., TWU) unions, and "pure" airline unions (e.g., AFA) versus unions with multi-industry jurisdictions (e.g., IBT). More important, and flowing from differences in the crafts they represent and the carriers that employ their members, these unions differ greatly in size, bargaining power, and status.[2] Within this structure of union representation, bargaining is conducted at the individual carrier level and on a craft-by-craft basis. The extent of national union control of bargaining varies considerably, but for the most part, carrier-level subunits are relatively autonomous (Cappelli 1985: 318).

The scheme of union representation in the airline industry, then, has several basic implications for inter-union relations. First, the number and variety of unions are considerable. This is not an industry where a single dominant union represents the vast majority of workers. Cohesiveness for airline labor necessarily involves relations that cross the organizational boundaries of unions. At the same time, these unions are likely to differ from one another in size, bargaining power, status, affiliations, and their extent of involvement within the airline industry, making inter-union relations more problematic. Second, the subunits of national unions in the airline industry, particularly such intermediate bodies as ALPA's master executive councils (MECs), have considerable discretion stemming from their leading role in bargaining. It is important to examine their role and not simply to assume that national union headquarters are the only relevant actors. Third, and finally, the representational structure of the airline industry makes craft and carrier the basic domains that define the jurisdictions of airline unions and differentiate their concerns and circumstances. Airline unions tend to have fairly narrowly defined constituencies and sets of immediate interests to represent. Although all airline unions share much in common (as does the entire labor movement), unions that represent the same category of workers or workers employed by the same carrier are especially apt to face common problems and to have their activities impinge upon one another.

Airline Unions

Although a number of unions represent airline workers, the majority are affiliated with one of the following inter/national unions: ALPA, AFA, the IAM, or the TWU.

Air Line Pilots Association

No discussion of airline unionism could proceed very far without mention of the Air Line Pilots Association. ALPA is the principal union representing pilots employed by commercial air carriers. Formed in the early 1930s as the pioneering union in the fledgling airline industry (Hopkins 1971: 59), ALPA counted some forty-two thousand pilots as members in 1989.[3] This relatively modest number obscures the leading role ALPA plays in bargaining, political action, and regulatory matters affecting the airline industry. Commensurate with this leadership role, ALPA has considerable resources at its disposal, including ample strike funds and staff, extensive research capability, and numerous lobbyists. ALPA pilots earn considerably more than the members of most other unions and pay 2.35 percent of their salaries in dues. Since 1985, part of this assessment has gone toward a "major contingency fund" designed to underwrite the cost of strikes and other actions. That this contingency fund accrued $44 million in the first two years of its existence but also expended $19 million to support strike-related activities at United, Continental, and Eastern (ALPA 1987: xv) demonstrates both ALPA's substantial ability to generate revenues and the increasingly burdensome resource demands faced by the association.

Within the organizational structure of ALPA, the units directly pertinent to this study are ALPA International headquarters in Washington, D.C., and the master executive councils. ALPA International includes the top International officers comprising the ALPA Executive Committee and a large number of staff members (approximately four hundred) employed in an array of staff departments. Master executive councils serve as coordinating bodies for the members at each carrier and are the principal locus of bargaining and decision making at those carriers. Serving on the MECs are the top officers of local executive councils (LECs), units responsible for representing pilots employed by a particular carrier and based in a particular city. In turn, MEC officers, in addition to International officers, make up the ALPA Executive Board and Board of Directors. The latter is the most inclusive forum within ALPA and is equivalent to a national union convention.

Association of Flight Attendants

The members of AFA, who numbered some twenty-six thousand in 1989, are flight attendants employed by commercial air carriers. AFA stands out as a leading example of a national union whose membership and leadership are largely female. Although it is still the largest union of flight attendants, AFA was hit hard by carrier mergers and bankruptcies in the 1980s. AFA is politically active and provides considerable support to its carrier-level subunits, but its resources, like those of other flight attendant unions, are relatively limited. Largely because AFA was formerly an affiliate of ALPA, the organizational structure of the two unions is very similar, save for AFA's more prominent emphasis on rank-and-file participation.

International Association of Machinists and Aerospace Workers

The IAM is a large international union that in 1989 had roughly 750,000 members employed in a variety of industries. The approximately ninety thousand IAM members employed by airlines or airline-related firms (e.g., service and fueling companies) make the airline industry a very significant jurisdiction for the union. The IAM has a lengthy history of representing airline workers, dating back to the late 1930s. Within the airline industry, the IAM represents a diverse group of workers, including mechanics, baggage handlers, office and clerical workers, stock and stores personnel, dispatchers, and, most recently, flight attendants. The IAM International has substantial resources at its command, including a sizable strike fund, a large research department, staff, Washington lobbyists, and a major PAC. Although its energies and resources are not focused solely on the airline industry, the IAM is the leading contender with ALPA for a leadership role among airline labor.

The structural units most relevant to this study are the IAM Airline Division and airline district lodges. The former is part of the international union and is headed by an international vice president. The district lodges are intermediate bodies responsible for coordinating the eighty-five or so IAM local lodges representing airline workers. The district lodges are relatively heterogeneous, typically incorporating workers from a variety of crafts and job groups, several different carriers, and other air transport–related firms. District lodges bear primary responsibility for bargaining with carriers, although international representatives are not shy about taking charge of negotiations deemed particularly significant.

Transport Workers Union

Of a total membership of about eighty-five thousand, almost half (forty-two thousand) of all TWU members were employed in air transport in 1989. Yet the core constituencies of the TWU in most respects remain its large units of public transit workers in New York City and Philadelphia. Like the IAM, the TWU has represented airline employees for some time (dating back to about 1946) and in a variety of crafts. The resources of the TWU are far more limited than those of the IAM, however, in part because the union does not maintain a strike fund.

The structural units of primary concern in this study are the Air Transport Division and the TWU locals. The breadth of the locals varies enormously. TWU Local 553, for example, represented all of the flight attendants at Eastern Airlines until the carrier's demise in 1991, regardless of where they were based. Local 540 represents dispatchers at numerous carriers. More akin to the usual scope of local unions, TWU Local 513 is among a number of geographically based locals representing mechanics and other job groups at American Airlines. A presidents' council, composed of the officers of all the locals representing workers at the carrier, functions to coordinate bargaining on a carrierwide basis at American.

A Closer Look—Inside ALPA

Capsule descriptions like the foregoing do not adequately convey the dynamics of a union and the manner in which formal structural arrangements come to life in actual relations between the union's affiliates. The relatively autonomous character of ALPA MECs and the consequences of a formal structure that segments pilots into carrier-specific groupings are emphasized in the following discussion.

Mark L. Kahn (1971: 488–90) once observed that elements of centralization and decentralization co-exist within ALPA. This observation continues to be valid. The centralized face of ALPA is manifested by the fact that the International, not the carrier-level MECs, is formally the authorized bargaining representative. ALPA members belong directly to the International and remit their dues to it. Each MEC receives an operating budget from ALPA International and is staffed in part by employees of the International. Contract administrators from the International are present at most negotiations. Consistent with its status as bargaining representative, ALPA International must approve all agreements (ALPA Constitution, Art. XVIII, Sect. 1).

These formal arrangements belie the substantial power of the MECs. By constitutional provision (Art. IV, Sect. 2C), and in practice, the MEC is the primary and usually final decision maker regarding the affairs of pilots employed at a given carrier. MECs are largely responsible for conducting negotiations, and the International's authority to reject agreements is, in fact, rarely employed. MEC officers serve on the ALPA Executive Board and Board of Directors, affording them considerable opportunity to influence the union's governance. Nor does the provision of staff and other resources appear to result in appreciable control being exerted over the MECs. Although contract administrators assigned to the MECs report to the International's Representation Department, they typically (at least at major carriers) provide services to a single MEC and have incentives to act more as MEC staff than as watchdogs of the International. Similarly, MEC budgets do not appear highly constraining, since cost overruns have been fairly routine.

ALPA MECs have very "pure" jurisdictions, representing the members of a single craft employed by a single carrier. This undoubtedly facilitates representation by providing MEC officers with a relatively narrow and homogenous set of interests to advance, but it also encourages an outlook in which the affairs and well-being of individual carriers become the paramount concern. This tendency is compounded by the importance of carrier-specific seniority in determining wages and working conditions and in curtailing the mobility of pilots (Kahn 1971: 566; Cappelli 1985: 332). The bargaining power of individual pilot groups, the identification of pilots with their "own" carriers, and the formal structure of ALPA all help ensure that MECs maintain substantial autonomy. The ability of the ALPA International to coordinate the activities of MECs closely, much less impose unwanted policies on them, is quite limited. Put differently, inclusion of most pilot groups within the formal structure of ALPA International is not, by itself, sufficient to ensure cohesion and coordination among pilots throughout the industry. It is striking that, despite the many accomplishments of his union, Henry A. Duffy, former president of ALPA International, conceded that

within the membership only a hazy awareness exists as to why a national union is necessary. At a time when most pilot energies have turned to coping with and solving deregulation-caused problems on individual properties, that the national perspective has been relegated to second position isn't surprising. Still, we must recognize that, to a degree, we have always been 'X' Airlines' pilots first and then members of ALPA (*Air Line Pilot*, Aug. 1988, 2).

Schisms along carrier lines have, in fact, been evident within ALPA. In the late 1980s, growing disparity in the financial status of carriers led to tensions between pilot groups employed by the "have" (e.g., Delta) and "have-not" (e.g., Pan Am) carriers. This split was partially cross-cut by a distinction between MECs that had been involved in recent conflicts with carriers (e.g., United) and those that had not (e.g., U.S. Air).

Tensions between ALPA pilot groups have been brought to the fore by several issues. One is the finances of the union. The "have" camp generally maintains that although it pays the lion's share of dues, it receives the least in return. Certainly, the major contingency fund expended large sums to support struggles at United, Continental, and Eastern, and some MECs consistently operated in the red during the 1980s (ALPA 1987: xiii, xv).

Another controversial matter is whether and for what reasons a nationwide suspension of service (SOS), in which all ALPA groups would engage in a job action in support of some cause, might be called. ALPA president Duffy was candid in acknowledging that the union had yet to prove that it could successfully employ this strategy: "While a certain romance surrounds the image of omnipotence in our being able to shut down the air transportation system, the truth is our past history in this area does not instill confidence" (*Air Line Pilot* Sept. 1989, 2). Assuming an SOS is feasible, the difficult problem remains of deciding which causes are sufficiently momentous to warrant its use. Again, as President Duffy has said:

> The possibility of using an SOS to settle a strike raises hopes and expectations in the minds of the striking pilots. The issue needs to be dealt with once and for all, for the tension has come close to tearing this association apart. Either an SOS is something that a striking pilot group can expect to be able to use as a weapon in a strike, or it isn't (*Air Line Pilot*, Sept. 1989, 2).

At various points in recent years, striking pilot groups at Continental, United, and Eastern each requested a nationwide SOS—and were rebuffed.

Few issues, however, have been more divisive than that of seniority list integration in carrier mergers. It is because location on the seniority list of a carrier affects so many facets of pilots' work lives and provides them with a clear sense of their standing relative to their peers in making a claim on the rewards of the profession that mergers requiring the reworking of seniority lists are enormously disruptive and threatening. "Have" pilot groups generally prefer the application of a formula in which greatest weight is placed on length of service with the surviving carrier, since their carriers are likely to be incorporating others and because they usually have experienced more rapid career advancement than pilots at carriers that are not growing. Mergers between Delta and Western, TWA and Ozark, and Northwest and Republic each entailed lengthy and often bitter negotiations between ALPA pilot groups over seniority list integration (*New York Times*, March 19, 1989, F-1). Despite calls for the creation of a single, nationwide pilot seniority list, only partial measures—including a first right-of-hire list (primarily applying to displacement caused by the sale of aircraft between carriers) and a pledge to negotiate for the preferential hiring (without retention of seniority) of pilots displaced through furloughs, bankruptcies, and strikes—have been achieved (*Air Line Pilot*, Jan. 1989, 34–6; Jan. 1987, 26).

In recent years, ALPA International has moved toward somewhat greater coordination and control of the MECs. ALPA's board of directors granted the executive board and executive committee greater leeway in making policy and interpreting ALPA's constitution (*Air Line Pilot*, Feb. 1988, 27). The major contingency fund was created with the stipulation that its use could be initiated only by the president or executive committee. There was a crackdown on excess expenditures by MECs (*Air Line Pilot*, Jan. 1989, 13), and changes were made in the procedures through which MECs procure the services of outside financial consultants and lawyers (*Air Line Pilot*, Feb. 1990, 32). The International has also employed various means to carry out its "Shared Vision Program," designed to "accentuate pilots' common identity in the association" (*Air Line Pilot*, Nov. 1988, 2). In the realm of bargaining, a tide of concession bargaining in the early 1980s, in which carriers successfully whipsawed individual pilot groups, prompted the International to promulgate guidelines for concession bargaining and to step up training of negotiators. Calls for "coordinated" or "pattern" bargaining have increasingly been voiced within ALPA (*Air Line Pilot*, April 1989, 34; Jan. 1989, 34). The Collective Bargaining Committee of ALPA is charged with the mission of investigating the possibilities for coordinated bargaining across carriers (*Air Line Pilot*, Jan. 1987, 36), and the "No B-Scale" Committee has the stated aim of eradicating two-tier wage provisions from ALPA contracts (*Air Line Pilot*, Jan. 1989, 34). Coordination of bargaining across MECs, however, is still far from being realized.

Efforts at exerting greater national-level control and coordination within ALPA, then, are an important part of the context shaping relations between ALPA MECs in recent years, but the fundamental autonomy of the MECs remains intact. Some of the tensions within ALPA became magnified by the challenge of dealing with the Eastern Airlines strike in 1989.

Federation Links between Airline Unions

The formal structuring of airline labor also includes a number of labor federations with which airline unions are affiliated. These federations potentially link airline unions to one another and to the larger labor movement, both nationally and internationally.

AFL-CIO

Most airline unions, at least at the national level, are affiliated with the primary labor federation in the United States, the AFL-CIO. In 1989, four unions that represent airline workers (IAM, IBT, TCU, AFA) had national officers who sat on the AFL-CIO Executive Council. Federation ties are less conspicuous at state and city levels. Of twenty-one subunits of AFL-CIO–affiliated national unions considered in this study, twelve (57 percent) reported that they were not connected to a state federation or local central body. Very likely, this reflects the fact that many of these subunits are intermediate bodies with jurisdictions not confined to single states or cities.

One vehicle within the AFL-CIO for promoting joint action by airline unions, particularly political action, is the Airline Coordinating Committee. Unions involved on a regular basis in the committee's activities include ALPA, AFA, the IAM, the IBT, FEIA, and the TWU. Meetings occur as needed and are attended by a combination of national officers, carrier-level officers, and, most often, staff from union and AFL-CIO legislative departments. Following the committee's deliberations, some combination of union personnel and staff of the AFL-CIO Legislative Department do the actual lobbying or testifying required. Exchanging views and positions appears to be the norm, rather than sharing actual testimony or drafting joint statements.

Several unions representing airline workers are also affiliated with the AFL-CIO's Industrial Union Department (IUD).[4] The IAM, IBT, and TWU are IUD affiliates, along with ALPA, which joined in 1988 (*Air Line Pilot*, Oct. 1988, 46). The activities of the IUD that are most distinct from those of AFL-CIO staff departments all have a patently inter-union focus: promotion of coordinated bargaining, joint organizing campaigns, and boycotts. The IUD's Jobs with Justice program was launched in 1987 with the broad aim of "mobilizing union members and community support in behalf of workers' rights" (AFL-CIO 1987). The program provides a network that can be drawn on to carry out a variety of activities, most often mass rallies and demonstrations. Thirteen IUD affiliates, including the IAM and TWU, were cited by the department as early and active participants in the program (*IUD Digest*, Oct. 1987, 1).

It is, of course, easier to identify formal federation ties than to discern the significance of those ties in producing inter-union coordination and unity. Certainly, the AFL-CIO is not the only, or under most circumstances the prime, locus for joint dealings between airline unions. Yet federation activities in the areas of limiting competition and handling disputes clearly affect airline unions, as does its coordination of legislative and legal activities. Mobilization of broad labor support for striking unions is another potential benefit of AFL-CIO affiliation, not often seen in the airline industry but central to the Eastern Airlines struggle.

International Federations

The International Transport Workers Federation (ITF) is one of eighteen international trade secretariats intended to coordinate the efforts of member unions in related trades or industries on an international level. In 1986, the ITF had about four hundred affiliate unions, located in ninety nations and representing more than four million transport workers (ITF 1986). ALPA, AFA, the IAM, the TWU, FEIA, and the TCU are among the U.S. unions that belong to the ITF. The federation's impact on inter-union relations stems from its occasional involvement in disputes between its U.S. affiliates and its support to striking unions. Although relatively little contact between U.S. airline unions involves ITF activities, the increasing globalization of the airline industry undoubtedly increases the ITF's relevance.

The same can be said for the International Federation of Airline Pilots Associations (IFALPA), representing some seventy thousand members in sixty-eight nations (*Air Line Pilot*, Sept. 1987, 20). ALPA, which is the only U.S. affiliate, has shown increasing interest in the affairs of IFALPA (*Air Line Pilot*, July 1989, 36). Traditionally, the federation placed primary emphasis on safety and flight operations issues, but the spread of deregulation world-wide has prompted IFALPA to become more concerned with industrial relations matters. A smaller federation of unions representing airline dispatchers, the International Federation of Airline Dispatcher Associations (IFALDA) also counts several U.S. affiliates among its members.

Labor Relations in the Airline Industry

That the U.S. airline industry is dynamic and has undergone profound changes in recent years hardly needs to be reiterated. Yet it is important to consider briefly, but explicitly, those facets of the changing character of the industry and its labor relations that have particular implications for inter-union relations. Even a cursory glimpse of the transformed and challenging environment airline unions faced in the late 1980s reveals that airline unions were contending with many difficult issues and had become increasingly interdependent.

Table 3-2 outlines significant developments in the airline industry in three periods: pre-1979, 1979–84, and 1985–90. These developments point to a relatively munificent preregulation era, to a period of intense upheaval in the immediate aftermath of deregulation, and to a somewhat more stable but transformed period in the second half of the 1980s. The turmoil of the early 1980s was replaced by a period of reconsolidation. There were mergers and acquisitions aplenty, and a small number of major carriers attained a collective market share in excess of their preregulation standing (Rosen 1988). With excess capacity and mounting carrier debt, however, making a buck in the airline industry continued to be difficult.

Chief among the interrelated set of problems or threats airline unions faced in the late 1980s, then, were financially troubled carriers, mergers and acquisitions, the prospect of permanent replacement in strikes, pressure for concessions, the activities of Texas Air Corporation, and adversity in political and regulatory forums. Airline unions were facing vastly increased pressure from carriers at a time when their political and regulatory support was also diminished. That airline union officers recognized this host of worri-

Table 3-2.   *Developments in the U.S. Airline Industry*

Pre-1979	1979–84	1985–90
1. Consistent growth in the demand for air travel	1. Deregulation is legislated (October 1978)	1. Reconsolidation of industry structure
2. Relative stability in industry structure	2. Inception and short-term success of some "new-entrant" carriers	2. Numerous mergers and acquisitions
3. Limited competition among carriers and minimal competitive pressure on labor costs	3. Fare wars among major carriers	3. Few "new-entrant" carriers remain
4. Relatively little differentiation in the financial circumstances of individual carriers	4. Severe recession and diminished demand for air transport (1981–83)	4. Resumption of trend of increasing demand for air travel
5. Carriers are largely protected from failure by the CAB	5. Poor financial performance by most carriers	5. Increased demand for pilots and mechanics
6. Labor protective provisions (LPPs) are stipulated as a condition for CAB approval of mergers or acquisitions	6. Employment threat is posed by bankruptcy, creation of alter-ego carriers, loss of market share, subcontracting	6. Increased sophistication in yield management techniques
7. Unions take initiative in bargaining, and substantial improvement from contract to contract is the rule	7. Growth of hub and spoke route systems	7. Consolidation of hub airports by major carriers
8. Unions look primarily to the same craft at other carriers in formulating bargaining demands and attempt to match or exceed those settlements	8. High turnover among top airline managers	8. Growth of interlining with regional and commuter carriers
9. Carriers usually do not attempt to operate during strikes	9. Widespread formation of airline holding companies	9. Indebtedness of many carriers sharply increases because of mergers and acquisitions
10. Until 1966, emergency boards are regularly appointed in airline strikes	10. Management seizes initiative in bargaining	10. Financially troubled carriers remain, with a growing gap between the have and have-not carriers
11. Airline unions enjoy considerable influence in both political and regulatory forums	11. Substantial concessions are demanded and received by carriers; quid pro quos sometimes negotiated	11. Largely nonunion Continental poses a serious threat to wages and employment at unionized carriers
	12. Carriers attempt to operate during strikes	12. Department of Transportation readily approves mergers; does not impose labor protective provisions as a condition
	13. Union political agenda is dominated by attempts to change bankruptcy laws and attempts to change bankruptcy laws and secure EPPs[a]	13. Management retains initiative in bargaining; continues to seek concessions
		14. Carriers attempt to operate during strikes; pretrain and hire permanent replacements
		15. Growing foreign ownership stake in U.S. carriers and increasing pressure for opening domestic market to foreign carriers
		16. Crowded union political and legal agenda, including random drug testing, FAR 145, emergency board in Eastern Airlines strike, Texas Air, LPPs, leveraged buyouts[b]

[a] EPPs are employee protective provisions under Section 43 of the Airline Deregulation Act of 1978. These provisions were intended to help individual employees deal with dislocation stemming from deregulation but were never fully implemented.

[b] These characterizations are drawn from multiple sources. Concerning the pre-1979 period, see Baitsell 1966; Kahn 1971, 1980; Northrup 1983; and Cappelli 1987. For the 1979–84 period, see Baily, Graham, and Kaplan 1985; Meyer et. al. 1981, 1984; Northrup 1983; Cappelli 1985; U.S. Civil Aeronautics Board 1984; *Air Line Pilot*, Jan. 1984: 10–11 (EPPs); *Air Line Pilot*, Aug. 1984: 24 (bankruptcy law); and *Daily Labor Report*, Nov. 22, 1985, A-8 (LPPs). For the 1985–90 period, major sources include James 1985; *Air Line Pilot*, May 1987; Rosen 1988; Cappelli 1988; *Air Transport World*, Aug. 1987: 48 (threat of Continental); *Air Transport World*, May 1986: 18 (mergers and acquisitions); *Air Line Pilot*, April 1986: 10 (management initiative in bargaining); *Air Line Pilot*, Feb. 1989: 31; *Air Transport World*, Nov. 1989: 24 (globalization, cabotage); *Air Transport World*, Dec. 1988: 58 (hubs); *Daily Labor Report*, June 29, 1989, A-7 (FAR 145); *Daily Labor Report*, March 16, 1988, E-1 (random drug testing); *Daily Labor Report*, Feb. 22, 1989 (emergency board); and *New York Times*, Nov. 3, 1988 (Texas Air).

some problems in the late 1980s is evident from the summary of their views in table 3-3.

Sources of Increased Union Interdependence

Mergers and Acquisitions

Mergers and acquisitions have reshaped the structure of the airline industry, the ownership of carriers, and the pattern of union representation. Although mergers and acquisitions have occurred in significant numbers throughout the history of the U.S. airline industry, the wave of transactions beginning in the late 1970s and reaching tidal proportion in the second half of the 1980s was unparalleled (Rosen 1988: 30; *Air Line Pilot,* May 1987). Major transactions finalized between 1987 and 1990 included the Delta-Western merger (April 1987), the American–Air Cal merger (July 1987), the Alaska–Jet

Table 3-3.   Airline Union Officers' Views of the Serious Problems or Threats Facing Their Unions, 1989 (N = 33)

	n	Percentage
Merger or acquisition of carrier[a]	27	81.8
Granting to foreign carriers increased access to domestic markets (cabotage)	21	63.6
Mismanagement of carrier	21	63.6
Imposition of random drug testing	20	60.6
Lack of statutory or regulatory protection in mergers (LPPs)	19	57.5
Carrier at which members are employed is financially troubled	18	54.5
Carrier demands for givebacks/concessions	18	54.5
Subcontracting of bargaining unit work	17	51.5
Permanent replacements in strike situations	17	51.5
Government not sufficiently concerned with safety	17	51.5
Absence of economic regulation of the airline industry	17	51.5
Spread of concessions across carriers	15	45.4
Disinvestment in carrier or sale of assets	15	45.4
Creation or purchase of a nonunion subsidiary by carrier	13	39.4
Inability to wield sufficient bargaining power	13	39.4
Existence of nonunion or largely nonunion carriers in the industry	11	33.3
Carrier not sufficiently concerned with safety	9	27.3
Inadequate recognition of the professional status of members	7	21.2
Other problems or threats[b]	7	21.2

[a] Percentage of respondents indicating this answer in response to the following question: "Which of the following do you regard as a *serious problem or threat* to your union? (indicate as many as apply)" (see appendix 1, item 26). The total number of problems or threats cited was 295, an average of 8.9 per respondent.

[b] The "other problems or threats" cited were the following: internal divisions within a union following a merger of carriers; technological displacement; Reagan court appointees; judicial and executive branch bias in favor of business; terrorism; failure of the courts and National Mediation Board to respect contractual LPPs; increasing foreign ownership stake in U.S. carriers; dominance of finance people within airline management; and low labor cost unionized carriers such as Braniff.

America merger (October 1987), U.S. Air's mergers with PSA (April 1988) and Piedmont (August 1989), the Federal Express–Flying Tiger merger (August 1989), and the acquisition of Northwest (September 1989).[5] The same period also saw serious, though unsuccessful, attempts by unions at Eastern (*Air Line Pilot*, May 1989, 36–39), Pan Am (*New York Times*, Nov. 25, 1987, D-3), and United (*New York Times*, Sept. 19, 1989, D-1) to buy out and/or locate new owners for those carriers. Additionally, several major transactions took place just before 1987 and continued to influence inter-union relations during the period on which this study focuses. These deals included the acquisition of Eastern by Texas Air Corporation (February 1986), the merger of Northwest and Republic (August 1986), and the merger of TWA and Ozark (October 1986). Concern over the effects of mergers or acquisitions easily topped the list of union officers' worries (see table 3-3), being cited as a serious problem by 82 percent of respondents.

Clearly, mergers and acquisitions are significant events of which the airline industry has seen more than its share in recent years. But what is the connection between merger activity and inter-union relations? One probable link is an increase in competition and conflict among unions. When carriers merge, the same national union does not always represent the same craft at both carriers. Long-settled representational rights can suddenly be thrown open to contest. Even when the same national union represents workers at both carriers, negotiations between affiliates over issues such as seniority list integration are apt to be highly contentious, as evidenced by the experience of ALPA. Conflicts between formerly separate unions are often perpetuated as rifts within merged units.

The prevalence of mergers also creates fundamental uncertainty for airline unions and heightens their need for timely and reliable information. Few unions could rest assured that the carrier employing their members would continue to operate in the same form, under the same ownership, and without the addition of crippling debt. This threat pervaded the industry in the latter 1980s but most directly linked the concerns of unions representing workers at the same carrier. Sometimes, of course, mergers and acquisitions are sought by unions. Whether wanted or unwanted, the fact that these transactions are in the works may require unions to join together in negotiating with prospective buyers or investors, in securing financial advice, and in deciding whether concessions should be promised and how any sacrifices will be distributed among employee groups.

Permanent Replacements in Strikes

The capacity to strike successfully, or at least mount a credible threat thereof, largely determines the bargaining power of unions. Though operating during strikes was relatively rare in the period before deregulation, doing so has become the norm since then. Hence, a review of strike activity between 1970 and 1979 shows that carriers ceased operations in twenty-five instances (64 percent) and continued to fly in only three cases (8 percent), while evidence could not be found regarding an additional eleven (28 percent) strikes.[6] In contrast, carriers attempted to operate in twelve of the fourteen strikes (86 percent) that occurred between 1980 and 1986.

Like firms in other industries, then, air carriers have increasingly used strike replacements, both temporary and permanent, and these personnel are sometimes recruited and trained before a strike is even called (Cappelli 1988: 54). The practice of using permanent replacements escalates the potential costs of a failed strike, from an inability to obtain desired bargaining outcomes and loss of income to loss of employment and the elimination of union representation. Recent court decisions are likely to further encourage carriers to operate during strikes.[7]

Confronted with the willingness of carriers to hire permanent replacements and operate during strikes, a premium is placed on inter-union support in strike or potential strike situations. This is especially the case for groups of workers whose skills are more widely available in the labor market and for whom replacements can quickly be brought into service (Lefer 1987). Vicki Frankovich, president of the Independent Federation of Flight Attendants and no stranger to the reality of permanent replacement, having faced it in a 1986 strike at TWA, observed:

> We now understand the importance of reaching out to help others, attending rallies, offering to help picket, etc., many things we, as flight attendants, never really did before. . . . In our case, the company [TWA] used no sympathy strike agreements and injunctions to divide the different unions on our property. It forced us to fight alone—obviously a very difficult position to be in (*Flightlog*, Spring 1988, 14).

The data in table 3-3 suggest that concern over the use of permanent replacements in strikes was fairly widespread among airline union officers (a "serious" threat for 52 percent of respondents), even as they were less apt to perceive insufficient bargaining power to be a problem (only 39 percent of respondents did).

Not all inter-union strike support is equally valuable, however. Although bargaining power is complex and variable, pilots and mechanics generally enjoy the greatest bargaining leverage among groups of airline workers (Cappelli 1985: 332–34; Kahn 1971: 500). Thus, obtaining the support of pilots and mechanics, whose skill and favorable labor market conditions make them critical to airline operations and relatively difficult to replace, has become particularly important.

Financially Troubled Carriers

Financial problems plagued numerous carriers throughout the 1980s. Although it can be arbitrary to designate some carriers as "financially troubled" and others as not, carriers such as Continental, Eastern, and Pan Am qualified handily for that label. From 1987 to 1990, these carriers were seriously in debt by any conventional measure, and they generally failed to produce a return on equity (ROE) or to maintain a positive cash flow.[8] Concern for the financial well-being of carriers extends beyond the most financially debilitated carriers, however. More than half (55 percent) of the union officers interviewed regarded the carrier at which their members were employed as financially troubled. The large debts assumed by some carriers in mergers and acquisitions was very much on the minds of these union officers.

Financial troubles lie beneath or compound many of the other problems facing airline unions. They present a shared problem for all the unions representing a carrier's work force, as the continued employment of each union's members hangs in the balance. A decision by one union at a financially struggling carrier to go on strike directly affects other unions if a consequence of that decision is that the financial situation of the carrier is worsened. Similarly, unions might be pressed to provide jointly a large amount in concessions to keep a carrier viable. Sometimes unions at financially ailing carriers are also in the position of proposing alternative business plans and/or seeking new owners for airlines. Such initiatives have a far better chance of succeeding if the major unions at the carrier are in accord.

Competitive Pressures and the Spread of Concessions

Contract terms negotiated by a craft at one carrier have always mattered to unions representing that craft at other carriers (Kahn 1971: 496). But political pressure on union negotiators to match or exceed gains made elsewhere is quite different from being whipsawed by carriers to make concessions as or more extreme than those negotiated at other carriers. The rapid proliferation of two-tier wage structures in the mid-1980s provides a good example of how quickly concessionary terms can spread throughout the airline industry (Walsh 1988). Peter Cappelli's (1985, 1987) cogent analysis of the decline of union bargaining power in the airline industry centers on this interdependence in bargaining outcomes. The decentralized, craft-based bargaining structure that was developed during a period of regulatory protection and that previously favored airline unions has become a liability, making it difficult to take labor costs out of competition and to resist matching concessions rendered elsewhere. The penalty for holding out against concessions can be loss of employment, since a labor cost edge gained by one carrier can now be used, via lower fares or other incentives, to win passengers away from carriers with higher labor costs. Cappelli (1988: 52) also emphasizes the importance of the early concessions won at the financially weak (but unionized) major carriers such as Pan Am and Braniff, as opposed to the competition from the "new-entrant" carriers, in generating the concessionary spiral in the industry.

Widespread concession bargaining in the airline industry during the first half of the 1980s has been well documented (Cappelli 1985; Nay 1991). At financially troubled carriers such as Pan Am and Eastern, management aggressively continued to pursue large-scale concessions thereafter. The sizable percentage (45 percent) of the union officers interviewed in 1989 who indicated that their apprehensions about carrier concession demands had not abated (see table 3-3) also speaks to the continuing pressure to render concessions. Concession bargaining in the airline industry is not a phenomenon that occurred in the immediate aftermath of deregulation and then disappeared. Even unions at more financially successful carriers were pressed to restrain bargaining demands or make further concessions. The bargaining climate in the late 1980s was perhaps best summed up by ALPA secretary Larry Schulte: "There is still a downward pressure on labor costs. Even though we make advances in contracts, that pressure remains (*Air Line Pilot*, Dec. 1989, 17).

Under these circumstances, information about what is being negotiated by other unions becomes particularly important. Some mechanism for "taking wages out of competition," or at least limiting that competition, is imperative (Moody 1987b). Formal change in the industry bargaining structure, such as toward multicarrier bargaining at the national union level, is an obvious, but improbable, option. Other mechanisms for coordinating bargaining—including sharing information, jointly devising strategy and proposals, establishing common contract expiration dates, and providing strike support—may be more readily attainable. Whatever the response, if any, to concessionary pressures, they represent yet another aspect of the airline industry context that links the fates of airline unions and calls for inter-union measures.

Frank Lorenzo and Texas Air Corporation

The name of Frank Lorenzo is virtually synonymous with all that is anathema to airline unions. Lorenzo and Texas Air Corporation authored some of the most egregious threats faced by airline unions in the 1980s.[9] An abbreviated listing of these affronts includes the following: a hostile takeover of Texas International in 1981 in which a buyout bid by the pilots was foiled (*Air Line Pilot*, Nov. 1983, 10); creation of nonunion alter-ego carrier New York Air (*Air Line Pilot*, Feb. 1981, 8); immediate contracting out of IAM work during its 1983 strike at Continental; declaration of bankruptcy at Continental in 1983 and abrogation of labor contracts (*Air Line Pilot*, Nov. 1983, 10–11); breaking of strikes by ALPA, UFA, and the IAM at Continental and refusal to recognize ALPA and the IAM despite their legal status as representatives (*Air Line Pilot*, Dec. 1988, 14–17); purchase of Eastern at a below-market price, once again over attempts by unions to arrange a buyout; disinvestment in Eastern, sale of assets, and exploitation of Eastern in financial dealings with Texas Air (*Air Line Pilot*, July 1989, 34–36; *New York Times*, March 2, 1990, 1); attempts to invalidate the ALPA contract at

Eastern; immediate and sweeping demands for concessions from the IAM (*New York Times*, March 8, 1989, B-5); a crackdown on workers at Eastern, including firings and disciplinary actions (*New York Times*, May 26, 1987, D-1); falsification of safety records and ignoring of necessary aircraft repairs by Eastern managers (*New York Times*, July 26, 1990, 1); and a second trip to bankruptcy court during the 1989 strike at Eastern, along with the hiring of permanent replacements (*New York Times*, March 10, 1989, 1).

Even a capsule description of the activities of Lorenzo and Texas Air conveys the gravity and breadth of the threat posed. Although these actions impinged most directly on the unions representing workers at Eastern and Continental, the harmful precedent that would be set by successful use of these tactics, as well as the increased downward pressure on wages throughout the industry, stood to affect airline unions much more broadly. Of innumerable statements by labor leaders attesting to the larger significance of the struggle with Texas Air, the following were typical:

> Frank Lorenzo's style of employee relations is a cancer that must be stopped at Eastern or it will spread to virtually every industry in the nation (IAM president George Kourpias, in *Daily Labor Report*, Dec. 1, 1989, A-6).

> For as certainly as there will be a dawn, we will be "next" if Frank Lorenzo succeeds in breaking the spirit of life at Eastern and in creating a robot-like workforce. In quick order, Lorenzo's work scales would be demanded by other chief executive officers using Lorenzo's tactics (ALPA president Henry A. Duffy, in *Air Line Pilot*, Summer 1989, 1).

Allowing for the rhetorical excess that inevitably surrounds such events, the depth of concern over the activities of Lorenzo and Texas Air, and the extent to which broad ramifications were seen, is still unusual. More than any other situation confronting airline labor in the late 1980s, the anti-union campaign of Frank Lorenzo afforded a potential basis for resolute and widely inclusive inter-union cooperation to deal with a serious problem.

Adversity in Political and Regulatory Arenas

The airline industry "grew up" with close governmental involvement (Baitsell 1966: 36). Gains made in the political and regulatory arenas have long been critical to the success of airline unions, especially ALPA (Kahn 1971: 461). The significance of politics for airline unions has not waned with the advent of deregulation (itself a political decision). Although the CAB is gone, public policy decisions remain critical to the industry and its workers. Safety, the operation of airports, and international air travel are three of the most obvious areas in which the government's role has been largely sustained (and in some respects expanded) in the wake of deregulation. Other key decisions, such as the appointment of emergency boards, the imposition of labor protective provisions, and the approval of mergers, also remain within the government's domain. That government officials in the 1980s regularly chose not to exercise authority affirmatively in these areas speaks not to the irrelevance of policy decisions but to a lack of concern for the interests of airline workers and greater adversity for airline unions as they attempt to advance those interests in political and regulatory forums. Nor can the political realm be neatly separated from union bargaining activities; the two are intimately intertwined (Cohen 1990).

In the late 1980s, the political agenda of airline unions was crowded and victories hard to come by. A plethora of issues surrounding Texas Air provided one major focus for political and legal activity. Other matters loomed large, however, including duty time regulations for flight attendants, FAR 145 (a Federal Aviation Administration [FAA] regulation that greatly expanded the ability of carriers to have maintenance work performed overseas), closer regulation of leveraged buyouts in the airline industry, foreign ownership shares and operation in the U.S. domestic market, and random drug testing. Random drug testing and cabotage (allowing foreign carriers increased access to routes within the United States) were each cited by more than 60 percent of the union officers interviewed as serious problems facing their unions. ALPA, in fact, takes such a dim view of cabotage that its board of directors voted in 1986 (and reaffirmed in 1988) that a policy shift in this direction would warrant a nationwide suspension of service by pilots.

Thus, numerous political and regulatory issues affecting a wide cross-section of airline unions were at stake in the late 1980s. The status of these issues as shared problems and the prevailing lack of receptiveness to union concerns in the political arena again suggest both a foundation and a need for broad-based inter-union political activity.

Conclusion

The relatively decentralized, craft-based representational structure of the U.S. airline industry has several basic implications for inter-union relations. Unity for airline labor necessarily involves ties extending across the boundaries of numerous unions, including carrier-level affiliates of national unions. Craft and carrier constitute the basic domains that bound the immediate concerns and interests of airline unions. The diversity of airline unions, in terms of such characteristics as their size, bargaining power, financial resources, status attached to members' work, organizational affiliations, and extent of involvement with the airline industry, is substantial. ALPA and the IAM stand out as unions with substantial resources and capabilities, enabling them to play (and sometimes contend for) the leading role among airline unions.

Although the representational structure of the airline industry determines which inter-union ties are possible, the environment within which airline unions operate shapes the need for such ties. The airline industry throughout the 1980s was marked by far greater threat to the effectiveness and existence of airline unions than in earlier periods. Aggressive strikebreaking, continuing pressure for concessions, numerous mergers and acquisitions (leaving carriers heavily in debt or with new owners whose intentions were suspect), the activities of Texas Air Corporation, and obstacles to success in traditionally important political and regulatory arenas all formed the backdrop for relations between airline unions in the period on which this study focuses.

Under these circumstances, airline unions experienced an increased need for support and resources from other unions, were subjected to common threats, and were affected by one another's actions (or inaction). In short, airline unions had become more interdependent. How they responded to this increased interdependence is the focus of the rest of this study.

Chapter 4

Inter-Union Relations
in Historical Perspective

T he airline industry and its labor relations have changed substantially over time. What about inter-union relations? Has the growing interdependence among airline unions prompted more widespread and intensive inter-union activity? The historical material in this chapter addresses this question for the period before 1987 and provides a useful baseline against which more recent inter-union activity can be compared. Overall, the historical evidence lends credibility to the notion that increased interdependence has led airline unions to form closer ties. Yet, even more so, the historical record makes it clear that as airline labor entered the late 1980s, it did so lacking any substantial tradition of inter-union support and cooperation on which to draw.

Organizational affiliations and disaffiliations, jurisdictional conflicts, competition for members, strike support, joint action, and coalition formation have been among the most interesting and consequential relations linking airline unions over the years. I consider each of these in turn.

Organizational Affiliations and Disaffiliations

ALPA and Its Affiliate Unions

At its 1944 board of directors meeting, the Air Line Pilots Association decided to create a number of affiliate unions that would represent, on a craft basis, all of the major crafts in the industry. Hence, over a period of several years, ALPA formed the Air Line Stewards and Stewardesses Association (ALSSA), the Air Carriers Mechanics Association (ACMA), the Air Line Agents Association (ALAA), the Air Carriers Flight Engineers Association (ACFEA), and the Air Carriers Communication Employees Association

(ACCEA) (Mason 1961: 235). Creation of the affiliate organizations was part of a broader scheme envisioned by ALPA in which all workers in each craft or class would be represented by a single national (industrywide) craft union. Following the model of the railroad industry, these national craft unions would be linked through participation in an "airline labor executives association," which would coordinate political action and decide policy matters (Kahn 1950: 307).

The ALPA Education and Organizing Department was charged with establishing the affiliates and attempted to propagate ALPA's vision of the optimal representational structure for the industry. In a telling statement, a longtime president of ALPA, David Behncke, was quoted as describing the function of the department as "'steering other organizations into sane and sensible bargaining channels'" (Kahn 1950: 309). Sanity and sensibility, in this case, referred to curtailing organization by militant industrial unions and installing a set of organizations likely to be more compliant with ALPA (Kahn 1950: 309; Nielsen 1982: 38).

Not surprisingly, ALPA's efforts were construed as the creation of a network of rival unions to encroach on the jurisdictions of established unions and prompted considerable competition and conflict. A 1946 TWU organizing pamphlet described ALPA affiliate ACMA as follows: "It is only the toy of a few Pilots who are laboring under the notion that they can hold on to their own wages by helping the companies keep down the wages of maintenance workers and other personnel" (*We Choose TWU* [1946], quoted in Kahn 1950: 285). Arguments of this sort were apparently convincing to workers because few of the ALPA affiliates enjoyed anything more than short-term success and most had disbanded by the early to mid-1950s (Kahn 1950: 309; U.S. NMB annual reports, 1946–55).

Although ALPA's grand design for the representation of airline employees was never realized, formulation of the plan was an early indication that ALPA would not be shy about assuming a dominant role in the industry or about promoting what it perceived to be pilots' interests, even when conflict with other unions was the likely outcome. One former ALPA affiliate, the Air Line Agents Association, changed its name to the Air Line Employees Association in 1965 and continues to operate (albeit marginally because of severe membership losses). It was ALPA's attempts to organize flight attendants, however, and place them in various affiliate organizations that enjoyed the most success and that had the greatest long-term impact on the structure of union representation in the industry.

ALPA, TWU, and the Flight Attendant Unions

Flight attendants organized their first union in 1945 at United Airlines (Nielsen 1982: 3). The unaffiliated Association of Air Line Stewardesses (AALS) (shortly thereafter changed to Air Line Stewardesses Association

[ALSA]) quickly found itself surrounded by flight attendant groups organized by ALPA's affiliate ALSSA, and at Pan Am, by the TWU. An unaffiliated flight attendant union faced severe obstacles at that time. Because of its members' low wages and relatively small numbers, ALSA was chronically short of funds and scarcely able to bear the cost of handling grievances. Largely because of its financial exigencies, ALSA merged with ALSSA in 1949.

The marriage between ALPA and its flight attendant affiliate, ALSSA, was stormy, marked by persistent struggles over the flight attendants' autonomy. The relationship culminated with all of ALSSA disaffiliating from ALPA and joining the TWU in 1961 (Nielsen 1982: 75–76). ALPA responded to this turn of events by creating another entity—the Stewards and Stewardesses Division, which immediately sought to regain representation rights from the now-TWU-affiliated ALSSA and was quite successful in doing so.

In 1973, the Stewards and Stewardesses Division of ALPA was made the Association of Flight Attendants, which became an "autonomous affiliate" in 1976. As of 1984, AFA had severed all formal ties with ALPA and had received its own AFL-CIO charter (Gifford 1984: 20). Flight attendants within the TWU were a little more satisfied with their subordinate status, but rather than join with AFA, which was perceived by some as too closely allied with ALPA, they formed several independent flight attendant unions in the mid-1970s (Nielsen 1982: 133).

The history of flight attendant unions, then, has been one of inclusion within male-dominated unions on a subordinate basis, struggles to obtain greater autonomy, and, eventually, the formation of numerous separate organizations. All current flight attendant unions have roots within ALPA and/or the TWU. This history has led to the relatively fragmented representation of flight attendants and an understandable sensitivity to issues of union autonomy. Unfortunately, autonomy is not only compromised by inclusion within subordinate organizations. Many flight attendant unions were just negotiating their first contracts as truly separate entities when deregulation occurred in 1978. Changes since then have arguably conspired to render their fragmentation a greater liability and to make flight attendant unions dependent once again on the likes of ALPA and the IAM—not for operating funds but for resources such as strike support and political clout. To the extent that this is true, the dialectic of autonomy and dependence that has long marked flight attendant unionism continues to be played out. Only now, this dialectic occurs in a more subtle form and on inter-union, rather than intra-union, terrain.

Disaffiliation of American Airlines Pilots from ALPA

Schisms have occurred among the pilot groups within ALPA as well. The disaffiliation of American Airlines pilots from ALPA and their formation of an independent union stands as an important example. Personal animosity between MEC chairman C. E. Gene Seal and ALPA International president Clarence Sayen, the denial of strike benefits to American pilots in 1958 under a newly promulgated ALPA policy, and sympathy on the part of American's pilots for flight engineers (see the discussion of the "crew complement" conflict below) had all served to heighten tensions between American Airlines pilots and ALPA International in the late 1950s. Matters came to a head when the American MEC signed a collective bargaining agreement that violated the ALPA crew complement policy by not requiring that existing flight engineers be retrained as pilots (Hopkins 1982: 226–38). Attempts by the ALPA International to nullify this agreement led to the American pilots disaffiliating from ALPA and forming an independent union, the Allied Pilots Association (Kahn 1971: 525).

The management of American Airlines was suspected of having a hand in fostering the breakup. George Hopkins (1982: 230) suggests, for example, that dissidents were given highly favorable work schedules, allowing them to conduct an effective disaffiliation campaign among pilots. Certainly, in its attempt to halt the disaffiliation by legal means, ALPA maintained that American Airlines' management had induced the pilots to leave and form a rival organization (*Daily Labor Report*, Feb. 17, 1964, A-17). Whatever its merits, however, the claim of carrier interference was ultimately to no avail and American's pilots remain the most significant exception to the industrywide representation of pilots by ALPA.

The case of the pilots at American is instructive. Whatever American's true role, it illustrates the potential for carriers to insert themselves into conflicts between unions (if not provoke them). More important, the American pilots' disaffiliation shows the limits of central authority within ALPA and the delicate balancing act that is required to accommodate the particular interests of pilots' groups at each carrier. The American Airlines disaffiliation occurred decades ago and has not been followed by other defections to date. But the breaking away of American's pilots continues to serve as a reminder of the substantial autonomy and relatively limited horizons of many pilot groups.

Jurisdictional Conflict and Competition

The Crew Complement Dispute

ALPA was again a central player in a protracted, often bitter struggle with the Flight Engineers International Association (FEIA) over who would occupy the third seat in the cockpit of the jet aircraft first introduced in the late 1950s. This complicated jurisdictional dispute spanned more than a decade and spilled over into labor-management relations on numerous occasions. Use of a three-person crew had been mandated on some larger planes before the advent of jets, but precise requirements for the training and background of the third crew member were never established. Consequently, some carriers used pilot-trained second officers, while others employed mechanic-trained flight engineers (Kahn 1971: 520). ALPA successfully campaigned for a three-person crew on all jets and then sought to ensure, through demands made in bargaining with carriers, that the third crew member be pilot-trained. The FEIA took the opposite position, maintaining that pilot certification should *not* be mandatory and that a mechanic's license was the requisite qualification. Fundamentally, the issue was whether all cockpit crew would be represented by a single union. Both unions pressed their contradictory demands in negotiations with carriers, resulting in several strikes in the latter half of the 1950s and leading some carriers to adopt four-member crews as a compromise (*Air Line Pilot*, Aug. 1961, 17).

When ALPA successfully petitioned the NMB to have its bargaining unit at United redrawn to include the second officer/flight engineer position, the gauntlet was thrown down and the flight engineers responded with a seven-carrier wildcat strike in February 1961. This strike, and the evident safety hazards emanating from the conflict between the pilots and flight engineers, led to the appointment of the Feinsinger Commission. On the core issue, the commission decided in ALPA's favor by maintaining that the third crew member in the cockpit should be trained as a pilot. The commission also echoed the AFL-CIO in calling for a merger of the two unions, stating that "neither peace nor safety on the airlines will be fully assured as long as there are two unions in the cockpit" (text of commission's report, reprinted in *Air Line Pilot*, June 1961, 19).

Throughout the conflict, FEIA sought the protection of the AFL and AFL-CIO, charging ALPA with encroaching on its jurisdiction (*Flight Engineer*, Feb. 1954, 1; June 1957, 1). Although FEIA eventually succeeded in having sanctions imposed against ALPA (*Daily Labor Report*, April 29, 1964, A-17), the principal recommendation of the federation throughout was to merge. The International Transport Workers Federation, by contrast, expelled ALPA in 1958 for violating FEIA's jurisdiction (*Daily Labor Report*, May 16, 1962, A-7). Although the Feinsinger Commission's report did not immediately end the conflict (it is doubtful that it is "over" today—it simply is no longer important because of the minimal presence of FEIA in the industry), the commission ratified the inevitable. Under continuing AFL-CIO pressure, ALPA and the FEIA entered into an agreement in 1978 to cease threats to each other's jurisdictions and to discuss the possibility of a merger (*Daily Labor Report*, Jan. 26, 1978, A5–7). That merger, however, has not been forthcoming.

Competition among Airline Unions

The foregoing is sufficient to show that there have been instances of intense competition between airline unions over members, especially when representation rights were not yet well established or when technological change played havoc with established jurisdictions. Kahn suggests that competition between airline unions has prevailed more generally: "Rival unionism has been a common phenomenon within many 'crafts or classes' and persists today as a factor affecting union behavior in collective bargaining" (1977: 109).

Competition among unions occurs in three basic situations: when one union attempts to remove the other as representative of a particular group of workers (raiding); when two or more unions contend for the right to represent a currently unorganized group of workers (multi-union election); and when a corporate merger places two or more unions into a contest for representation of a merged unit. It appears that obtaining members the "old-fashioned way," by raiding, has been an attractive option for airline unions. Joseph Krislov (1988: 244) concluded from his analysis of Railway Labor Act representation elections between 1955 and 1984 that "unions in the railroad and airline industries are active in efforts to displace an incumbent union as the bargaining agent, i.e. raiding." Airline unions have been adept as well as active at raiding, supplanting the incumbent union in 76 percent of elections between 1955 and 1984 (Krislov 1988: 245).

Data on airline representation elections for the period 1970–86 reinforce Krislov's more general findings.[1] Of fifty-nine representation elections between 1970 and 1986 *in which more than one union participated,* forty-four (75 percent) involved raids, twelve (20 percent) stemmed from carrier mergers, and only three (5 percent) concerned previously unorganized units. Almost all (ten) of the representation elections held in conjunction with carrier mergers occurred since 1979, suggesting that corporate mergers had become increasingly important in precipitating competition among airline unions. The IBT was a party to no less than thirty-three (75 percent) of the raids during this period. The other prime competitor for already organized bargaining units was the IAM, which was involved in nineteen raids between 1970 and 1986, many of them contests with the IBT. Virtually all the raids took place between AFL-CIO affiliates and independent unions.[2] The number of units transferred between unions under competitive circumstances is shown in table 4-1.

What conclusions can be drawn regarding competition among airline unions before 1987? The available data suggest that it was relatively commonplace and that it most often took the form of raiding. The implications of this finding for inter-unions relations more recently are not straightforward, however. First, although competition occurred, it hardly amounted to a free-for-all. Instead, the competition was fairly structured, especially along the lines of craft and AFL-CIO affiliation. Given the IBT's reaffiliation with the AFL-CIO in 1987, the threat of raids on established units has diminished. Second, some of the most virulent competition and conflict occurred in earlier years when the structure of union representation was not

Table 4-1. Units Gained and Lost under Competitive Circumstances, 1970–86

		Units Lost								
Units Gained	ALPA	FEIA	AFA	IAM	IBT	TWU	ALEA	TCU	Other	Total
ALPA	—	N.E.ᵃ	N.E.	N.E.	6	1	N.E.	1	0	8
FEIA	N.E.	—	N.E.	N.E.	N.E.	N.E.	N.E.	N.E.	N.E.	0
AFA	N.E.	N.E.	—	N.E.	2	1	N.E.	N.E.	0	3
IAM	N.E.	N.E.	N.E.	—	12	0	2	N.E.	1	15
IBT	2	N.E.	3	10	—	1	4	N.E.	1	21
TWU	1	N.E.	1	2	0	—	N.E.	1	0	5
ALEA	N.E.	N.E.	N.E.	0	0	0	—	0	N.E.	0
TCU	N.E.	N.E.	N.E.	N.E.	N.E.	0	1	—	N.E.	1
Other	2	N.E.	2	0	0	4	N.E.	N.E.	N.E.	8
Total	5	0	6	12	20	7	7	2	2	61

Source: U.S. National Mediation Board, Determinations of the National Mediation Board, vols. 5–13.

Note: Table is read as follows: row entries indicate the number of elections that the union in that row *won* from the union in each column. The figures include raids, multi-union elections, and merger-related elections. The "other" category includes APA, APFA, UFA, IUFA, and IFFA. The total number of bargaining units transferred (61) is greater than the number of elections (59) because two elections involved more than two unions.

ᵃ N.E. = No election in which these unions competed.

clearly established and major technological change was afoot. Neither of these conditions pertains now. Third, to the extent that competition stemming from carrier mergers has become increasingly prevalent, competition in recent years may have become less predictable, while the stakes (large, established units in jeopardy) are higher.

Support in Strikes

Support in strikes is one of the most meaningful forms of inter-union activity. Genuine strike support entails real costs and risks for the supporting unions but also has the potential to alter labor relations outcomes. A number of writers have commented on the very limited support from airline unions in strike situations. Cappelli has written that "unions in air transport have historically offered each other little cooperation, in particular, by routinely crossing one another's picket lines" (1987: 171). Similarly, Charles Craypo has observed that "airline unions have not normally cooperated with one another. Their independent bargaining power made cooperation unnecessary, and law and contract prohibitions made it illegal to conduct sympathetic job actions in support of other airline unions" (1986: 117).

The data presented in the previous chapter showed that the most common scenario prior to 1979 was for a struck carrier to shut down, rendering the question of inter-union strike support moot. This places the issue of noncooperation in a somewhat different light, pointing more to prior lack of necessity than to unwillingness on the part of airline unions. However, there were several "early" (prior to 1979) strikes in which carriers either deviated from the standard script of ceasing to operate or in which larger issues were involved for labor. Examining the record of inter-union strike support in these early strikes and in a number of strikes during the 1980s throws further light on the availability of strike support in the airline industry. Against the general backdrop of limited need for strike support prior to deregulation, the actions of airline unions have been somewhat more varied than generalizations about nonsupport might allow.

Early Strikes

The National Airlines strike of 1948 was the first protracted strike in the industry and also the first serious attempt by a carrier to operate with replacements (Kahn 1952: 11). The strike was actually two strikes: an initial six-month walkout by the IAM and a subsequent nine-month strike by ALPA. IAM office and clerical workers struck the carrier, and their picket lines were respected by IAM mechanics at National. Shortly thereafter, over an unrelated issue, ALPA pilots also went out. Kahn (1950: 339) is emphatic that "in no sense was the ALPA's action a sympathy strike." National accepted the recommendations of a presidential emergency board regarding the IAM but rejected them concerning its dispute with ALPA. The carrier was reasonably successful in maintaining operations with replacement pilots but eventually settled because of intense political pressure in the form of a threatened CAB investigation of National's fitness to operate (Kahn 1952: 24).

The Southern Airways strike of 1960, mentioned in the introduction to this book, was another early and significant conflict involving ALPA. The Southern strike had much in common with the National Airlines struggle. Both strikes featured staunchly anti-union managements, carriers that operated successfully with replacements, and outcomes largely decided in the political arena. In contrast to the National strike, however, inter-union solidarity played a prominent role in the successful resolution of the Southern Airways conflict.

Following a successful campaign in 1958 to break the mechanic's union, Southern Airways president Frank W. Hulse reportedly set out to provoke a strike with ALPA in order to replace the unionized pilots (Hopkins 1982: 187). That confrontation began in June 1960 and lasted for almost two years. The outcome of the strike stood to affect ALPA's position at other regional carriers, and there was speculation that Hulse enjoyed their covert support in taking on ALPA (Hopkins 1982: 191). The pilots ultimately won out through the use of a large purchase of Southern's stock to exert pressure on management and by obtaining a favorable CAB (by then replete with Kennedy appointees) decision to cease subsidies to the carrier, overturning an earlier adverse decision.

The level of inter-union support in the Southern Airways strike surpassed that of any airline strike before and many since then. Support was not quick in coming, however. ALPA's publication *Air Line Pilot* made no mention of the strike until early 1962, more than a year and a half after it had started. On January 22, 1962, some five thousand ALPA pilots from forty-seven carriers gathered at twenty-three airports to engage in informational picketing designed to draw government and public attention to the situation at Southern (*Air Line Pilot*, Feb. 1962, 25). The action, although lasting only one day, carried out by off-duty pilots, and apparently initiated at the rank-and-file level, was unprecedented. Support from the AFL-CIO and its affiliates was also more conspicuous than in the past, especially at the state and city levels. George E. Hopkins (1982: 196) refers to the initiation of a "Labor Contact Program" through which "practically every labor organization in America except the Teamsters had applied pressure in support of the SOU [Southern] strikers." Hopkins's claim regarding the breadth of support for the Southern strikers is difficult to verify. What is clear, however, is that there were numerous offers of legislative assistance, picketing help, and funds and that the AFL-CIO's Memphis Labor Council (Southern Airways was based in Memphis) was especially supportive of the pilots (*Air Line Pilot*, May–June 1962, 12). An added ingredient in this situation was Jim

Harper, leader of the pilots at Southern. Harper was unusual among pilots in his strong sense of connection to the broader labor movement:

We realize that our goals are ultimately the same as those of automobile workers, electrical workers, rubber workers and steel workers. The status friendships we've lost [he is referring to community hostility toward the strikers] are now replaced by enduring friendships with union brothers. We are revitalized by joining in Labor's eternal quest, human dignity (quoted in *Air Line Pilot*, May–June 1962, 9; explanation in brackets is mine).

One of the largest strikes in the history of the airline industry was a forty-three-day strike by the IAM against five carriers in 1966 (*Annual Report of the National Mediation Board* 1967: 11). By mutual agreement and contrary to the usual industry practice, the IAM was negotiating jointly on behalf of employees at all of the carriers. ALPA, FEIA, TWU, and BRAC were said to have pledged support to the IAM, although that support was not tested because the carriers did not attempt to operate during the strike (*Machinist*, July 14, 1966, 1). Despite its magnitude, the strike was essentially a conventional one. It assumed larger dimensions only when a Senate resolution was passed that would have ordered an end to the strike and set an ominous precedent for government intervention. The AFL-CIO became more involved at that juncture, but the strike was ultimately settled before the legislation could be acted upon.

The AFL-CIO also intervened in a 1973 strike by flight attendants (at that time represented by the TWU) at TWA. Again, larger issues were involved. A statement released by the AFL-CIO imputed broad anti-union designs to the carrier: "If the airline can make an example of the flight attendants, an example dictated by 19th Century labor-management relations, then it will not be hesitant to break the Machinists or the Pilots" (*Daily Labor Report*, Nov. 8, 1973, A-11).

An underlying concern of the unions was that the recently formed Airline Industrial Relations Conference (AIRCON), created by carriers to coordinate their bargaining activities, was behind TWA's bargaining stance and that AIRCON would encourage similar actions elsewhere (*Daily Labor Report*, Nov. 8, 1973, A-12). Picket lines were extended to Pan Am and American, where the TWU also represented workers, on the grounds that these two carriers were participating in the strike by making support payments to TWA through the carriers' Mutual Aid Pact (MAP). Pan Am and American were grounded for a day until the carriers obtained temporary restraining orders against the pickets (*TWU Express*, Dec. 1973, 20). Support also came from the International Transport Workers Federation and was cited as an important factor in shutting down the international traffic of TWA (*TWU Express* Dec. 1973, 20). With comparatively broad inter-union support, the strike was settled after about a month and a half.

More Recent Strikes

Given the increased importance of inter-union support in strikes after carriers began to regularly use replacements, how did airline unions respond? The initial response to the routine strikebreaking attempts of the 1980s reflected the prior history in which regular support was not required and the consequences of lack of support were less severe. Hence, a brief mid-contract strike by the TWU in protest of layoffs of its members at Pan Am received little attention from other unions at the carrier (*New York Times*, Jan. 26, 1980, 8). Likewise, other unions at Continental Airlines declined to honor Union of Flight Attendants picket lines in a 1980 strike, thereby allowing the carrier to continue operating half its flights (*Annual Report of the National Mediation Board* 1981: 42). A 1982 strike at Northwest by the IAM went much the same way. The IAM received some support from the TWU and the International Transport Workers Federation, but none from ALPA or the IBT, allowing Northwest to maintain partial operations (*Daily Labor Report*, June 9, 1982, A-11).

Although the dearth of inter-union support diminished the effectiveness of the aforementioned strikes, the consequences were not severe. The strikes at Continental in 1983 were a different story. In August 1983, the IAM went on strike against the carrier. The other unions at Continental did not support the action, and many IAM jobs were either contracted out or turned over to permanent replacements. Following a three-day cessation of service in late September 1983, during which Continental filed for bankruptcy, the carrier returned to the air. With the bankruptcy court's blessing, the carrier unilaterally devised "emergency work rules," abrogating the collective bargaining agreements that were in place.

On October 1, 1983, both ALPA and UFA struck in response to the carrier's actions. A few days earlier, the ALPA Executive Council had met to "'consider extraordinary measures for an industry-wide pilot response to both Continental and the growing anti-labor activity within the industry'" (*Daily Labor Report*, Sept. 27, 1983, A-11), but no such measures were forthcoming. The IAM and UFA strikes continued until April 1985, and the ALPA strike until October 1985, but large numbers of workers crossed picket lines and the strikes were ineffectual (*Daily Labor Report*, April 19, 1985, A8–9; Nov. 4, 1985, A11–12).

The Continental Airlines debacle may have prompted a growing realization of the importance of inter-union strike support in the airline industry. Support activities were a conspicuous element in several strikes during 1985. The TWU struck Pan Am on February 28, 1985, over several issues, including the carrier's failure to fund the pension plan adequately. For about ten days, all of the other unions at Pan Am respected the TWU's picket lines and the carrier was shut down. Pilots and flight engineers went back to work on March 8, 1985, largely out of concern that a prolonged strike would push the financially moribund airline over the edge. As ALPA president Henry Duffy put it, "Continuation of the strike posed a serious threat to the long-term viability of the airline" (*Daily Labor Report*, March 8, 1985, A-9). The director of the TWU International's Air Transport Division shared this concern (*Daily Labor Report*, March 26, 1985, A-5) and is believed by some to have encouraged the other Pan Am unions to return to work as a means of ending the strike. IUFA flight attendants sustained their sympathy action until just before a tentative settlement was reached on March 23, 1985. The 1985 TWU strike, then, illustrated both the potency of unified (at least initially) strike action, but also the manner in which the effects of a strike become a critical concern for all the unions at financially troubled carriers.

At about the same time, a strike by IAM mechanics was under way at Alaska Airlines. Office and clerical workers, also represented by the IAM, joined the strike, despite the presence of a no-strike provision in their contract. AFA flight attendants launched their own sympathy strike[3] for several weeks (*Flightlog*, Spring 1985, 4-5), but ALPA pilots crossed the IAM picket lines. Absent pilot support, the hiring of permanent replacements was effective and the two-month strike ended in defeat (*Daily Labor Report*, June 4, 1985, A-8).

The largest and most celebrated strike of 1985 occurred at United Airlines, where ALPA pilots walked out on May 17 in the face of insistent concession demands and determination by the carrier to continue operating during any strike. ALPA picket lines were respected by AFA, some management flight instructors, and most of the five hundred trainee pilots who had been enlisted as strikebreakers. The IAM, however, did not join in the strike, apparently because of the no-strike clause in its contract. The carrier was effectively shut down, and the strike was settled in slightly less than a month. Although United received some concessions in the settlement (e.g., a two-tier wage structure), the strike was generally viewed as a victory for ALPA because the union had blunted many of the carrier's demands and served notice that it was prepared to be more militant in the future.

Final agreement between United and ALPA was delayed because ALPA insisted that AFA members, the trainee pilots and the flight instructors receive satisfactory back-to-work guarantees (*Daily Labor Report*, June 13, 1985, A-12). Eventually, however, ALPA members ratified their contract even though the back-to-work provisions for the AFA sympathy strikers had not been ironed out. Negotiation of these provisions was far from routine in this case, and Pat Friend, Chair of the AFA MEC, charged United with "'persistent efforts to negotiate a punitive back-to-work agreement'" (*Daily Labor Report*, June 18, 1985, A-8). Although the pilots did not go the full distance in linking their contract ratification to a suitable back-to-work agreement for flight attendants, the monetary assistance ALPA provided to AFA was substantial, with $500,000 going to defray costs of the sympathy strike and an additional $600,000 placed in a special hardship fund for individual flight attendants (*Daily Labor Report*, July 3, 1985, A-11).

That the United pilots sought the support of flight attendants is noteworthy. It signaled the realization that even though the pilots could shut down the carrier by themselves, the action would enjoy greater legitimacy if it were supported by other groups. Rather than "rich pilots" trying to get more for themselves, it became clear that matters of principle were involved and that all workers at United held a significant stake in the outcome of the strike.

In contrast to the encouraging signs of 1985, the 1986 strike by flight attendants at TWA showed that inter-union strike support is still very much an open question. Flight attendants at TWA, represented by the Independent Federation of Flight Attendants, went on strike on March 7, 1986. The walkout occurred after protracted negotiations in which IFFA believed that it was being pressured to make concessions more severe than those agreed to by ALPA and the IAM in conjunction with Carl Icahn's acquisition of the carrier. TWA moved quickly to hire permanent replacements for the flight attendants. ALPA pilots at TWA, who as a condition of Icahn purchasing the carrier had agreed to the only no-strike clause in an ALPA contract, crossed the IFFA picket lines (*New York Times*, March 8, 1986, 8). A sizable number of IAM mechanics, particularly those based in Kansas City and St. Louis, initially stayed out in sympathy with IFFA. The IAM International took no official position on support, however, and there is reason to believe that it sought to make any pledge of support contingent upon IFFA formally affiliating with the IAM. In any event, the limited IAM sympathy action ended with the carrier obtaining an injunction a few days into the strike (*New York Times*, March 12, 1986, A-17).

After a little more than two months, during which TWA was able to keep flying with replacement flight attendants, IFFA ended its strike with an unconditional offer to return to work. The statement of IFFA vice-president Karen Lantz that "'when we went out, we went out planning to fight it ourselves'" (*New York Times*, April 9, 1986, B-2) provided an apt commentary on the fact that support from other airline unions in a strike was still not something to be expected, or perhaps even hoped for, in many situations.

What conclusions can be drawn from this review of inter-union support in strikes prior to 1987? It was a lack of need for and opportunity to engage in active strike support that best characterized the period prior to deregulation. In at least a few situations when support was required, however, airline unions, with the help of the AFL-CIO, were able to pull together. It is only since deregulation that carriers have routinely sought to operate with replacements during strikes and that the availability of meaningful support from other unions has been truly tested. The results of these early tests were mixed. Despite growing recognition that a "go-it-alone" strategy was wanting and the existence of a few successful instances of inter-union cooperation during strikes, the availability of strike support remained a very large open question.

Joint Action by Airline Unions

The line between joint action and support in strikes is not a firm one, but the emphasis here is on situations in which unions have worked together to deal with common problems, rather than to help other unions prevail in strikes. Significant historical instances of joint action by airline unions can be found in the collective responses of unions to attempts by carriers to band together, in efforts to get the government's attention on issues of safety, in labor's respose to deregulation, and in attempts to deal with the problems of particular carriers and crafts.

Responses to Organizing by Carriers

A major stimulus for joint action by airline unions was several attempts by carriers to band together to strengthen their hand in dealing with labor. The Mutual Aid Pact in particular was the target of joint political and regulatory activity for some twenty years. The MAP was originally devised in 1958 by six carriers to provide subsidies to airlines that were being struck and could not operate. The basic scheme remained in place until 1978, but a series of revisions expanded the number of participating carriers and the level of benefits offered (Unterberger and Koziara 1980; Kahn 1980: 354–55).

The CAB, which was vested with the authority to approve or strike down the carriers' agreement, was a focal point in union efforts to combat the MAP. Shortly after the pact was initiated, the IAM and BRAC jointly petitioned the CAB to disapprove it. A union spokesman explained what was at stake:

> Obviously, no organization representing employees can sit idly by and do nothing while a dispute it is having with one carrier is financed and supported by a group of other carriers with whom it may or may not have disputes. Self-defense would ultimately require action with respect to the whole group to the extent permitted by law (*Daily Labor Report*, Nov. 18, 1958, A-2).

In September 1959, a plan for creating a coordinating committee of airline unions within the AFL-CIO was announced (*AFL-CIO News*, Sept. 26, 1959, 2). Dealing with the carriers' MAP was prominent among the areas of "immediate concern" to be addressed by the committee.[4] In November 1959, the Association of Air Transport Unions was created as the formal outgrowth of the earlier agreement (*AFL-CIO News*, Nov. 14, 1959, 2). The association was headed by IAM president Al J. Hayes and included the IAM, TWU, ALPA, FEIA, BRAC, ALDA (Air Line Dispatchers Association), ALSSA, and the UAW. The stated aims of this body were reasonably expansive: "to provide union employees on the airlines with improved facilities for mutual cooperation and more effective coordination in economic, legislative, and industry activities" (*Daily Labor Report*, Nov. 10, 1959, A-2).

In fact, the association and its successor, the Airline Coordinating Committee, have had a political focus and have concentrated on a few issues, especially the MAP. The legislative and regulatory campaign against the MAP waged on throughout the 1960s and 1970s (*Daily Labor Report*, June 14, 1963, E1; *TWU Express*, Feb. 1974, 14), culminating with the passage of the Airline Deregulation Act of 1978, which, for all practical purposes, outlawed the pact (Unterberger and Koziara 1980: 87).

Labor's response to the creation of the Airline Industrial Relations Conference by carriers was similar in character to that evoked by the MAP, although more short-lived. AIRCON (originally referred to as AIRCO) was established in 1971 as part of a "three-pronged" approach for contending with labor (the other prongs being the MAP and legislative activity). It had the basic purpose of "'promoting a more consistent position on issues in pending labor negotiations'" (*Daily Labor Report*, April 9, 1971, AA–2). But a far more ambitious role was outlined in the agreement forming the conference: "AIRCO will act as exclusive representative of member carriers in collective bargaining, mediation, arbitration and conciliation with such labor organizations as specified by each carrier. It will appear and act on behalf of member carriers" (*Daily Labor Report*, April 9, 1971, AA–2).

Insofar as bargaining with individual carriers favored airline unions at that time, there was strong labor opposition to what was viewed as a thinly disguised attempt to force multi-employer bargaining on the unions. Numerous unions collaborated in presenting a joint petition to the CAB to have AIRCON disbanded (*Daily Labor Report*, Dec. 4, 1972, A-7). Additionally, the wide support for the flight attendants' strike at TWA in 1973, mentioned above, largely revolved around concern over the role of AIRCON in the negotiations. Whatever the carriers' intent in forming AIRCON, by 1978 they had scaled back its functions to those of researching collective bargaining agreements and disseminating information to carriers (*Daily Labor Report*, Nov. 20, 1978, A-3).

Getting the Attention of Government

The airline industry has always been directly affected by government action and inaction. In the midst of an alarming increase in "skyjackings," the International Federation of Airline Pilot Associations called for a twenty-four hour worldwide suspension of service by pilots on June 19, 1972. Statements by ALPA president J. J. O'Donnell made it clear that the aim of the action was expressly political, to gain the attention of governments worldwide, rather than to put pressure on carriers (*Daily Labor Report*, June 16, 1972, A-2). Despite support for the initiative by ALPA International, however, only three pilot groups in the United States and eighteen worldwide actually stayed on the ground (*Air Line Pilot*, Sept. 1989, 2).

A second instance of a broad job action with primarily political objectives nearly occurred in 1981, when ALPA threatened an industrywide suspension of service in the United States (*Air Line Pilot*, Jan. 1981, 12). ALPA was concerned with a number of adverse proposals and decisions being made by the FAA, but particularly with the union's exclusion from the process of certifying new aircraft. These actions had the consequence of limiting ALPA's ability to influence decisions regarding the proper crew size for new-generation jets (*Air Line Pilot*, Feb. 1981, 6). In the words of ALPA president O'Donnell: "I share the strong feeling of your Board of Directors that this deplorable record of the federal government, and FAA in particular, fully justifies our planning a total suspension of service to make the public aware of our deep feelings on these issues and to bring about needed reforms" (*Air Line Pilot*, Feb. 1981, 38).

The plan was dubbed "Operation USA," an acronym for "Unity for Safe Air Travel." On February 11, 1981, however, about two weeks before the walkout was set to occur, it was canceled. In return, when the secretary of transportation, Drew Lewis, promised that the safety concerns raised by ALPA would be examined and that a presidential commission would study the crew complement question (*Air Line Pilot*, March 1981, 3).

Even though the incidence and impact of "political strikes" in the airline industry have thus far been minimal, the apparent willingness of the courts to allow such actions on First Amendment grounds and because they do not present a labor-management dispute cognizable under the Railway Labor Act has made them a source of concern to management advocates (Conway 1988: 214).

Deregulation

Not surprisingly, airline unions were opposed to the legislative proposals that ultimately led to the deregulation of the airline industry in 1978 and engaged in concerted activity to defend their interests. But given the magnitude of the threat posed by deregulation (apparent in hindsight at least), union opposition was somewhat belated and limited. ALPA, apparently acting on its own, argued against deregulation in comments submitted to the CAB in early 1976 (*Daily Labor Report*, Jan. 19, 1976, A-7). The AFL-CIO Executive Council issued a statement endorsing ALPA's opposition to deregulation legislation on February 25, 1977, and the Airline Coordinating Committee was prompted into greater activity (Brown 1987: 145; *Machinist*, May 1977, 3). Coalition-building also occurred to some extent, as several non-AFL-CIO unions (IBT and APA) and a number of carriers joined with Airline Coordinating Committee member unions to form the labor–air Carriers Committee to combat deregulation legislation (*Machinist*, June 1977, 10).

It is difficult to judge whether the joint efforts of the unions were ineffectual or whether the pro-deregulation forces, including a broad array of backers from corporations, government, academia, and within the CAB itself (Brown 1987: 102–3; Moody 1987b: 8), were simply too strong to overcome. There are some reasons to believe that a less than all-out effort was launched, however. For one thing, it has been suggested that ALPA members tended to favor deregulation because of their conservatism and belief in the promises of deregulation advocates (Hopkins 1982: 289). Additionally, labor was tossed a few bones in the form of the employee protective provisions (section 43) of the Airline Deregulation Act and the outlawing of the carriers' Mutual Aid Pact, both of which arguably softened union resistance to the legislation (Brown 1987: 146). Finally, the AFL-CIO had bigger fish to fry at the time deregulation was being considered. The federation's political energies were absorbed in an ultimately unsuccessful quest to obtain labor law reforms. In any event, the deregulation battle did relatively little to instill confidence in the ability of airline unions to form the kind of broad and effective coalitions needed to contend successfully in a political arena that would grow far more inhospitable during the 1980s.

Airline Union Coalitions

The formation of coalitions by airline unions dates back to at least the 1940s. The Flight Radio Officers Air Safety Committee, in which both AFL and CIO unions representing flight radio officers joined in an effort to preserve their craft, and the Allied Trade Union Council of Pan American Workers, a coalition of unions representing all crafts at that carrier, were two early union coalitions (Kahn 1950: 313). There appears to have been little further coalition activity in the industry until a coalition reemerged at Pan Am in the mid-1970s. Arguing that Pan Am was disadvantaged by government policies and concerned that the carrier might fail, the ALPA, FEIA, TWU, and IBT units at Pan Am, with the aid of the Industrial Union Department, joined in a broad campaign to obtain the likes of better mail-carrying rates and access to domestic routes for Pan Am (*Daily Labor Report*, Nov. 26, 1974, A11–12).

In the 1980s, an array of coalitions appeared, most among unions at financially troubled carriers. Carriers where coalitions emerged (or were reactivated) included Pan Am, Frontier, Republic, Ozark, TWA, Eastern, Piedmont, and U.S. Air (*Flightlog*, Summer 1984, 4). Several of these coalitions engaged in some form of joint concession bargaining (e.g., Republic, TWA) or attempted to influence acquisitions by outside buyers (TWA, Frontier) (*Air Transport World*, Feb. 1985, 51; *Daily Labor Report*, Oct. 11, 1985, A-3; June 20, 1985, A-10).

Not all financially distressed carriers saw the formation of union coalitions, of course. Western Airlines, for example, experienced several rounds of concession bargaining and union representation on the board of directors, with little cooperation being evident among its unions (Wever 1988). Nor did each of the above-mentioned coalitions include all of the unions at the particular carrier. For example, the IAM distanced itself from the coalitions at Republic and Frontier, refusing to join in offering concession packages (*Daily Labor Report*, Sept. 5, 1985, A-7; *Business Week*, April 9, 1984, 33). Lastly, a number of the coalitions formed in the early to mid-1980s were short-lived. The coalitions at Republic, Frontier, and Ozark ceased to exist when these carriers were merged, while the coalition at TWA dissolved following purchase of the carrier by Carl Icahn. The joint efforts at Piedmont and U.S. Air were relatively informal, were prompted by the initial turmoil following deregulation, and lapsed prior to 1987.

Two other efforts at coalescing, one successful, the other not, should be noted. In 1984, a group of six flight attendant unions (APFA, IUFA, IFFA, UFA, TWU Local 553, and the IBT Airline Division) formed the Joint Council of Flight Attendant Unions, "a coalition of labor organizations that works collectively on issues affecting flight attendants particularly in the areas of air safety, flight attendant health, and labor legislation" (*International Teamster*, June 1987, 16). The Joint Council remains active and is discussed at some length in chapter 7.

More novel, but ultimately fruitless, was a proposal generated in 1985 by the IBT Airline Division to form a coalition of unions whose members worked in and around JFK Airport in New York City. Using common employment site as a basis for coalition-building has some merit, particularly in light of the strategic advantage to be gained from such an arrangement when carriers concentrate much of their traffic in a few large hubs. The coalition failed to get off the ground, however, falling victim to disagreements over who would lead it.

There is historical precedent, then, for airline unions, both at the national and carrier levels, to engage in joint action around common problems. At the national union level, political activity through the AFL-CIO has occurred. This activity was especially intense in response to the carriers' Mutual Aid Pact and AIRCON. There was a sharp upturn in joint activity, particularly the formation of coalitions, in the early 1980s. Most often, the coalitions were formed by unions representing workers at carriers facing severe financial problems and changes of ownership. Although a number of these coalitions had already disappeared by 1987, those at Pan Am and Eastern, as well as the Joint Council of Flight Attendant Unions, remained and became an important part of the story of airline labor in the latter 1980s.

Conclusion

Before deregulation, airline unions appear to have been involved with each other only sporadically. That engagement sometimes took an antagonistic form, such as the representational and jurisdictional battles in which ALPA became embroiled. Collaboration was most evident among AFL-CIO affiliates and in response to carrier initiatives, such as the MAP. Substantial strike support was occasionally rendered, but most often the need for such support was obviated because carriers ceased operation during strikes. The clearest indication that the increasing interdependence of airline unions had begun to affect inter-union relations is found in the sharply increased volume of coalition activity in the 1980s. Increased collaboration in strikes during the 1980s is arguable, but the consequences of failing to garner support certainly became evident. At best, then, inter-union relations in the period with which this study is most concerned would reflect ongoing attempts by airline labor to organize itself, rather than stable, well-established patterns of cohesive action.

Chapter 5

Interdependence and the Presence of Inter-Union Ties: A Quantitative Analysis of Union Pairs

Although in the previous chapter a general picture of inter-union relations before 1987 was pieced together by relying on union publications and other published sources, the questions raised in this study require more systematic data. This chapter reports on the methods used to obtain these data and the results of a quantitative analysis of the relations among pairs of airline unions. This analysis addresses the questions of which airline unions maintain particular kinds of ties with one another and why. The findings generally support the propositions that inter-union ties are established to deal with interdependence and that relations differ qualitatively depending on the nature of the interdependence.

Methodology

Data

One of the first choices to be made in designing a study of inter-union relations is which unions and pairs of unions to consider. This analysis examines relations among unions that represented workers at nine major U.S. air carriers in the period from 1987 to mid-1989: American, Continental, Delta, Eastern, Northwest, Pan Am, TWA, United, and U.S. Air.[1] Counting separately national unions and their subunits having primary responsibility for bargaining, a total of thirty-seven unions represented workers at these carriers (not all for the entire period). Data were successfully gathered for thirty-three of these unions. These included six inter/national unions, six independent unions,[2] twelve intermediate bodies, and nine locals.

The dyad or union pair, rather than the individual union, is the unit of analysis. All possible pairs of these thirty-three unions are considered, with the exception of pairs constituted by a national union headquarters and one of its own subunits (e.g., the ALPA International and an ALPA MEC).[3] This results in a total of 1,024 pairs whose relations are analyzed.[4]

Data were gathered by means of telephone interviews conducted with union officials. These interviews proceeded from a survey instrument developed for this study (see appendix 1). This instrument was pretested and refined through interviews conducted with three airline union officers whose unions were not included in this study. Copies of the survey instrument were mailed to potential respondents with a cover letter explaining the research project before any attempt to make telephone contact. Potential respondents were subsequently called and asked to participate in the study. The interviews, which were conducted between May and September 1989, generally lasted for about an hour.

The survey instrument focused on specific types of inter-union relations (e.g., information exchange, agreements, disputes) and asked, for each type of relation and every other union, whether or not these ties were present at any point during the approximately two and a half years between the beginning of 1987 and when the interview was conducted. This time span did not unduly tax the memory of respondents and provided a fairly unambiguous indication of whether any meaningful connection existed. Respondents had both the questions and a list of unions in front of them. For each type of relation, respondents were urged to go through the list of other unions and to designate those with which the specified tie existed. If respondents answered in blanket terms such as "all of them" or "none of them," they were asked whether there were any exceptions among the listed unions. To obtain richer data and to provide a check on responses, respondents were also asked to provide examples of the content of the ties (e.g., if there was joint action with another union, what was done?).

Interviewing multiple respondents from each union would have been optimal, but in practice it was necessary to rely on a single respondent. On the premise that the top officers of unions are the persons most likely to handle boundary-spanning activities with other unions, particularly in important instances, these individuals were sought as respondents. Top officers were, in fact, interviewed in twenty of the thirty-three cases. In the remaining instances, interviews were conducted with four vice presidents, three secretary-treasurers, one senior general chairman, two contract administrators, two staff department directors, and an assistant airline coordinator. All of the interviewees had held union office during the entire span about which they were being asked, although some had attained their current position during this period.

How reliable were respondents' reports? One limited form of corroboration came from published sources, with which respondents' reports were quite consistent. Another important check was the extent of agreement between respondents. Some relations (e.g., direct communication), although by no means all (e.g., received substantial support from), are inherently symmetrical.

Both parties in a given pair had to engage in the relation if the tie existed. Reports on inherently symmetrical relations were reasonably consistent. Thus, for the relations "had direct communication or contact" and "engaged in joint action," just short of 80 percent of reported ties were agreed upon. Since there was not complete agreement regarding inherently symmetrical relations, ties were treated as existing only if *both* parties reported them.[5]

Operationalization of Variables

The model of inter-union relations presented in chapter 2 (Fig. 2-1) suggests a number of variables that might account for the presence or absence of ties between unions. Broadly speaking, these factors are various forms of interdependence,[6] domain/ideological consensus, and organizational characteristics.

Because measures of interdependence are not well established and are central to this study, a brief introduction will clarify the operational definitions that follow. Craft and carrier are the basic categories that define the jurisdictions of airline unions. Thus, they are used to assess whether or not particular unions operate in common domains. They are also used in constructing other measures of interdependence. Government data on representation cases provide a means of identifying unions that compete. Comparable data are not available to document other forms of interdependence; however, the importance of bargaining power and political capacity as resources and their unequal distribution among unions suggest a measure of resource dependence based on asymmetrical ties between unions with high bargaining power or political capacity and unions with less bargaining power or political capacity.

Financially troubled carriers present a number of shared problems for unions with members at those carriers. Thus, employment of members by a financially struggling carrier is used as the basis for one measure of common problem interdependence. The broad threat posed by the activities of Frank Lorenzo and Texas Air Corporation at Eastern Airlines is used as the basis for a second measure of common problem interdependence.

The premise for the measure of workflow interdependence is that the in-flight crafts (pilots, flight engineers, flight attendants) work most closely together, while other employee groups tend to be more dispersed.

Lastly, bargaining outcome interdependence is assessed indirectly by identifying carriers that are the closest competitors. With a craft-based bargaining structure, unions representing the same crafts at competing carriers are the most likely to be affected by one another's negotiations and to attempt to take wages out of competition.

The operational definitions and sources for all the variables used in the dyadic analysis are specified below:

CRAFT (shared domain—craft): Coded 1 if both unions represent the same craft, 0 otherwise. *Sources*: U.S. NMB, *Annual Report of the U.S. National*

Mediation Board 1986; "Airline Labor Contract Status," *Air Line Pilot,* June 1989: 28. See table 3-1.

CARRIER (shared domain—carrier): Coded 1 if both unions represent workers employed by the same carrier, 0 otherwise. *Sources*: U.S. NMB, *Annual Report of the U.S. National Mediation Board* 1986; "Airline Labor Contract Status," *Air Line Pilot,* June 1989: 28. See table 3-1.

NATIONAL (national union affiliation): Coded 1 if both unions are affiliated with the same inter/national union, 0 otherwise. *Source*: U.S. NMB, *Annual Report of the U.S. National Mediation Board* 1986.

AFLSTAT (AFL-CIO affiliation status): Coded 1 if both unions have the same AFL-CIO affiliation status (i.e., they are both affiliates or both independents), 0 otherwise. *Source*: Gifford, *Directory of U.S. Labor Organizations, 1988–1989.*

COMPETE (competitive interdependence): Coded 1 if the unions were both parties to the same NMB representation case between January 1987 and September 1989, 0 otherwise. *Source*: U.S. NMB, *Determinations of the U.S. Mediation Board,* vols. 14–16.

BARGAIN (bargaining outcome interdependence): Coded 1 if both unions represent the same craft and their members are employed by carriers that are "prime competitors," 0 otherwise. Competing carriers are identified by determining, for each carrier, how many times other carriers overlap in carrying 1 million or more passengers in a market. The markets considered were the top twenty-eight U.S. cities in passengers enplaned in 1987 and three broad international markets (Atlantic, Pacific, Latin American). The two other carriers that overlap with a carrier in the largest number of markets were designated its "prime competitors." In the case of ties, more than two carriers were so designated. *Sources*: U.S. Department of Transportation, *Air Carrier Traffic Statistics Monthly,* Dec. 1986–87; FAA, *Airport Activity Statistics of Certificated Route Air Carriers,* Dec. 1987. See appendix 2 for a list of competing carriers.

RESDEP (resource dependence): Coded 1 if both unions represent workers at the same carrier and one union has relatively high bargaining power and the other does not. Unions representing either pilots or mechanics are designated as having relatively high bargaining power. Coding is asymmetrical, so that if union i has less bargaining power than union j, $A\_i\_j = 1$ and $A\_j\_i = 0$. For national-level unions, unions with lower political capacity (in terms of PAC size and number of Washington lobbyists) are coded as depending on unions with higher political capacity. *Sources*: Zuckerman 1988; Close, Bologna, and McCormick 1989. See appendix 2 for a list of high bargaining power and political capacity unions.

WORKFLOW (workflow interdependence): Coded 1 if both unions represent in-flight personnel (pilots, flight engineers, or flight attendants) at the same carrier, 0 otherwise. *Source*: U.S. NMB, *Annual Report of the U.S. National Mediation Board* 1986.

FINPROB (common problem interdependence—financially troubled carrier): Coded 1 if both unions represent workers at the same financially troubled carrier, 0 otherwise. Financial standing is assessed in terms of debt, ROE, and cash flow. *Sources*: *Standard & Poor's Industry Survey*, July 1989; ALPA 1988a. See appendix 2 for a list of financially troubled carriers.

EALPROB (common problem interdependence—Eastern Airlines): Coded 1 if one or both of the unions represents workers at Eastern Airlines, 0 otherwise. *Source*: U.S. NMB, *Annual Report of the U.S. National Mediation Board* 1986. See appendix 2 for a list of unions representing workers at Eastern Airlines.

LEGITMCY (domain consensus—legitimacy): Coded as the least number of years that either union has continuously represented workers in the airline industry. The year in which representation began is subtracted from 1989. *Sources*: U.S. NMB, *Annual Report of the U.S. National Mediation Board*, various years; Hopkins 1971.

EMPLOWN (ideological/tactical consensus—employee ownership): Coded as the absolute difference in responses to a survey item tapping prevailing attitudes among the union leadership toward employee ownership. Difference scores can range from 0 to 5. *Source*: Appendix 1, survey item 27.

STAFFING (organizational characteristics—staff size): Coded as the least number of full-time staff available to either union. Staff includes officers and all others performing paid work for the union that is not secretarial or clerical in nature. Part-time staff were added to produce their full-time equivalent. *Source*: Appendix 1, survey item 2.

ACTIVITY (organizational characteristics—breadth of activity): Coded as the fewest number of activities in which either union had engaged, ranging from 0 to 5. *Source*: Appendix 1, survey item 4.

ORGLEVEL (organizational characteristics—level): Coded 1 if both unions are located at the same organizational level (i.e., local, intermediate body, inter/national union), 0 otherwise.

DIRCOMM (direct communication/contact): Coded 1 if both unions report having had direct communication/contact, 0 otherwise (symmetrical). *Source*: Appendix 1, survey item 6.

FREQUENT (frequent contact): Coded 1 if both unions reported having contact at least once per month, 0 otherwise (symmetrical). *Source*: Appendix 1, survey item 6a.

TURNSTRK (would turn to first in a strike): A_i_j is coded 1 if union i reported that union j is among the first unions it would turn to in a strike, 0 otherwise (asymmetrical). *Source*: Appendix 1, survey item 11c.

KEYREL (highly instrumental relationship): A_i_j is coded 1 if union i reported receiving substantial support from union j and/or if union i included union j among those unions that are most important to it, 0 otherwise (asymmetrical). *Source*: Appendix 1, survey items 11, 24.

JOINTACT (joint action): Coded 1 if both unions reported having engaged in joint action, 0 otherwise (symmetrical). *Source*: Appendix 1, survey item 14.

DISPUTE (dispute/disagreement): A_i_j is coded 1 if union i reported having a dispute or disagreement with union j, 0 otherwise (asymmetrical). *Source:* Appendix 1, survey item 21.

EXPSUPP (expect support from): A_i_j is coded 1 if union i reported expecting support from union j, 0 otherwise (asymmetrical). *Source:* Appendix 1, survey item 8.

EALCOMM (communication/contact related to the Eastern Airlines strike): Coded 1 if either union indicated that there was communication/contact related to the strike, 0 otherwise (symmetrical). *Source:* Appendix 1, survey item 18.

Means and standard deviations for the variables used in this analysis are listed in table 5-1.

Analysis

The task at hand is to sort out the relative influence of a number of factors that might account for the presence or absence of ties between unions. A multiple regression analysis is clearly appropriate, but there is a hitch. It is a fundamental assumption of regression techniques that observations on the dependent variable are independent of one another or, equivalently, that error terms are

Table 5-1.   Means and Standard Deviations of Variables

Variable	Mean	Standard deviation
CRAFT	0.297	0.457
CARRIER	0.244	0.430
NATIONAL	0.068	0.252
AFLSTAT	0.578	0.494
COMPETE	0.023	0.151
BARGAIN	0.075	0.264
RESDEP	0.076	0.265
FINPROB	0.121	0.326
EALPROB	0.266	0.442
WORKFLOW	0.041	0.198
LEGITMCY	22.623	13.538
EMPLOWN	2.248	1.662
STAFFING	5.822	5.962
ACTIVITY	2.703	1.095
ORGLEVEL	0.348	0.476
DIRCOMM	0.225	0.418
FREQUENT	0.053	0.224
KEYREL	0.059	0.224
TURNSTRK	0.053	0.234
JOINTACT	0.068	0.252
DISPUTE	0.048	0.214
EXPSUPP	0.306	0.461
EALCOMM	0.141	0.348

not correlated (Aldrich and Nelson 1984: 49). With dyadic relational data of the sort used in this study, however, the assumption of independent observations becomes very dubious, since the same union is involved in multiple pairings with other unions (Lincoln 1984: 58; Krackhardt 1988: 361). This is the problem of "network autocorrelation." It has been shown in a number of simulation studies that even moderately high levels of network autocorrelation can render tests of significance meaningless, especially for ordinary least squares (OLS) regression (Dow, Burton, and White 1982; Doreian, Teuter, and Wang 1984). Although there is agreement that the consequences of network autocorrelation can be serious, there is a lack of consensus as to how to deal with the problem (Wasserman and Weaver 1985: 408; Lincoln 1984; Mizruchi 1989). Fortunately, David Krackhardt (1988) has developed a method for analyzing such data that combines OLS regression and the quadratic assignment procedure (QAP) (Hubert and Baker 1978). The details of Krackhardt's procedure are discussed in appendix 3. Here, it is sufficient to note that Krackhardt's method is a form of regression analysis that does not rely on estimated standard errors for tests of significance. Hence, it permits the desired regression analysis while circumventing some of the potential technical problems posed by dyadic relational data.

Hypotheses

Several major hypotheses guide this analysis. The first concerns the factors predicting the presence or absence of ties among unions generally:

Hypothesis 1: Inter-union relations are more likely to be present among unions that are interdependent, that share basic agreement regarding domains and ideology, and that have organizational characteristics facilitating the maintenance of inter-union ties.

This hypothesis follows from the model of inter-union relations depicted in figure 2-1. It asserts that positive relationships exist between inter-union ties and variables capturing the presence of interdependence, domain/ideological consensus, and organizational characteristics.[7]

Qualitative differences in the kinds of ties established, depending upon the type of interdependence present, are also expected.

Hypothesis 2: Relations between unions representing the same craft (e.g., competitive, bargaining outcome interdependence) are likely to be characterized by both collective action and conflict.

Hypothesis 2 is grounded in the fact that airline unions representing the same craft draw upon the same membership base. They are also likely to be similar in size, resources, and capabilities because of the roughly comparable scale of the major carriers. These unions are apt to perceive common interests around craft- or industry-related issues and a need to pool individually limited resources to deal successfully with these matters. Unions representing the same craft are also affected by one another's bargaining outcomes and have reason to share information. Yet, to the extent that there is active competition for members, conflict is also likely to occur.

Hypothesis 3: Relations between unions representing different crafts (e.g., resource dependence, workflow interdependence) are likely to be both highly instrumental and conflictful.

Unions representing different crafts, particularly when they also represent workers employed by the same carrier, impinge upon each other in a variety of ways. Because crafts differ substantially in their numbers, criticality to the work process, and ability to draw on strong national unions, relations across crafts are likely to reflect inequality, dependence, and power dynamics. Unions representing other crafts are capable of providing meaningful support in strike situations and are likely to possess information different from that circulating among unions representing the same craft. Relations also assume particular importance when other crafts are closely related in the work process. Thus, cross-craft relations are likely to be among the most highly instrumental for airline unions (hypothesis 3). Yet cross-craft relations should also be conflictful, as common interests are less readily identified, support is rendered only conditionally, and workplace conflicts become inter-union conflicts.

Hypothesis 4: Relations between unions that are common problem interdependent are likely to evidence collective action and relatively high intensity (frequency of contact).

The basis for hypothesis 4 is simply that the collective nature of common problem interdependence calls for a joint response. Engendering collective action is always difficult, but faced with sufficiently compelling common problems, unions will have a strong incentive to submerge (at least temporarily) their differences, relinquish some of their autonomy, and do what is necessary to deal with the shared threat. The seriousness of problems, the need for an immediate response, and the inherently time-consuming nature of joint endeavors all point in the direction of contact between unions that is frequent and intensive.

Hypothesis 5: Relations between unions that are affiliated with the same larger organization (e.g., national union, AFL-CIO) are likely to feature direct communication and expectations of support.

Hypothesis 5 asserts that organizational affiliations, particularly among subunits of the same national union, will lead to a much greater likelihood of communication because of the common organizational identity and established lines of communication. Similarly, formal organizational boundaries provide a clear indication of which unions are in one's own camp and from which support can most readily be expected.

Findings

Results from the multiple regression-QAP analysis are listed in table 5-2. The findings are discussed separately for each of the relations considered and are then summarized in terms of the theoretical framework. Models assess— for pairs of unions—the effects of variables capturing interdependence, domain/ideological consensus, and organizational characteristics on the presence or absence of direct communication, frequent contact, readiness to turn to another union for strike support, "key" ties, joint action, disputes, expectations of support, and communication related to the Eastern Airlines strike. The ties that serve as dependent variables in this study reflect qualitative differences in form. Specifically, highly instrumental relations are captured by the variables TURNSTRK and KEYREL, collective efforts by JOINTACT, intensive relations by FREQUENT, conflict by DISPUTE, and formalization by EXPSUPP.[8]

Direct Communication/Contact

The existence of direct communication between two unions is a basic indicator of their relevance to one another. A major reason for communicating is to obtain or provide information. The union officers interviewed cited a variety of information that was received from other unions. Mentioned most often was information pertaining to bargaining matters, including the progress of negotiations, contract language and outcomes, and copies of collective bargaining agreements. Contract administration also occasioned information exchange, as grievance outcomes and arbitration cites or awards were made available. Several respondents referred to a flow of information concerning safety issues, including information regarding the status of members involved in an accident, discussion of a National Transportation Safety Board (NTSB) investigation, and sharing of a safety manual. Union newsletters, minutes of union meetings, and union policy statements were also exchanged.

Which unions had direct contact with one another? The regression results listed in the first column of table 5-2 provide a relatively clear picture of the lines of communication. Common national union affiliation (NATIONAL) and workflow interdependence (WORKFLOW) stand out as bases for contact. Unions affiliated with the same national union or linked by close contact between their members in the work process were much more likely than other unions to have had direct contact. Affiliation with the same national union provides ready entrée to other affiliates; established lines of communication, including formal meetings; and a variety of internal governance and external issues around which communication can usefully occur. Workflow interdependence makes it difficult for other unions to be regarded as "out of sight and out of mind," since issues of joint concern arise regularly.

Lines of communication extend throughout the domains of unions, insofar as other unions representing the same craft (CRAFT) or workers employed by the same carrier (CARRIER) were also more likely to be in contact. Within-

Table 5-2. OLS Regression with QAP Estimates for Models Predicting Inter-Union Relations (p-values in parentheses)

Variables	Direct communication	Frequent contact	Turn to first in strike	Key ties	Joint action	Disputes	Expect support from	Contact re Eastern strike
CRAFT	0.201***	0.029	0.031	0.013	0.055*	0.040*	0.162*	0.048
	(.002)	(.148)	(.088)	(.311)	(.050)	(.026)	(.014)	(.174)
COMPETE	0.128	0.015	-0.010	0.003	0.064	0.131*	0.032	0.001
	(.156)	(.409)	(.477)	(.407)	(.202)	(.022)	(.375)	(.475)
BARGAIN	0.091	0.056	0.036	0.061*	0.094*	0.030	0.136*	0.055
	(.106)	(.068)	(.136)	(.032)	(.020)	(.168)	(.036)	(.235)
CARRIER	0.149*	0.007	0.051*	0.047	0.024	0.068**	0.295***	-0.064
	(.032)	(.327)	(.046)	(.072)	(.251)	(.004)	(.002)	(.228)
RESDEP	0.048	-0.014	0.088*	0.090**	-0.039	0.099***	0.011	-0.021
	(.164)	(.275)	(.014)	(.006)	(.074)	(.002)	(.437)	(.335)
WORKFLOW	0.471***	0.189**	0.081*	0.116*	0.286***	0.093*	-0.007	0.103
	(.002)	(.008)	(.049)	(.024)	(.002)	(.022)	(.453)	(.140)
FINPROB	0.154*	0.094*	0.023	0.056	0.178**	0.017	-0.052	0.015
	(.040)	(.014)	(.251)	(.088)	(.004)	(.279)	(.295)	(.453)
EALPROB	-0.022	-0.046	-0.019	-0.019	-0.098	-0.089	0.012	0.242**
	(.377)	(.066)	(.214)	(.218)	(.006)	(.002)	(.429)	(.006)
NATIONAL	0.464***	0.030	0.068	0.098*	-0.146	0.053	0.373***	0.169*
	(.002)	(.275)	(.058)	(.012)	(.002)	(.074)	(.002)	(.050)

AFLSTAT	-0.053 (.168)	0.053* (.028)	0.007 (.345)	-0.013 (.291)	0.050 (.082)	-0.055*** (.002)	0.028 (.305)	-0.025 (.333)
LEGITMCY	0.000 (.387)	-0.002 (.042)	0.000 (.375)	0.001 (.054)	-0.001 (.218)	0.002 (.002)	-0.003 (.180)	0.002 (.303)
EMPLOWN	0.000 (.478)	-0.008 (.122)	-0.006 (.092)	-0.016*** (.002)	-0.003 (.341)	0.003 (.219)	-0.001 (.489)	-0.005 (.305)
STAFFING	0.009* (.034)	0.006** (.010)	0.007*** (.002)	0.007*** (.002)	0.009** (.004)	0.002 (.089)	0.002 (.307)	0.010* (.014)
ACTIVITY	0.019 (.257)	0.017 (.104)	0.004 (.361)	-0.003 (.395)	0.009 (.307)	-0.005 (.301)	0.055* (.046)	0.026 (.213)
ORGLEVEL	0.133** (.009)	0.083*** (.002)	0.064*** (.002)	0.011 (.297)	0.080** (.006)	0.028 (.062)	0.037 (.186)	0.052 (.102)
Intercept	-0.079	-0.044	-0.052	-0.010	-0.052	-0.012	0.029	-0.107
R-squared	.424*** (.002)	.175*** (.002)	.147*** (.002)	.160*** (.002)	.273*** (.002)	.124*** (.002)	.201*** (.002)	.257*** (.002)

N = 1,024 for all models. Standard errors are not listed because they may be biased for these data and are not used in the QAP significance test. Five hundred permutation trials are used in the QAP significance test. Therefore, the minimum possible p-value is .002. *p ≤ .05. **p ≤ .01. ***p = .002 (one-tailed test).

carrier contact was probable overall, but this was especially likely to occur between unions confronted with the common problem of a financially troubled carrier (FINPROB).

Lastly, organizational characteristics also affected the probability of inter-union contact. Contact was more common among unions located at the same level within their respective national unions (ORGLEVEL) and among those with larger staffs (STAFFING). Contact was not confined to horizontal linkages between counterparts, but similarity in authority and scope of responsibility favored the maintenance of relations. Likewise, larger staff size facilitated monitoring the environment and engaging in potentially time-consuming inter-union meetings.

Frequent Contact

That there is direct communication between two unions tells us little about the "strength" (Granovetter 1973) of that tie. Frequent contact often indicates a stronger, more meaningful relationship. The frequency of contact between airline unions in the period from 1987 through mid-1989 varied considerably. Among unions that had any contact at all, frequent contact (at least once per month), infrequent contact (no more than once or twice per year), and intermittent contact (between the two extreme categories) were about equally prevalent. Although a few unions reported communicating at least once a week, they were the exception. Other than unions affiliated with the same national union, contact between unions tended to occur on an "as needed" basis, rather than in regularly scheduled meetings.

From column 2 in table 5-2, it is apparent that one circumstance under which frequent contact tended to occur was when unions represented workers at the same financially troubled carrier (FINPROB). Joint action to deal with the threat to members' continued employment required relatively close, intensive contact. Frequent contact was also more common among unions representing employees linked in the work process (WORKFLOW), presumably because opportunities for contact between work groups were rife and issues arose on an ongoing basis. Somewhat surprising, frequent contact was more prevalent between unions with the same AFL-CIO affiliation (either both affiliates or both non-affiliates) (AFLSTAT). This reflects contact between AFL-CIO affiliates at the national level and a considerable amount of interaction between independent flight attendant unions. Unions were most likely to have frequent contact with other unions located at the same organizational level (ORGLEVEL) and when a sufficient number of staff were available to carry out the dealings (STAFFING).

High Instrumentality Relations

Some ties are especially important for goal attainment. Columns 3 and 4 in table 5-2 pertain to two such high instrumentality relations: unions seen as prime sources of strike support (TURNSTRK) and "key" relations (KEYREL) (a composite of those unions that had provided "substantial support" in the past and/or that were seen as the "most important" ties).

The airline industry bargaining structure renders other unions representing workers at the same carrier critically important in determining the outcome of a strike, particularly for unions with limited ability to shut down a carrier on their own. This is reflected in the propensity of union officers to cite other unions at the same carrier (CARRIER, RESDEP, WORKFLOW) as those they would turn to first in the event of a strike. Having a large staff size (STAFFING) and congruence with respect to organizational level (ORGLEVEL) also made other unions more attractive as sources of strike support.

That the willingness to provide information and support is a large part of what makes other unions important and helpful was evident in the findings regarding bases for "key" ties (KEYREL). Relations with more powerful, politically capable unions (RESDEP) and between unions linked by workflow (WORKFLOW) again stand out as strategically important. Relations between unions representing the same craft were less likely to be cited, with the important exception of unions interdependent with respect to bargaining outcomes (BARGAIN). Unions linked by common national union affiliation (NATIONAL) also tended to be seen as important and/or as having provided substantial support. Interestingly, union officers tended to designate as key those unions whose views regarding employee ownership (EMPLOWN) were closer to their own. This presumably reflects the high salience this issue had for airline unions in the late 1980s and the active involvement of a number of unions in buyout efforts.

Comments by union officers in responding to these questions reinforce the aggregate findings regarding high instrumentality relations. The examples of "substantial" support (defined for respondents as help that made a real difference in enabling the union to attain its goals) centered on resources. Support received from other unions in actual or potential strike situations was mentioned most frequently. This aid took a number of forms, including sympathy strikes, assistance in strike preparation, contributions to strike funds, and pledges of support in impending strikes. Two respondents cited as instances of substantial support situations in which another union at the same carrier involved itself in the negotiations of the respondent's union by attending negotiating sessions to intimidate management or by threatening to make treatment of the respondent's union an issue in its own negotiations with the carrier. In other cases, substantial support involved aid in achieving legislative ends and in locating an organizing target. In one instance, substantial support was rendered by backing a union's position on a matter before a national union.

Statements concerning reasons for designating particular relationships as "most important" are less easy to summarize. The largest number of responses related to the resources and capacities of the union seen as most important— the other union has high bargaining power, is the major representative of a craft, has political clout, is a valuable source of information, has provided support in the past, and so forth. Other respondents alluded to more general grounds for attributing importance, particularly overlaps in carrier and national union affiliation. Several officers mentioned the effect of other unions on negotiations as a basis for regarding those unions as important actors. This finding is consistent with the quantitative results linking bargaining outcome interdependence and "key" ties. Finally, and in line with the aggregate findings concerning views on employee ownership, several respondents mentioned similarity in philosophy and politics as the basis for their most important relationships.

Joint Action

Cooperation between unions sometimes takes a collective form, involving joint efforts toward a common goal, rather than one union helping another achieve its particular ends. This distinction between working together and helping out was emphasized in asking respondents to indicate other unions with which they had engaged in joint action. The union officers interviewed cited a variety of instances of joint action. Joint political and legal action were mentioned most often, involving issues such as flight attendant duty time, FAR 145, random drug testing, the activities of Texas Air Corporation, the privatization of TWA, and state-level legislation concerning employee stock ownership plans (ESOPs).

Several instances of joint action respondents cited concerned financially troubled carriers. Unions representing workers at these carriers were often involved in collaborative efforts to locate buyers, to develop plans for financial restructuring, to reach agreements regarding concessions to be offered to prospective owners, and to share the costs of legal and financial advisers. Other examples of joint action cited were collaborative efforts to have safety-related changes made in a particular type of aircraft; the composition of a professional standards letter, which called for unions to work out disputes arising on the job among crafts rather than hand them to management as grievances; sharing of responsibility for coordinating a United Way campaign; and a joint effort to improve medical benefits for all workers at a carrier. Much, though not all, of the joint action the airline unions engaged in took place within coalitions.

The aggregate results from the regression analysis (see table 5-2, column 5) point to several grounds for collective action by unions. Unions representing the same craft (CRAFT, BARGAIN) tended to engage in joint action. Consistent with the examples of joint action cited by respondents, unions contending with financially struggling carriers (FINPROB) were more likely to have acted in concert. Joint action was also more common among unions representing in-flight personnel (WORKFLOW). Safety issues were one of the main foci for joint activity by flight crew unions. Consistent with the notion that joint action is most likely between unions that are relative equals or that are thrust into circumstances that promote common interests, joint activity occurred most often between unions at the same organizational level (ORGLEVEL).

Once again, having a larger staff (STAFFING) facilitated contact, in this case engaging in joint action.[9]

Disputes

The discussion to this point has focused on essentially cooperative relations. What about conflict? The aggregate findings (Table 5-2, column 6) suggest a number of lines of interdependence along which disputes emerged but no dominant explanation. Conflict extended throughout the domains of unions, occurring generally between unions representing the same craft (CRAFT) and between those whose members were employed by the same carrier (CARRIER). Among unions representing the same craft, competitive interdependence in the form of representational contests for members (COMPETE) was especially likely to result in conflicts. By contrast, common AFL-CIO affiliation status (AFLSTAT) was associated with an absence of conflict, presumably because of the prohibitions against raiding affiliated unions and mechanisms within the federation for dispute resolution. In cross-craft relations, resource dependence (RESDEP) stands out as a basis for conflict, most likely resulting from unilateral actions or incursions on the autonomy of less powerful unions by more powerful unions. Consistent with the classic image of multiple crafts employed at the same work site, workflow interdependence (WORKFLOW) precipitated several disputes.[10]

The aspect of competition mentioned most often as a source of disputes was the transfer of bargaining units in mergers. Officers of unions that had represented workers at carriers that merged consistently reported that their former members were not treated fairly in the process, particularly with respect to the combining of seniority lists. The co-existence of cooperation and conflict among unions in coalitions, particularly unions with differing capacities to affect outcomes unilaterally, was also apparent in the disputes cited. In one case, contention arose because a pilots union broke away from the rest of a coalition and settled on concessions, thereby effectively forcing the hand of the other members of the coalition. Although there was no statistically significant effect overall, several disagreements were rooted in the interdependence of bargaining outcomes for unions. The negotiation of concessions by one union was seen as establishing an undesirable precedent that hampered the bargaining efforts of other unions. Two-tier wage structures were mentioned several times in this context.

Several disputes also grew out of the workflow interdependence of flight crew members, particularly flight attendants and pilots. But unlike intercraft jurisdictional disputes of the sort typified by the struggles between pilots and flight engineers in earlier years, more recent disputes between flight crew members have centered on issues of authority. Pilots hold ultimate authority over aircraft operations in an otherwise largely unsupervised work setting, and disputes over the use of this authority are apparently fairly common, leading to grievances and affecting relations between pilot and flight attendant unions.

Expectations of Support

Respondents were also asked to indicate those unions from which they expected at least mild support (defined as any helpful action). This relation is of particular significance because it is an indicator of the extent to which the existence of a labor movement is important. If being part of a larger social movement counts for anything in terms of inter-union relations, then unions should have a fairly large number of potential allies on which to draw and grounds for claiming at least minimal assistance from them.

Which unions were viewed as prospective sources of support? One of the clearest findings regarding expectations of support (Table 5-2, column 7) is that other unions affiliated with the same national union (NATIONAL) were seen as allies to be counted on. Being part of the same larger organization carries with it a common identity and a sturdy basis for making claims on the support of other unions. As one officer of a pilots union put it, "support from other MECs for a particular action may be absent, but in general, it's likely to be there." Expectations of support extended more broadly throughout the domains of airline unions, with officers generally anticipating assistance from other unions representing the same craft (CRAFT, BARGAIN) or workers at the same carrier (CARRIER). Lastly, support was more likely to be anticipated from relatively active unions (ACTIVITY). The size of the union and of its staff was less important than its level of activity in identifying it as a prospective source of support.

Belonging to the same national union was prominent among the rationales mentioned for respondents' expectations of support. Several respondents also referred to federation membership as a basis for expecting help from other unions. Solidaristic rhetoric was not conspicuous in the statements of the union officers interviewed, but respondents did speak of support received in the past *by other unions* (suggesting generalized, rather than specific, reciprocity), the existence of common problems, similar interests and goals, the commonality of representing airline workers, working "side by side," "union brotherhood," and "solidarity among unions" as grounds for expectations of support.

Contact Related to the Eastern Airlines Strike

The interviews with union officers occurred shortly after the onset of the major strike at Eastern Airlines in March 1989. This strike was clearly an important focus for inter-union activity, and claims were made regarding the unusual breadth of involvement in the struggle. To what extent did the pattern of strike-related communication differ from the lines of communication generally occurring this period?

The regression estimates listed in table 5-2, column 8, suggest that contact related to the Eastern strike did indeed deviate from the usual contours of inter-union activity. The variable capturing common problem interdependence with respect to events at Eastern (EALPROB) has the largest coefficient and is one of only three variables showing a statistically significant effect. Recall that the coding of common problem interdependence with respect to Eastern takes into account ties among all the Eastern unions, regardless of craft or organizational level, and all other airline unions. Thus, contact related to the Eastern strike reached outside the domains of craft and carrier and other interdependencies that usually bound relations among airline unions.[11] More consistent with the findings throughout this analysis, unions affiliated with the same national union (NATIONAL) were more likely to have had strike-related contact, as were unions with larger staffs (STAFFING).

Discussion

Table 5-3 summarizes the regression results in a manner conducive to comparisons across variables. Explanatory variables are grouped into the broad categories of interdependence between unions representing the same craft,

Table 5-3. Summary of Findings

	DIRCOMM	FREQUENT	TURNSTRK	KEYREL	JOINTACT	DISPUTE	EXPSUPP	EALCOMM
Intracraft Interdependence								
CRAFT	+				+	+	+	
COMPETE						+		
BARGAIN			+		+		+	
Cross-Craft Interdependence								
CARRIER	+		+			+	+	
RESDEP			+	+		+		
WORKFLOW	+	+	+	+	+	+		
FINPROB	+	+			+			
EALPROB								+
Organizational Interdependence								
NATIONAL	+		+				+	+
AFLSTAT		+				−		
Consensus								
LEGITMCY								
EMPLOWN				−				
Organizational Characteristics								
ACTIVITY							+	
STAFFING	+	+	+	+	+			+
ORGLEVEL	+	+	+		+			

interdependence across crafts, and interdependence based on organizational affiliations, domain and ideological consensus, and organizational characteristics. These groupings are not dimensions or factors in a statistical sense but nonetheless help relate the findings to the study's theoretical framework.

A basic conclusion is that the factors incorporated in the theoretical model of inter-union relations outlined in chapter 2 do, in fact, contribute to an understanding of the presence or absence of a variety of relations between airline unions. Ties between unions are not established randomly or for reasons so particularistic as to defy generalization. Instead, ties tend to follow coherent lines of interdependence (hypothesis 1). Further, multiple forms of interdependence, rather than any single or dominant type, constitute the grounds for inter-union relations.

Much remains to be accounted for regarding the formation and maintenance of inter-union ties. Particularistic explanations based on the histories of unions and personal connections between leaders are undoubtedly significant pieces of that story. This analysis demonstrates, however, that a systematic and theoretically meaningful pattern does exist with respect to relations between airline unions. It also establishes that there are some broad, qualitative differences in these relations depending on the manner in which the unions are interdependent. Without pushing this claim too far, meaningful differences can be discerned between intracraft, cross-craft, and formally organized relations.

Intracraft Relations

Relations between unions representing the same craft typically incorporate several elements. Insofar as these unions draw on the same membership base, competitive interdependence may be present. The craft-based bargaining structure of the airline industry renders comparisons with the same craft at different carriers a basic yardstick for assessing a union's bargaining outcomes. Hence, unions representing the same craft may also be linked by bargaining outcome interdependence. More generally, intracraft relations are marked by overlapping concerns with craft issues, a common craft identity, and relatively similar resources and capabilities (particularly, as is the case here, when employers are similar in scale).

The findings clearly support the notion that common craft constitutes an important basis for inter-union relations in the airline industry (as, of course, it does for intra-union relations). Qualitatively, intracraft relations evidenced the confluence of collaboration and conflict that was hypothesized (hypothesis 2). Hence, whereas there was conflict between unions that had actively competed for members, the relative similarity of unions representing the same craft was conducive to joint action.

Intracraft interdependencies were less useful in accounting for high instrumentality ties. To be sure, the centrality of bargaining as a union endeavor makes other unions with which there is bargaining outcome interdependence important actors. Unions representing the same craft at competing carriers also have a good deal of information to offer. Yet, despite the usefulness of pooling similar but limited resources in a collective manner, individual unions representing the same craft do not stand out in strategic importance in the same manner as, for example, a union with sufficient bargaining power to make a carrier think twice about taking a strike. Lastly, the bond of common craft generally is sufficiently meaningful to lead union officers to expect support from other unions representing the same craft (even controlling for national union affiliation).

Cross-Craft Relations

In segmenting the airline work force into bargaining units based on the type of work performed, craft organization also generates interdependence between unions representing different crafts. The interconnection of members of different unions in the work process creates workflow interdependence between unions. That crafts differ in numbers and strategic importance to the work process is a fundamental basis for resource dependence between unions with differential bargaining power and political capacity. More generally, craft organization in the airline industry results in several unions representing different crafts at the same carrier and having a mutual interest in the affairs of that employer.

Cross-craft interdependencies proved to be a very significant basis for inter-union ties in this study. Resource dependence between more and less powerful unions, workflow interdependence between unions representing in-flight crafts, and the shared domain of representing workers employed by the same carrier all accounted for multiple ties. These forms of interdependence were especially prominent as bases for high instrumentality relations and for conflict (hypothesis 3). Resource dependence, capturing relations between unions possessing unequal amounts of scarce resources and capabilities, was a basis for both types of instrumental ties. To the extent that unions rely on resources and support from one another, unions with greater ability to provide these resources stand out as strategically important. That these relations are also fraught with problems is reflected in the association between resource dependence and conflict. Disputes become likely when needed support is not forthcoming or attempts to influence less powerful unions are resisted. Inequality also makes joint action, particularly in the absence of compelling common problems, more difficult to achieve. Powerful unions have less incentive to join in collective efforts from which they may gain little and that threaten to curtail their autonomy.

Workflow interdependence provided grounds for a wider range of ties (including joint action) than resource dependence. Insofar as unions are rooted in the workplace and the employment relationship, it makes sense that the nature of the production process has a substantial impact on inter-union relations as well. Still, the centrality of workflow interdependence as an explanatory variable was somewhat surprising and requires further investigation. One caveat is that the crude measure of workflow interdependence employed also captured the prevalence, complicated history (including prior organizational affiliations), and unique character of pilot union–flight attendant union relations.

Lines of common problem interdependence also crossed craft boundaries (although this is not inherently a feature of common problem interdependence). Common problem interdependence related to events at Eastern Airlines entailed interdependence across both crafts and carriers. The measures of common problem interdependence differed from other cross-carrier relations in that they involved a specific problem impinging on a set of unions. The finding that unions at financially struggling carriers were more likely to have had direct contact, to have communicated frequently, and to have engaged in joint action is quite consistent with the fundamental expectation that common problem interdependence would be associated with intensive and collective relations (hypothesis 4). Serious common problems, such as the threat of a carrier going under financially, stand to affect all unions at a carrier equally and to call for joint actions, such as deciding whether to render concessions, hiring financial consultants, and seeking prospective buyers. But despite indications of widespread and grave concern about the potential impact of the situation at Eastern, this form of common problem interdependence did not lead to joint action, at least as it was measured here. The most likely reason is that collective action took place at the level of the AFL-CIO and individual unions focused on support activities. Although actual communication related to the Eastern strike conformed only partially to the pattern that would be expected if every union had contact with every Eastern union, the measure of common problem interdependence related to Eastern was one of the primary (and few) variables accounting for the actual pattern of strike-related communication.

Formally Organized Relations

The structure of union representation in the airline industry includes numerous unions affiliated with the same national unions or with the AFL-CIO. The organizational boundaries of some unions (e.g., ALPA, AFA) correspond with craft lines, since these unions represent workers of a single craft. There are, however, theoretical grounds for suspecting that relations occurring within the boundaries of larger organizations may be qualitatively distinct, regardless of whether or not there is also homogeneous craft representation. A common organizational identity, established lines of communication, joint decision-making forums, and a national headquarters with explicit responsibility for coordination are all likely to shape relations between affiliates.

Affiliation with the same national union was quite important in determining the nature of inter-union ties. As hypothesized (hypothesis 5), unions affiliated with the same national union were especially likely to have had direct contact with one another. Some of this contact occurred in the process of conducting the affairs of the national union, but much of it transpired directly between affiliates. Common national union affiliation led to expectations of support as well. Being part of the same larger organization establishes a claim on other affiliates that can be asserted with relative confidence. A common identity, past instances in which support has been rendered to other affiliates, and, if need be, the ability of the national headquarters to prod reluctant affiliates into action all undergird expectations of support.

Findings concerning the instrumentality of the ties between national union affiliates are somewhat less clear. Other unions affiliated with the same national union were no more likely to be cited as prime sources of strike support. Nor was contact with other affiliates of the same national union more apt to be frequent. Undoubtedly, some of the contact between affiliates of the same national union took place in the context of routine and mundane governance activities. Yet unions affiliated with the same national union were more likely to be seen as key ties, and the comments of interview respondents generally suggested considerable reliance on their counterparts within the same national unions. The failure to cite other affiliates among the unions that would be turned to first can plausibly be viewed as the result of a reliance on the national union as a whole (recall that ties between union headquarters and their affiliates were not among the union pairs considered) to provide resources (e.g., information through its research department) and to coordinate support activities. That common national union affiliation was one of the lines along which support was mobilized during the Eastern Airlines strike also speaks to the at least potential instrumentality of these ties.

Having a common AFL-CIO affiliation had a more limited impact on interunion relations. Disputes were less likely between unions with the same AFL-CIO affiliation status than they were between affiliated and independent unions. This makes sense in light of the dispute resolution and jurisdictional maintenance functions of the AFL-CIO. Although it was expected that federation membership would provide a vehicle for contact, the association between frequent contact and shared AFL-CIO affiliation status was somewhat surprising. This finding may reflect the intensive coalitional activity involving independent flight attendant unions more than anything else.

Also somewhat surprising, expectations of support were not any more common among unions with the same AFL-CIO affiliation. That a more pronounced influence was not apparent is attributable to several factors. First, federation membership is much more inclusive than national union affiliation and clearly is a more remote connection. Since the great majority of unions studied were AFL-CIO affiliated, that status did not differentiate the unions to any great extent. Second, especially when one moves down from the national union level, AFL-CIO activity does little to foster ties or coordination between airline unions per se (ties to unions in other industries may be a different story). Third, the coding of the variable capturing affiliation status was crude; for example, a pair of AFL-CIO affiliates and two independent unions shared the same affiliation status.

Other Variables

The domain and ideological consensus variables generally did not account for the presence or absence of ties between unions, save for the interesting relationship between consensus on the value of employee ownership as a strategy and "key" ties. The variables investigated were quite limited, however, and sweeping generalizations about the relevance of consensus to inter-union relations are not warranted.

Organizational characteristics were more telling. In particular, the size of a union's staff was associated with the presence of numerous ties. Having a larger staff facilitates working together with other unions, monitoring the environment, and being able to provide support. Since staff size and number of members represented are positively correlated, this measure captures a more general organizational size effect as well.

The range of activities in which unions engaged was less important but did serve as a basis for identifying unions likely to provide support. Organizational level also proved to be a relevant characteristic, insofar as unions tended to have ties with other unions at the same level. This tendency reflects the similarity in authority and scope of responsibility among unions that are counterparts within their respective national unions.

Conclusion

A basic reason unions establish ties is to deal with their interdependence. When the decisions and actions of some unions affect other unions, those unions are likely to communicate and interact. Thus, the regression analysis in this chapter showed substantial correspondence between lines of interdependence and the presence of inter-union relations.

The relations between unions differ qualitatively depending on the nature of their interdependence. The confluence of collaboration and conflict among unions representing the same craft, the high instrumentality and conflict-prone nature of relations across craft, the intensity of contact between unions linked by the common problem of a financially failing carrier, and the formality of relations between affiliates of the same national unions demonstrates the linkage between types of interdependence and relational forms.

Chapter 6

The Structure of the Airline
Union Network

I f we take seriously the notion that the labor movement is an inter-union
network, then it is insufficient to limit analysis to union pairs. Ties
between pairs of unions combine to form a larger system of relations that
is more than the simple aggregate of pair-wise ties. The patterning or
structure of that network is crucial, affecting the outcomes of individual
unions and shaping the capacity of airline labor as a whole to mobilize and
act cohesively. The network analyses reported in this chapter address several
basic questions. How prevalent are particular relations between airline unions?
To what extent is the airline union network centralized, and which unions
are most central within it? How coherent is the structure of this network, and
how can it best be described?

A picture emerges of a network in which most airline unions are at least
minimally involved and communication flows quite freely but where substantial support and resources are difficult to come by; of a network that is
relatively decentralized but in which unions facing serious threat become
central; and of a network in which relational patterns are not rigidly defined
but where the underlying craft organization of the airline industry and
associated differences in the characteristics of unions representing different
crafts have a pervasive effect on relations.

Networks and Structural Analysis

Although the industrial relations literature has been essentially devoid of
network-level analyses, organizational researchers have increasingly recognized the importance of networks (Lincoln 1982; DiMaggio 1986; Laumann
and Knoke 1989). A network can be understood to be all the links of a

specified type among a given set of actors. Thus, a network consists of the entire pattern of relations, including indirect ties, among those actors. The relations may be anything from intimate friendships to arms shipments. Actors may be individuals, groups, nations, or, as in this case, organizations.

A defining feature of network analyses is that the relations among the actors, not their attributes, are of prime concern. Actors are viewed as thoroughly embedded in a larger social context (Granovetter 1985), rather than as atoms whose behavior can be adequately understood in terms of their individual attributes. Attributes are important in interpreting the structure of a network, but it is the web of relations in which actors are located that is key. Moreover, a network is not a simple aggregate of pair-wise relations between actors. The patterning or structure of a network is an emergent property. The same dyadic relation can have very different implications depending on the structure of the surrounding network. It can, for example, be one of many ties among a set of closely interconnected actors (and therefore be essentially redundant) or a critical link between two distinct factions, the removal of which would seriously disrupt the larger system.

What difference might the structure of a union network make? A dense network implies more alternative sources of information and support than a sparse network. A more highly centralized network lends itself to coordination, but also to domination. Unions positioned centrally within a network stand to have greater access to information, more influence, and to play a critical role in producing unified action. A network structure in which unions form numerous internally cohesive but provincial "cliques" bodes ill for broader labor unity. These are only some examples. The essential point is that a network analysis invites us to think of airline labor as a whole and to examine the place of individual unions within that larger system.

Findings of Network Analyses: Density, Reciprocity, and Centrality

Network Density

This study examines relations among airline unions only. The results of any network analysis are heavily dependent on whether or not all of the most relevant actors are included in the network that is being studied (Laumann, Marsden, and Prensky 1983). The inter-union ties of airline unions are, in fact, confined primarily to other unions in the industry. Seventy-one percent of respondents reported that "almost all" of their contact was with other airline unions, 19 percent said "more" contact was with airline unions than with nonairline unions, and only 10 percent reported that the amount of contact with nonairline unions was equal to or greater than that with airline unions. Focusing on an airline union network thus captures most, although not all, of the inter-union activity of these unions.

The density of a network is the proportion of all possible ties of a specified kind that are actually present among the actors in that network. Density thus gets at the prevalence of a particular kind of relation. How dense is the airline union network? The answer depends very much on the particular tie being considered.[1] Network densities for the relational contents examined in this study are shown in table 6-1.[2]

Overall, relatively superficial ties, which either do not entail actual contact or which do not require a large sacrifice of autonomy or resources, are the most prevalent. Conflict and "high cost" relations are considerably less common. Thus, the airline union network was densest during the period studied for the relations "know of a contact person," "expect at least mild support," and "received/exchanged information of any kind." The network was least dense for the ties "had a written/oral agreement," "belonged to the same coalition," "had a dispute/disagreement," "received substantial support," and "perceived competition."

That respondents tended to be aware of the names of particular individuals at other unions, even in the absence of actual contact with those unions, suggests that establishing contact with a wider circle of airline unions is not very difficult for those unions inclined to do so. Officers also reported expecting at least mild support from a fairly large number of other unions. Although not all other airline unions were seen as prospective providers of support and the degree of support expected was not necessarily great, being

Table 6-1.   Density and Reciprocity of Inter-Union Relations

Relation	Density	Percent of ties reciprocated
Know of a contact person	.390	71.36
Expect support from	.327	51.01
Direct communication/contact	.248	SYMM.
Received information from	.230	60.08
Perceive interdependence with	.185	42.05
Engaged in joint action with	.097	SYMM.
Turn to first for information[a]	.069	21.92
Turn to first in strike[a]	.066	17.14
Received resources from	.058	55.74
Most important tie(s)[a]	.050	22.64
Received substantial support	.047	20.00
Had disagreement or dispute	.046	24.49
Belong to the same coalition	.042	SYMM.
Have written/oral agreement	.036	SYMM.
Perceive to be a competitor	.027	7.14

N = 1,056

[a] Densities for these relations are less meaningful because the survey item constrained the number of nominations that could be made.

SYMM. = Relation was regarded as inherently symmetrical and the data were symmetrized (by intersection) to conform with this.

part of a larger labor movement and representing workers in the same industry was sufficient to engender relatively broad expectations of aid. Information flows were also relatively dense. As one respondent put it, "Information is shared much more readily than other things."

In contrast with the tendency to be aware of the names of union officers and to have loose expectations of support, explicit written or oral agreements between airline unions were largely absent. Other than agreements between national unions and their subunits, few formal accords were reported. Indeed, several respondents seemed surprised that the issue was even raised. Nor are perceptions of competition and conflict widespread. The reality of competition and conflict was certainly acknowledged, but most respondents appeared to have glossed over minor tensions and reported what they took to be more serious conflicts. Receiving support regarded as "substantial" was also rare. This is an important finding if this analysis is to be kept in proper perspective. Although there were a number of instances of support that "really made a difference," most contact was more mundane.[3]

Perceptions of interdependence occupy the middle ground in terms of density. Airline union officers clearly perceive that the actions and outcomes of other airline unions affect their own unions, but this perception extends to only a relatively few unions. To the extent that relations are premised on interdependence and perceptions of it, this implies there are real limits to the density of the airline union network, unless union officers come to view more unions as consequential to their own.

The density figures, then, depict an airline union network that is neither intensely cooperative nor conflictful. Airline union officers tend to be aware of one another and to maintain a number of loose alliances and contacts. They realize that their fates are intertwined with those of other airline unions, albeit a fairly select subset of them. Other than dealings between affiliates of the same national union, relations are quite informal, and there are few written agreements or regular meetings. Access to substantial resources and support is limited and not part of the experience of many airline unions.

Reciprocity

Density figures provide a useful starting point for network analyses by showing which relations are most common. The same density of ties can be arranged into any number of structural configurations (Barnes 1979: 407) however. A second important property of networks, more revealing of network structure, is the extent to which ties are reciprocated. That is, if union A cites union B with respect to a given relation, how often does union B cite union A with respect to that same relation?

In general, reciprocation suggests a relationship between relative equals. The relationship is of similar importance to each party, produces acceptable outcomes for each, and is relatively free of constraint. The absence of reciprocation, by contrast, often indicates a lack of parity between actors and that power and dependency relations may be involved.

On the whole, the ties between airline unions tend to lack reciprocity. Lack of reciprocation is especially evident regarding several of the more select, instrumentally oriented ties, such as "would turn to first in a strike" or "received substantial support from." A plausible interpretation, compatible with the regression findings, is that more powerful, resource-rich unions tend to be designated as important by less powerful unions but usually do not reciprocate in the relation. Consistent with this interpretation, the number of times unions representing pilots or mechanics were cited as the most important tie (26) was more than twice that of unions representing other groups of workers (11).[4]

Greater mutuality is evident in the awareness of contact persons, receipt of information, and expectations of support. Presumably, support is more likely to be forthcoming if both parties view each other as allies. The very limited correspondence in perceptions of competition is surprising but most likely reflects differences in the propensities of unions to expand their jurisdictions and, perhaps, a tendency to see competition as present only when one's own union comes out on the losing end. The extent of disagreement on disagreement is also striking. There were a significant number of instances in which the issues of aggrieved parties were not acknowledged by the offending parties. The systematic nature of this asymmetry and of the overall tendency toward lack of reciprocation is illuminated in the blockmodeling analysis reported below.

Network Centralization and Union Centrality

Looking at airline labor as a system or network, it is useful to ask whether one or a few unions are focal points in the flow of communication, resources, and influence. To what extent are certain unions more "in the middle of things"? Put differently, how centralized is the airline union network, and which unions are most central?

At least three distinct conceptions of centrality are commonly employed: centrality as the extent to which a given actor has direct ties to numerous other network actors (degree); centrality as the extent to which a given actor occupies a position in the network that affords ready access to numerous other actors (closeness); and centrality as the extent to which an actor is positioned to mediate the contact of numerous other actors (betweenness) (Freeman 1978–79). Substantively, these three forms of centrality imply: (1) the amount of activity within the network (actors that are most central in terms of degree have the most extensive ties); (2) the degree of independence (actors that are most central in terms of closeness can communicate or exchange resources with other actors without going through a large number of intermediaries; and (3) the ability to exert control within the network (actors that are most central in terms of betweenness can potentially use their positioning to decide which network actors get information or other resources) (Freeman 1978–79: 221–26). Regardless of the specific type of centrality considered, the centralization of a network as a whole is derived from a comparison of the centralities of individual network actors. In a highly centralized network, one actor will be far more central than most of the other actors.[5]

Network Centralization

To determine how centralized the airline union network was during the study period, centralization scores were computed for the networks formed by each of the following ties: "had direct communication/contact," "received/exchanged information," and "engaged in joint action."[6] Centralization scores for the networks formed by each of these relations are listed in table 6-2.

Overall, the centralization scores are low to moderate. Scores for centralization based on betweenness are particularly low. No single union stands out as being readily positioned to mediate the flow of information or joint action among other unions. Since centrality based on betweenness is the form that most readily lends itself to exerting control within a network (Freeman 1978–79: 221), the limited extent of centralization in this regard is significant. The higher degree centralization scores indicate greater disparity across unions in the number of other unions with which they had direct contact or communication. Some unions are clearly more active than others in maintaining lines of communication, but this is far from the scenario in which a single "hub" union maintains ties with a set of otherwise isolated actors (which is the underlying model of a completely centralized network).

The moderate degree centralization of the network based on information flows is consistent with the notion that information circulates relatively freely among airline unions and no single union has a monopoly on it. The slightly higher centralization figure for in-degree, however, suggests that sources of information (the substantive interpretation of in-degree because

Table 6-2. Network Centralization Measures (in percents)

Relationship	Degree	Closeness	Betweenness
Direct communication/contact	40.12	42.62	17.75
Receive/exchange information	35.38[a] (42.06)	32.04	9.43
Joint action	25.20	6.55	27.54

Note: Centralization measures were computed using UCINET IV (version 1.0) (Borgatti, Everett, and Freeman 1992).

[a] Because receive/exchange information is a nonsymmetrical tie, measures of degree centralization according to both out-degree and in-degree (in parentheses) are shown.

of the wording of the item) were a somewhat more select group than recipients. The lower centralization scores for the network based on joint action suggest that involvement in joint action was spread fairly evenly across unions. Unions entered into collective efforts as necessary and with a set of other unions sharing some immediate concern, but were not likely to do so in a number of different instances and with different partners.

The measures of closeness tell a similar story. The lengths of the shortest paths (geodesics) connecting airline unions are relatively short and do not vary much. The maximum geodesic in terms of direct communication/contact, for example, was a path length of four. Eighty percent of all pairings were separated by path lengths of two or less, meaning that the unions either had direct communication or had both been in contact with the same other union. There were no isolates (unions that did not maintain a specified tie with any other unions) in the network based on direct communication/contact but a few in the other two networks. Simply put, the findings on closeness suggest that airline labor is a "small world." Unions not in direct contact with one another are still able to establish most desired links through a set of relatively immediate contacts and to have access to essential information.

The picture that emerges, then, is of a relatively decentralized airline union network. Results vary somewhat depending on the relation considered and the specific centralization measure employed, but there is little evidence that one or a few unions dominate inter-union communication.

Union Centrality

Even if the airline union network as a whole is not highly centralized, some unions are still likely to be more central than others. Which unions are the most central?

One way to approach this issue is to ask which characteristics are likely to confer higher centrality on unions. Each of the hypothetical networks outlined in chapter 2 provides a different answer to this question. In a craft-centered network, unions with jurisdictions encompassing multiple crafts might be expected to have the highest centrality. These unions share this bond with a number of other unions with which they may either compete or cooperate. The logic of a resource-centered network points to higher centrality for those unions most able to provide meaningful resources and support. A problem-centered network is likely to revolve around unions enmeshed in some problem or crisis affecting a significant number of other unions within the network. High centrality would be conferred on the basis of unions located "in the eye of the storm" being the recipients of support and requests for information from other unions in the network. Lastly, within an organization-centered network, national union headquarters would be expected to be most central. Higher centrality would accrue to national-level unions as a result of their links to multiple subunits and the likelihood that other unions would tend to deal with them as authoritative decision-making bodies.

To assess empirically the sources of centrality within the airline union network, OLS regression models predicting the centrality of individual unions in the network defined by direct communication/contact were estimated. The hypothesized sources of centrality were represented in this analysis by variables capturing breadth of jurisdiction (JURIS), possession of high bargaining power or political capacity (HIPOWER), representation of workers at Eastern Airlines (EALUNION), and national union status (NATLSTAT). Models were estimated for both degree (DCENTRAL) and betweenness centrality (BCENTRAL) (closeness centrality was highly correlated with degree centrality). Operational definitions, means, and standard deviations for these variables are listed below. Note that the unit of analysis here is the individual union and that variables consequently differ from those used in the dyadic analysis.

EALUNION: Coded 1 if the union represents workers at Eastern, 0 otherwise (mean = 0.15, s.d. = 0.36).

JURIS: Number of different job groups the union represents (from an eight-category NMB classification of job groups) (mean = 2.00, s.d. = 1.44).

HIPOWER: Carrier-level unions that represent pilots or mechanics and national unions with high political capacity (in terms of number of lobbyists, size of PAC) are coded 1; otherwise a 0 is assigned (mean = 0.48, s.d. = 0.51).

NATLSTAT: Coded 1 if the union is a inter/national union with subunits considered in this study, 0 otherwise (mean = 0.18, s.d. = 0.39).

DCENTRAL: Normalized degree centrality score for each union (mean = 24.81, s.d. = 13.30).

BCENTRAL: Normalized betweenness centrality score for each union (mean = 3.07, s.d. = 4.32).

The results (see table 6-3) indicate that unions representing workers employed by Eastern Airlines were among the most central in terms of both degree and betweenness, but especially the former. These unions were directly involved in a problem of great concern to the larger network and actively solicited and obtained support. The only other statistically significant effect was the greater betweenness centrality of national-level unions. By being linked to their own subunits and to other national-level unions, these unions are positioned to mediate communication and exchange within the network. This lends considerable power to the national headquarters and gives them an important role in affecting coordination among airline unions. Inspection of the individual betweenness centrality scores for national unions shows them to be quite low, however. The findings regarding union centrality, then, are still consistent with the notion of a fluid, decentralized network, albeit one in which national union headquarters are moderately central.

An analysis of centrality shows the airline union network to be relatively decentralized overall but centering on unions in need of support and (less so)

Table 6-3.   OLS Regression Models Predicting Union
Centrality (t-ratio in parentheses)

Variables	Degree centrality	Betweenness centrality
Intercept	20.896 ***	0.703
	(5.53)	(0.74)
JURIS	-1.014	0.507
	(0.55)	(1.09)
HIPOWER	5.427	-0.410
	(1.08)	(0.33)
EALUNION	19.942 *	6.081 **
	(2.73)	(3.32)
NATIONAL	1.636	3.476 *
	(0.26)	(2.21)
F	3.662 *	10.765 ***
Adjusted R-squared	.250	.550
N	33	33

Note: Results are based on the relation "had direct communication/contact."
***$p \le .001$.   **$p \le .01$.   *$p \le .05$ (one-tailed test).

national-level unions. The relative decentralization of the airline union network corresponds with the decentralized bargaining structure of the airline industry. When unions below the national level retain important functions and autonomy, ties should be more evenly distributed across union organizational levels than when national unions have fuller control over bargaining. With considerable decision-making ability and a relatively broad scope of responsibilities, intermediate bodies and locals in the airline industry are likely to be involved in situations in which other unions find reasons to consult with them. The centrality of the Eastern unions demonstrates the fluidity of the airline union network and its ability to respond when critical situations arise. Yet the combination of fluidity and decentralization also raises questions about the capacity of airline labor to work together in a consistent and coordinated fashion. If coordination cannot be readily orchestrated from above and inter-union activity is focused on putting out fires, achieving unified action becomes a complicated process subject to the vagaries of circumstances.

Findings of Network Analyses—CONCOR Blockmodeling

Background

A fuller and more systematic description of network structure can be obtained through a CONCOR blockmodeling analysis. A description of how CONCOR works is provided in appendix 3. It is sufficient here to note that the purpose of this procedure is to reduce the large set of pair-wise relations between the unions studied to a parsimonious and meaningful network structure. Structure can be understood as patterned, recurring relations among a set of actors (White, Boorman, and Breiger 1976: 733).

The structure revealed by CONCOR represents the typical relations among and between the occupants of network positions. These positions are defined on the basis of similarity in patterns of ties with other actors. Stated differently, blockmodeling involves an attempt to identify positions (roles) occupied by structurally equivalent actors and to describe the relations within and between these positions as a depiction of network structure. The grouping of actors in this form of structural analysis is based not on their closeness in terms of direct ties with one another (i.e., positions are not necessarily the equivalent of "cliques") but rather on the similarity in their pattern of ties with other actors in the network (White, Boorman, and Breiger 1976; Knoke and Kuklinski 1982).

An example may help clarify the logic of blockmodeling. Suppose that you have no information about a group of individuals in an organization other than knowledge about the relationship "gives/receives orders." You observe that one individual gives orders to others but receives them from no one. A larger group of individuals both give and receive orders. A still larger group only receives orders. Based only on this relational data, a plausible structural inference can be made that this is a hierarchy of authority and individuals can be assigned to the positions (roles) of top management, middle management, and rank-and-file worker.

Because the relationship chosen for this illustration usually corresponds closely to formal organizational structure, a similar structure could be discerned on the basis of attributes (e.g., job titles). However, the informal structure emerging when there are multiple and more subtle relations among a group of unions is far less likely to be isomorphic, with formal categories or a priori groupings based on shared attributes. In any event, the degree of correspondence between formal and informal structure is an empirical question that blockmodeling can help answer. The fundamental point is that CONCOR blockmodeling derives structure from the actual relations among a set of actors (in the example, relations of authority), and it does so on the basis of the similarity in relational patterns (in the example, similar patterns of order taking and giving). Consistent with the sociological underpinnings of blockmodeling, roles or positions in a network are defined by the relations actors have and with which actors they have them.

The following relations were analyzed in the CONCOR procedure: "received from/exchanged information," "would turn to first in a strike," "engaged in joint action," "expect at least mild support from," "perceive to be a competitor," "had a disagreement or dispute with," "perceive interdependence with," and "received or exchanged resources other than information." It is similarity across unions in the other unions with which they maintained these ties that identified positions of structurally equivalent unions. Partitions of the network into two through eight positions were examined. The choice of the number of network positions is ultimately left to the researcher. Four positions were selected because they capture the structural essence of the network without introducing inordinate complexity into the analysis.

Network Positions

If the attributes of actors are not the primary basis for structural analysis, they nonetheless aid in the interpretation of network structure. Table 6-4 compares the unions assigned to different positions by the CONCOR procedure on a number of attributes.[7] These characteristics, including the predominant craft, carrier, and national union affiliation for unions in each position, size, the range of activities in which unions engaged, and several indicators of bargaining power, flow from the theoretical concerns of the study.[8] Because of the relatively small number of unions occupying each position, statistical tests to identify differences between positions can only be suggestive. Nevertheless, the data in table 6-4 point to a number of characteristics that tend to differentiate the occupants of the four network positions and that help make sense of the distinct relational patterns across network positions.

For position 1 unions, the attributes that stand out are their small size, limited involvement in political action, relatively high bargaining power, tendency to be affiliated with the TWU, and employment of members at American Airlines. Position 1 unions are a less active and elite group than position 3 unions but still quite effectual. The apparent lack of concern regarding bargaining power may reflect the relative insulation of position 1 unions from some of the problems that afflicted unions at less well-off carriers than American. Their eschewing of political activity suggests a primary focus on bargaining. The attributes and relational pattern (discussed below) of unions occupying this position suggest the label of "detached" position for this group.

Position 2 is occupied wholly by flight attendants unions. These unions engaged in a more restricted range of activities than other unions, but they were all involved in politics. This lesser range of activity is most likely attributable to their limited resources and consequent constraints in undertaking the likes of organizing and litigation. The importance of political activity to flight attendants unions stems from their vital concern with safety and regulatory issues and perhaps also from their need to pursue gains in the political arena that cannot be extracted through bargaining. Serious and near-unanimous concern with their lack of sufficient bargaining power clearly distinguishes position 2 unions. Position 2, without any invidious intent, is labeled a "power-deficit" position.

Table 6-4. Attributes of Network Position Occupants

Attribute	Position				Chi-square/Kruskal-Wallis H	p ≤
	1	2	3	4		
n	7	8	10	8	n.a.	n.a.
Predominant craft	Mechanics	Flight Attendants	Pilots	Mechanics	n.a.	n.a.
Proportion	.29	1.0	.80	.50	n.a.	n.a.
Predominant carrier	American	Mixed	Eastern	Mixed	n.a.	n.a.
Proportion	.57	n.a.	.40	n.a.	n.a.	n.a.
Predominant union	TWU	AFA	ALPA	Mixed	n.a.	n.a.
Proportion	.43	.38	.80	n.a.	n.a.	n.a.
Median size	650	7,500	5,300	5,500	4.482	.25
Median range of activity (0–5)	3.0	2.5	5.0	4.0	8.897	.05
Proportion politically active unions	.29	1.0	.90	.50	12.51[a]	.01
Proportion craft unions	.57	.88	.80	.14	11.79[a]	.01
Proportion with high bargaining power/political capacity	.43	0.0	1.0	.38	18.50[a]	.005
Proportion citing lack of bargaining power as a serious problem	.00	.88	.30	.38	12.69[a]	.01

Note: Statistics test the null hypothesis that each variable originates in the same population across network positions. Kruskal-Wallis H (chi-square distribution, 3df) is used for interval- and ordinal-level measures (size, range of activity), and chi-square (3df) is used to evaluate the same hypothesis for nominal level variables.

[a] Low expected values for the chi-square tests make these results only suggestive.

n.a. = not applicable.

Position 3 is an elite position in many respects. Its occupants are all high in bargaining power and political capacity, are affiliated primarily with ALPA (the leading representative of pilots in the industry), and engage in a wide range of activities, including political action. That occupants of this position indicated greater concern with their insufficient bargaining power than position 1 unions reflects the experience of the Eastern strike, in which a number of position 3 unions were principals, and the greater likelihood that the more active position 3 unions would be called upon to use their leverage. Position 3 is labeled an "elite" position.

Position 4 unions are the most difficult to characterize. They tend to represent mechanics and to have an industrial union orientation (i.e., they represent more than a single craft). Position 4 unions occupy an intermediate ground; they are less elite than position 3 unions but more so than most others, particularly in their activity and bargaining power. Position 4 unions are referred to as in a "linking" position, primarily because of their pattern of relations, rather than their attributes.

Multi-dimensional Scaling Representation of Network Structure

Multi-dimensional scaling (MDS) makes the network structure being described more concrete by providing a spatial representation of similarity across unions in relational patterns. An MDS plot of CONCOR correlations is shown in figure 6-1.[9] The location of each union is indicated by a letter. Unions located closer to one another in the plot are more alike in their ties with other unions. They may or may not be directly linked themselves. Curved, solid lines enclose all of the unions assigned to the same network position by CONCOR. Dotted lines enclose those unions affiliated with the same inter/national union. Thus, the MDS plot allows one readily to envision the contrast between the formal and informal structuring of this network.

The MDS spatial representation of the data largely coincides with the CONCOR partitioning, at least to the extent that positions can be enclosed without any overlap. Consistent with the more homogeneous nature of positions 2 and 3, the unions within them are clustered considerably closer than the unions in other positions, especially position 4. Thus, although the CONCOR positions are not the only groupings that could reasonably be superimposed on the MDS representation, the two methods generally converge in identifying clusters of actors that are similar and proximate.

How closely do the formal structure reflected in common affiliation with a particular national union and the informal structure revealed by CONCOR correspond? ALPA and AFA units (including the national levels of these unions) are entirely contained within single positions (3 and 2 respectively). Even within positions, units of these two unions are clustered fairly closely and apart from other position occupants. The various units of these unions, then, exhibit substantially similar patterns of relations with other unions and are quite interchangeable in this respect. Two units of the Flight Engineers

Figure 6-1.   MDS Plot of CONCOR Initial Correlations

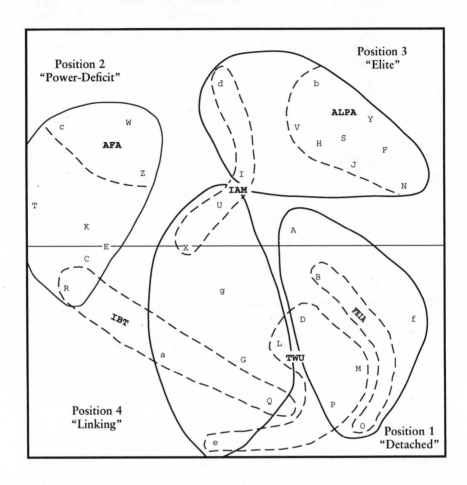

International Association (points B and O in position 1) are also located within the same position but are spatially more distant. Unions affiliated with the IAM are split between two different positions, as are affiliates of the TWU and IBT. The reason for this difference between these unions in the match between structural equivalence and formal organizational affiliation is not entirely clear. That ALPA, AFA, and FEIA are completely homogenous in terms of craft, however, while the other unions are not, is no doubt pertinent. When craft and organizational boundaries, both important determinants of inter-union relations, coincide, unions are more likely to exhibit the same interdependencies and to become enmeshed in similar relational patterns.

Overall, there is a significant degree of correspondence between organizational boundaries and network positions, but formal and informal structure are by no means isomorphic. Subunits of several national unions are split between network positions, and even for those national unions whose subunits all occupy the same network position, that position is generally shared with other unions.[10] To grasp the structure of the airline union network more fully, then, we have to look beyond the formal organizational affiliations of airline unions to more subtle patterns based in craft, the distribution of resources, and the ebb and flow of shared problems. More immediately, we need to look at the relational patterns that distinguish unions occupying different network positions.

Relations within and between Network Positions

Identifying groups of structurally equivalent actors is only one part of a blockmodeling analysis. It is also necessary to examine ties within and between network positions. Doing so clarifies the distinctive relational patterns of network positions and allows them to be articulated with the characteristics of position occupants. Table 6-5 displays block density and image matrices for the airline union network.

Block density matrices indicate the density of ties within the four network positions identified above (main diagonal cells) and between those positions (off-diagonal cells) for each of the eight distinct relations analyzed. Density has the same meaning here as earlier (the number of ties actually present out of the maximum possible number) but is applied to subgroups based on position, rather than the network as a whole.[11] Image matrices reduce block densities to an essential network structure by representing them dichotomously. Cells in the block density matrices with a density higher than the overall density (alpha) for that relation are assigned a "1," while cells with lower density are assigned a "0."[12]

The typical relations of position 1 ("detached") unions are captured in the first row and column of the block density and image matrices. The most striking feature of their relational pattern is the prevalence of "0" cells in the image matrices. Position 1 unions send and receive relatively few ties. Not only do position 1 unions maintain few ties in a relative sense (as indicated in the image matrices), but they also tend to have low density ties in an absolute sense (as indicated by the block density matrices), including a number of instances in which no ties at all are maintained. Position 1 unions are especially unlikely to have ties with position 2 unions. Most important, to the limited extent that position 1 unions are involved in this network, their engagement centers on competition and conflict. Even so, the Eastern Airlines strike occasioned contributions of resources other than information by position 1 unions to position 3 unions.

The airline union network, then, includes a number of unions that are relatively isolated, sending and receiving few ties. Limited connectedness to other unions is roughly consistent with the impression gleaned from an

Table 6-5.   *Block Density and Image Matrices*

Block density matrices				Image matrices			

Receive/Exchange Information

Alpha = 0.230

0.214	0.054	0.171	0.089	0	0	0	0
0.089	0.714	0.237	0.156	0	1	1	0
0.143	0.125	0.667	0.162	0	0	1	0
0.143	0.109	0.262	0.196	0	0	1	0

Turn to First in a Strike

Alpha = 0.066

0.024	0.036	0.029	0.089	0	0	0	1
0.000	0.161	0.087	0.063	0	1	1	0
0.014	0.038	0.256	0.036	0	0	1	0
0.036	0.016	0.063	0.036	0	0	0	0

Engage in Joint Action

Alpha = 0.097

0.048	0.018	0.014	0.071	0	0	0	0
0.018	0.536	0.087	0.047	0	1	0	0
0.014	0.087	0.267	0.075	0	0	1	0
0.071	0.047	0.075	0.036	0	0	0	0

Perceived Competitor

Alpha = 0.027

0.000	0.000	0.043	0.071	0	0	1	1
0.036	0.143	0.025	0.031	1	1	0	1
0.057	0.000	0.000	0.000	1	0	0	0
0.018	0.000	0.013	0.018	0	0	0	0

Expect Support From

Alpha = 0.327

0.286	0.196	0.257	0.196	0	0	0	0
0.196	0.750	0.313	0.234	0	1	0	0
0.200	0.237	0.778	0.200	0	0	1	0
0.286	0.281	0.363	0.321	0	0	1	0

Disagreement/Dispute

Alpha = 0.046

0.024	0.000	0.014	0.054	0	0	0	1
0.054	0.161	0.050	0.047	1	1	1	1
0.043	0.025	0.111	0.038	0	0	1	0
0.036	0.016	0.050	0.000	0	0	1	0

Perceive Interdependence

Alpha = 0.185

0.024	0.000	0.086	0.071	0	0	0	0
0.179	0.446	0.250	0.156	0	1	1	0
0.071	0.075	0.500	0.087	0	0	1	0
0.232	0.188	0.250	0.196	1	1	1	1

Receive/Exchange Resources Other Than Information

Alpha = 0.058

0.000	0.018	0.057	0.054	0	0	0	0
0.000	0.161	0.025	0.000	0	1	0	0
0.071	0.013	0.244	0.063	1	0	1	1
0.054	0.016	0.038	0.036	0	0	0	0

examination of the attributes of position 1 occupants, particularly their restricted range of activity. Yet position 1 unions are hardly nonentities. They have the capacity to make their presence felt, most often, it appears, through antagonistic relations with other unions.

Position 2 ("power-deficit") unions maintained high levels of within-position ties across all of the relations examined, as indicated by the prevalence of 1s in the second cell on the main diagonal of the image matrices. Indeed, ties among these flight attendants unions are consistently among the densest within the network. Position 2 unions are especially likely to share information, engage in joint action, and expect support from one another. This cohesiveness, however, co-exists with relatively high levels of perceived competition and disagreement.

Position 2 unions are also the most outward-looking, sending high density ties to a number of other positions, especially the "elite" position 3 unions. Position 2 unions report disputes at an above-average level with occupants of all three other positions. Yet these conflicts are often not acknowledged by unions in other positions. This asymmetry is in keeping with the overall finding that position 2 unions receive dense ties from none of the other positions, except perceived interdependence by position 4 unions, which perceives interdependence with all other positions as well.

Overall, position 2 encompasses a set of unions whose relations with one another are relatively intensive, incorporating both collaboration and conflict. These flight attendants unions are also oriented toward relations with other unions, even as those other unions tend to overlook them. The cohesiveness and lack of reciprocation characterizing the relations of position 2 unions are consistent with the limited resources of flight attendants unions.

More than most other airline unions, flight attendants unions appreciate the importance of inter-union support and the difficulty of going it alone. To a considerable extent, they have been able to put aside conflicts to gain the benefits of pooling resources and information. Yet the limited ability of flight attendants unions to influence outcomes decisively on their own necessitates relations with other unions. The fairly dense but not frequently reciprocated ties sent by position 2 unions to the primarily pilot unions of position 3 especially fit this pattern. Overlaid with a history of unsatisfactory organizational affiliations, workflow interdependence, occupational status differences, and gender issues, relations between pilots and flight attendants unions derive their particular character from the unequal bargaining power and resources of these groups—resulting in relations shaped by the dynamics of power.[13]

Position 3 unions are also quite cohesive. With the exception of perceptions of competition, position 3 unions maintain the bulk of their ties with other unions occupying the same position. This reflects a concentration of ties among ALPA MECs, as well as with two units of the IAM. Notably, these ties include a higher than average amount of conflict. The other salient feature of the pattern of relations of position 3 unions is that, although they are often the recipient of ties, they send relatively few ties to other positions. This is seen in the fairly large number of "1" cells in column 3 of the image matrices compared with row 3.

Position 3 unions are preferred sources of information for unions in other positions, are most often among those unions that would be turned to first in a strike, tend to be seen as parties to conflict, and, very significantly in light of the theoretical framework of this study, generally are viewed as affecting the actions and outcomes of other unions (interdependence is perceived with them). For both position 2 and position 4 unions, there is a pronounced tendency to send ties to position 3 unions. Such is not the case with position 1 unions, for which mutual perceptions of competition provide the major link with unions in position 3. The primary exception to this self-reliant, aloof pattern of ties is the receipt of resources other than information by position 3 unions. This is accounted for by funds sent to the striking Eastern Airlines unions, several of which were located in position 3.

The relational pattern of position 3 unions fits with their casting as elite within the airline union network. Position 3 unions relate primarily to each other and are seen by unions in other positions as unions to turn to in a strike, for information, and so forth. At the same time, their superior resources and bargaining power afford them the luxury of concentrating on their relations with one another. The elite unions also have the means to contest one another, so that conflicts among ALPA MECs and between ALPA and the IAM are relatively common. The advent of the major conflict at Eastern Airlines, however, necessitated a departure from business as usual, at least to the extent of receiving strike funds and other material support from throughout the network.

Position 4 unions, similar to position 1 unions, maintain few dense ties among themselves and tend to be seen as competitors or disputants by unions in other positions. They differ from position 1 unions in having more extensive ties throughout the network, especially with position 3 unions. Most strikingly, position 4 unions perceive interdependence to exist far more widely throughout the network than do other unions, perhaps because of the predominance of industrial unions in this group.

Although the relational pattern of position 4 unions is not clear-cut, terming it a "linking" position is justified insofar as the ties of position 4 unions are spread relatively evenly (if not always densely) across positions. Position 4 unions are more fully engaged in the network than position 1 unions, and unlike unions in positions 2 and 3, the ties of position 4 unions are not concentrated among themselves. Their more diverse jurisdictions are matched by greater breadth to their ties, particularly their grasp of interdependence with other airline unions. This places position 4 unions in an important position in terms of potentially linking together the airline union network as a whole.

The airline union network, then, manifests the following basic structure: a group of "detached" unions having relatively little to do with one another and even less with unions in other positions, save for perceived competition and conflict; a group of flight attendants unions that are cohesive and very active within the network but whose ties are often not reciprocated by occupants of other positions; a number of "elite" unions, representing pilots and mechanics, whose ties are heavily concentrated within their own position and that tend not to reciprocate ties sent by other positions; and a fourth group of unions that maintain relatively sparse ties among themselves but whose ties are distributed more evenly throughout the network.

Discussion

The web of relations connecting airline unions has a number of basic structural features. Airline unions have most of their contact with one another (rather than with unions in other industries). Bonds between airline unions tend to be relatively loose and informal. Establishing contacts and procuring at least certain kinds of information is relatively easy; firm commitments, resources other than information, and strong support are more difficult to come by. Although some unions are more central than others, the network as a whole is relatively decentralized and is fluid enough to reflect circumstances as they arise. Two groups of unions, composed of flight attendants and (primarily) pilots unions respectively, exhibit cohesiveness in their high level of ties among themselves. Although the flight attendants unions also have links with unions in other crafts, the pilots unions interact more as a clique, remaining somewhat aloof from the rest of the network. Limited reciprocation, especially for instrumentally oriented ties and involving the more "elite" unions, is an essential structural feature of the airline union network.

If interdependence is a basic condition generating ties between pairs of unions, then this should also be apparent in the network as a whole. The structure described in this chapter does, in fact, reflect underlying interdependencies among unions. Again, the picture is one of multiple grounds for inter-union relations, rather than a single, dominant explanation.

That the structure of the airline union network is more subtle and complex than that which would be inferred strictly from formal organizational affiliations should not obscure the considerable correspondence between national union boundaries and network structure. Affiliates of three national unions (ALPA, AFA, and FEIA) exhibit patterns of ties similar enough to warrant their location in the same network positions. Put differently, the units of these national unions play the same roles within the network and are largely interchangeable in that respect. That the national headquarters of unions enjoy higher betweenness centrality is also consistent with the influence of formal structuring. Although this is not a highly centralized network in which national union headquarters call all the shots, national unions are well positioned to mediate the flow of resources and information.

The structural relevance of craft is also evident in this network. Two of the network positions (2 and 3) are largely homogeneous with respect to craft. Affiliates of national unions that represent a single craft are the most alike in their relational patterns. Position 2 unions, in particular, are linked by the bond of representing the same craft (but, for the most part, are not affiliates of the same national union) and manifest a distinctive relational pattern incorporating substantial degrees of both collaboration and conflict.

Craft organization is meaningful not only because of the links between unions representing the same craft at different carriers but also because it opens up the possibility of relations crossing the boundaries of unions representing different crafts, especially at the same carriers. In the airline industry, the numerous crafts differ substantially in number, strategic importance to the production process, national union affiliation, and the ability of their members to provide financial support for union activities, among other things. Relations across crafts, then, typically occur on less than equal footing. The structural impact of differences in resources and capacities is quite evident in the airline union network. The tendency toward limited reciprocation of ties is probably best accounted for in these terms. The relational profile of the elite unions is also indicative of the distribution of resources and capacities. Position 3 unions can all be regarded as relatively powerful but are not all representatives of the same craft or affiliates of the same national union. Other unions see them as influential and as important sources of information and support, but the elite unions are most interested in maintaining ties (not necessarily cooperative) with one another.

Circumstances creating common problems for unions also shape the structure of relations. This is clearest in the high centrality of the unions representing workers at Eastern Airlines, whose location in the "eye of the storm" placed them in the middle of support activity and information flows. Significantly, the Eastern Airlines struggle also accounted for a departure from the norm in that the elite unions, a number of which represented workers at Eastern, became recipients rather than providers of resources (strike contributions).

Given that the structure of the airline union network partly reflects the ebb and flow of circumstances, just how established and recurrent are relations? The issue of network stability is an important one (Aldrich and Whetten 1981: 391), because it is when relations are relatively stable and enduring that a network structure is most meaningful. Ultimately, longitudinal data are needed to demonstrate continuity in network structure. Nonetheless, there are good reasons to believe that the essential features of the structure of the airline union network tend toward stability. To the extent that relations are grounded in interdependencies stemming from the distribution of resources and capacities among unions, the nature of the production process, union jurisdictions, the decentralized bargaining structure of the industry, and formal organizational affiliations—conditions not likely to change rapidly or often—those relations should also evidence essential continuity. More generally, the weight of expectations and a tendency toward inertia in interorganizational relations (Laumann, Galaskiewicz, and Marsden 1978: 470) also promote stability. At the same time, the relative ease of establishing at least superficial relations among airline unions, the limited formal authority relations or binding agreements between most airline unions, the considerable turnover among union officers, the somewhat indefinite and situation-specific resource needs of unions, and a rapidly changing and threatening industry environment all portend a significant amount of dynamism and fluidity in the structure of the airline union network.

Practical Implications of Network Structure

The network structure described here has a number of implications for the manner in which airline unions deal with one another and, ultimately, for airline labor relations. This is a network in which it is relatively easy to establish at least superficial ties. Communication links are moderately dense, and most airline unions can be reached either directly or through a single intermediary. The union that makes a concerted effort to obtain information, for example, will often secure it, although generating strike support may be more difficult.

The airline union network is basically decentralized. Consequently, top-down efforts to mandate greater coordination and cooperation are apt to meet with only limited success. Certainly, national union headquarters and the AFL-CIO are necessary starting points if one wishes to orchestrate broad inter-union collaboration, but the substantial autonomy of carrier-level unions means that they may have to be sold individually on the benefits. A decentralized network also implies that airline labor as a whole is less likely to be drawn into particular conflicts or problems. The advantages of this situation are that it allows different strategies to be tried out (rather than necessitating agreement by all) and conserves resources (not everyone is involved in every battle). But such "loose coupling" can easily shade over to lack of solidarity, parochialism, and an inability to recognize the fundamental interdependence of unions in the industry.

The structure of the network has some further implications for concerted action by airline labor. Those unions occupying the "detached" position would be least readily brought into active, joint efforts. Nevertheless, the financial and other support that was enlisted from several of these unions during the Eastern Airlines strike suggests that there may be relatively few "lost causes" in terms of potential support. Because of their high internal cohesion, unions in the "secondary" and "elite" positions are more readily organizable and apt to enter into struggles as a group. At the same time, the concentration of ties within these positions, especially for unions in the elite position, reinforces a parochial outlook. As a group, position 4 unions, with their relatively wide-ranging ties, varied jurisdictions, and broad perceptions of interdependence, are the best positioned to bring together a diverse group of airline unions.

Attempts to promote unity have to be pursued with an awareness of several basic lines of conflict among airline unions made clearer by the network analysis. One such antagonism is among the flight attendants unions, reflecting competition and tensions arising out of efforts to work together. The elite unions are a focal point for perceptions of conflict. Tensions between these unions and the flight attendant unions are both job related and a result of the elite unions taking actions that have had detrimental effects on the flight attendants. Conflicts among the elite unions themselves, particularly between ALPA pilot groups and IAM mechanic units (the latter located in both positions 3 and 4), center on these powerful groups vying for influence, each intent on pursuing its own interests.

Lastly, this network analysis makes it clear that relations between airline unions are largely affected by their power dynamics. Airline unions differ substantially in size, resources, bargaining power, and political wherewithal. They are not interchangeable entities, but rather have widely varying abilities to affect outcomes, provide meaningful support, and make decisions that affect other airline unions. This stratification among the unions is not always acknowledged, but understanding the resultant differences in outlook and interests is critical to any realistic effort to forge labor unity in the industry.

Conclusion

This chapter has considered the "big picture"—airline labor as an interunion network. The web of relations among airline unions exhibits a distinct structure. The airline union network is relatively decentralized and fluid but clearly reflects the influence of craft, organizational boundaries, and differences in resources and capacities across unions. Airline unions interact primarily with other airline unions, and their bonds are relatively loose and informal. Limited reciprocation of ties, especially instrumentally oriented ones, is evident. The most cohesive groups within the network are composed of the flight attendants unions and some of the pilots and mechanics unions. Members of the latter elite group are sought out for information and support but primarily attend to one another. This network structure reveals lines of cohesion and cleavage within airline labor and suggests problems in engendering broad-based collaboration.

The following two chapters describe efforts by airline unions to join together and affect labor relations outcomes collectively. More so than the foregoing analyses, the qualitative material in these chapters gets close to the actors, their actions, and specific circumstances in order to capture the dynamics of relations among airline unions. Yet these efforts take place within the structural context outlined here and are shaped by the same underlying forces.

Chapter 7

Dynamics and Outcomes of
Inter-Union Relations:
Airline Unions in Coalition

T his chapter uses case studies of several airline union coalitions to examine the dynamics and outcomes of inter-union relations. The increase in the number and activities of these coalitions is one of the clearest indicators that inter-union relations have assumed greater importance in the airline industry. It is the essence of coalitions[1] that, at least at certain times and for specified purposes, they subsume their constituent unions and are able to speak with a single voice, make commitments, and engage in concerted action. Coalitions are thus especially instructive in assessing the capacity of airline unions to work together and the potential impact of such efforts. Airline labor successfully formed and maintained coalitions in the late 1980s, but the workings of these coalitions were affected by the unequal resources of their member unions and other obstacles to unified action. The impact of coalitions was limited by the imposing nature of the problems that prompted their formation.

The coalitions of airline unions in the late 1980s linked unions representing either workers of the same craft or workers employed by the same carrier. The primary example of a craft-based coalition was the Coalition of Flight Attendant Unions. There was also an attempt in 1987 to bring together pilot groups, both union and nonunion, throughout the industry. Although this initiative did not result in the formation of a coalition, it provides an instructive contrast to the flight attendants' experience.

Coalitions composed of unions representing workers employed at the same carrier have been more common over the years than craft-based coalitions. A number of the carrier-based coalitions formed during the first half of the 1980s at financially troubled carriers (e.g., Frontier, Republic) had disappeared by 1987—along with the carriers, which were merged or acquired. Previously formed coalitions at Pan Am and Eastern became highly active, however, and a coalition of unions emerged at United Airlines in early 1990. The coalitions at Pan Am and United are considered in this chapter, while discussion of the joint activity of Eastern Airlines unions is reserved for chapter 8.

Craft-Based Coalitions

Coalition of Flight Attendant Unions

The Coalition of Flight Attendant Unions had its inception in 1984 and was originally known as the Joint Council of Flight Attendant Unions. The members of the original Joint Council were the Association of Professional Flight Attendants; the Independent Union of Flight Attendants; the Union of Flight Attendants, Local 1; the Independent Federation of Flight Attendants; the Transport Workers Union, Local 553; Teamsters Local 2747; and the Teamsters' Airline Division. The Association of Flight Attendants joined the group in 1987, at which point it became known as the Coalition of Flight Attendant Unions. The change in name was more than a matter of semantics. It signified that the inclusion of AFA was a meaningful event that altered the character of the coalition. As of 1989, the Coalition of Flight Attendant Unions incorporated unions representing approximately seventy thousand members (*Flightlog*, July 1989, 11).

The issue that prompted the formation of the coalition, and that has remained its principal focus, is duty time and rest provision regulations for flight attendants (*Flightloq*, Spring 1988, 10). The FAA stipulated maximum work hours and minimum rest periods for other in-flight crafts, but not for flight attendants. Consequently, flight attendants would often end up working long shifts with little rest in between, especially when delays prolonged flights. Contractual provisions in this area proved difficult to enforce and did not provide uniform protection for all flight attendants, particularly those working at nonunion or regional carriers. More than anything else, though, the strategy of seeking FAA regulation reflected a desire to have the status of flight attendants as professionals with important safety responsibilities legitimated through the promulgation of the same kind of regulations that apply to other in-flight crafts.

The coalition has taken action on other legislative and regulatory issues, including the ban on smoking during flights, ozone monitoring, and the safe storage of carry-on baggage (*International Teamster*, June 1987, 16). Less emphasis has been placed on bargaining-related matters, although corporate campaigns have been discussed and promises of support were elicited for an APFA corporate campaign against American Airlines in 1987 (Moody 1987a: 11).

A capsule description of the coalition's activities does not adequately capture its salience for its member unions, the relatively high level of joint activity (not always involving the entire coalition), and the considerable extent to which coalition members look to one another as sources of support. Without overstating the degree of solidarity or its potency (both of which have serious limits, discussed below), this coalition is arguably the best example of coalition-building that airline labor has to offer. The number of unions involved, the coalition's longevity, and the fact that an impending crisis has not been required to sustain activity are all particularly impressive. Consistent with this view, most interview respondents expected the coalition to continue in some form, even if its current goals were attained.

Concrete gains have proven hard to come by, however. The coalition was on the winning side in supporting the ban on smoking on most domestic flights, passage of which was no minor accomplishment (*Flightlog*, Jan.–March 1990, 12–13). But regarding its central goal, the establishment of duty time regulations, progress has been very slow. For almost five years, the FAA and the Department of Transportation (DOT) made repeated promises to study the matter, but little happened. Finally, in January 1989, the unions' petition was denied (*International Teamster*, July 1989, 10). The coalition then turned to legislative means to force the FAA to establish duty time standards. A bill (H.R. 638) introduced in 1989 by Democratic Congressman Norman Mineta of California would have automatically established maximum duty and minimum rest periods if the FAA refused to write its own rules. AFA president Susan Bianchi-Sand sized up the accomplishment the bill represented: "This is the first time in my memory that a piece of aviation safety legislation which solely relates to flight attendants has been introduced in Congress. . . . It is a testimony to the combined power of one flight attendant voice that we have been able to accomplish this" (in *Flightlog*, July 1989, 11). It would be several more years and several more proposed bills, however, before the coalition's persistent efforts would come to fruition.[2]

The coalition's path has not been a smooth one. Many of the tensions within the coalition stem from AFA's joining in 1987. As a national union with flight attendant bargaining units throughout the industry, with the legitimacy that accompanies AFL-CIO affiliation, with Washington headquarters, and with greater financial resources and lobbying capacity than possessed by other flight attendant unions, the addition of AFA was important to the coalition's effectiveness. Yet, as one officer from a union that was an original member of the Joint Council put it, the coalition "does not work the same with AFA." An example was cited of a situation in which AFA wanted to use the AFL-CIO's facilities to produce a teleconference while some other coalition members were more inclined to use alternative facilities. The implication was that AFA's relationship with the AFL-CIO determined the choice, rather than criteria of more importance to other member unions. Another respondent indicated that AFA's goal of being the one union for flight attendants "gets in the way of trust." Additionally, there were objections to what was seen as AFA's propensity to claim to speak on behalf of *all* flight attendants, when, in fact, it represented only a portion of them. Intent on ensuring that their voices continue to be heard and that AFA does not dominate the coalition, some of the original Joint Council unions maintain close ties and communicate frequently outside of the formal coalition.

The claim that AFA has a goal of bringing about a single flight attendants union (presumably AFA itself) is essentially accurate. Hence, even as it was taking strides to develop closer working relationships with other flight attendant unions, forming a single union remained the preferred option: "'A single flight attendant union, while not the only way, still remains the best way to protect the flight attendant career and keep control of our destiny. AFA's Board of Directors supported this long-term goal in 1986, and it remains a top priority for 1987'" (Susan Bianchi-Sand, in *Flightlog*, May 1987, 2).

AFA nearly took a large step toward realizing this goal in 1987, when it reached an agreement with the leadership of APFA, the largest independent flight attendants union, to merge (*Daily Labor Report*, Aug. 18, 1987, A-11). But the merger was voted down by the membership of APFA, an action interpreted by some as a general expression of membership disapproval of APFA's leaders (*Wall Street Journal*, Sept. 23, 1987, 14). The charge that AFA attempts to speak on behalf of all flight attendants also has some validity, as evidenced by statements such as "We [AFA] are recognized on Capitol Hill as the flight attendants' spokesperson" (*Flightlog*, Fall–Winter 1986, 10). At the same time, if AFA cannot claim to speak for all flight attendants, then surely no other single union can either.

From AFA's perspective as well, participation in the coalition has been trying. It requires submergence of the goal of a single union and implicitly lends legitimacy to the independent unions. Further, AFA's autonomy is constrained. The coalition's reliance on consensus decision making means that a slow, complex process often precedes the taking of an action. AFA has also encountered difficulty in convincing other coalition members that an ultimate aim of the coalition should be the establishment of procedures for the certification of flight attendants (*Flightlog*, Spring 1988, 2).

Why did AFA join the coalition then? AFA's choice appears to have been predicated on several considerations. First, a change of leadership within the union facilitated joining. AFA's participation in the coalition began shortly after Susan Bianchi-Sand became national president in 1987. Her public statements clearly articulate a desire to foster better relations with other flight attendants unions. Second, through mergers, acquisitions, and bankruptcies, AFA lost representation rights at a number of carriers during the 1980s. Third, even as a national union, AFA has limited resources and encounters many of the same difficulties in bargaining as other flight attendants unions do. These circumstances makes joint political activity more attractive, if not essential. Hence, at the eleventh meeting of the AFA Board of Directors in 1986, Bianchi-Sand pointed squarely to the interdependence of flight attendants unions and their consequent need to join forces:

> In this era of deregulation every flight attendant group is affected by what other flight attendant groups do and when there is a weak link anywhere in the industry, we all suffer. . . . We sent a message at this Board of Directors to all the independent unions: "Where we have differences of substance, let us talk together and try to iron them out. Where we are divided only by personalities or history, let us put those concerns aside" (*Flightlog*, Fall–Winter 1986, 10).

Thus, a combination of statesmanship and necessity born of interdependence has led flight attendants unions to embrace each other in joint effort. Their coalescing is consistent with theoretical arguments that resource scarcity (in this case a shortage of political and bargaining clout) promotes the formation of coalitions (Bacharach and Lawler 1980: 82) and that parties are more likely to join coalitions when those parties do not possess a large amount of resources and influence relative to other partners in the coalition (Bacharach and Lawler 1980: 83).

The Coalition of Flight Attendant Unions is both aided and hindered by the relative equality of its members.[3] On the one hand, the absence of a highly dominant flight attendants union means that a fairly broad coalition can be maintained that offers similar rewards to all parties and is not readily controlled in the interest of one party. The similarity of these unions makes it possible to discern common interests and to combine efforts in the manner required for effective political action. On the other hand, the somewhat limited and similar resources of the flight attendants unions, even when combined, do not compensate for the liabilities of individual unions in situations when complementary, and not simply aggregated, resources are required, as in strikes. Joining together commensally interdependent unions, the Coalition of Flight Attendant Unions is also susceptible to competitive tensions and the allure of incorporating (e.g., by merger), rather than working with, coalition partners. Coalitions with low power differentiation are also subject to instability over time because this condition necessitates continual compromise.

For the time being, however, the coalition's focus on issues of genuine common concern to its member unions and the impossibility of achieving desired ends in isolation provide sufficient grounds for the unions to work together. The following discussion of "pilot dialogues" offers a marked contrast, demonstrating what can happen when a highly dominant union is present during an attempt to coalesce along craft lines.

Pilot Dialogues

During 1987, three meetings of pilot groups from numerous carriers and with different union affiliations (including some nonunion) took place. The idea appears to have originated with the TranStar Pilots Association, an independent union representing pilots at a subsidiary of Southwest Airlines. At the time of the first "dialogue" (April 1987), the TranStar pilots were in the process of affiliating with ALPA (*Air Line Pilot,* June 1987, 6). The initial meeting was sponsored by the TranStar Pilots Association and drew participants from twenty different pilot groups. Among the issues discussed at this gathering were the effects of deregulation, legislation, integration of seniority lists in mergers, and safety (*Air Line Pilot,* July 1987, 32–33). ALPA executive administrator (subsequently International president) Capt. Randy Babbitt, described the first dialogue as an attempt to "establish a forum whereby we pilots can get to the core of a lot of common issues, regardless of affiliation" (in *Air Line Pilot,* July 1987, 32).

The second dialogue occurred in July 1987 and was hosted by the Allied Pilots Association, the representative of pilots at American Airlines. This meeting had seventy-six attendees and saw agreement on a "7 point priority plan" (*Air Line Pilot,* Oct. 1987, 36).[4]

A third, and final, session was hosted by ALPA in October 1987. It drew representatives from fifteen pilot groups and was described as a "workshop on professional standards" (*Air Line Pilot,* Oct. 1987, 18). The low-key description of this third meeting and its confinement to professional issues provides a hint that ALPA was wary of the concept of a pilot dialogue by then, if not from the outset. The meetings ceased and are not likely to be reinitiated anytime soon.

Of the nine pilot groups considered in this study, seven reported having sent representatives to at least one of the dialogues. Their perspectives on the proceedings are enlightening. Not surprisingly, the one non-ALPA group was the most enthusiastic about the meetings, viewing them as a useful forum that should be sustained in some fashion. Officers from two ALPA MECs offered lukewarm assessments, indicating that the meetings may have helped them improve their relations with other pilots unions in some diffuse manner. In the main, however, the judgments of ALPA officers were quite negative. The complaint registered most frequently was that other pilot groups were using these meetings as a device to obtain some of the benefits of association with ALPA without incurring the costs of joining.

Several officers of ALPA MECs indicated that they were careful to send as representatives to the dialogues union members who were not officers. This reflected a desire to avoid the impression that the legitimacy of the other groups was being recognized, that anything more than an informal exchange of ideas was taking place, and that the capacity to enter into any commitments existed. The comment by one ALPA officer that the meetings started to "take on governing body aspects" is also quite telling. The crux of the matter was stated succinctly by another ALPA officer, who opined that the other unions "were interested in creating another umbrella group. We weren't interested. We are the umbrella group." If any ambiguity remained regarding ALPA's position on the pilot dialogues, it was removed by ALPA vice-president Roger Hall in remarks made during the fifty-third meeting of the ALPA Executive Board:

> We clearly indicated that ALPA would not be participating in any efforts to establish a congress of pilots' representation organizations. [ALPA would] continue to participate in the dialogues on a limited basis as long as we felt there was value in pilots getting together and talking, but that we would not undercut the efforts of our organization (*Air Line Pilot*, July 1988, 26).

ALPA's dominance allows it to control its participation with other pilots unions and to insist that they affiliate with ALPA if they want to partake of its benefits. With the possible exception of APA, there is little that the other pilot groups have to offer ALPA, other than the prospect that they might affiliate at some point or follow ALPA's lead on industry issues, thereby enhancing its standing as the primary representative of pilots. Whether or not the dialogues actually had the potential to co-opt ALPA and limit its autonomy by committing it to some kind of joint decision-making process, they came to be viewed in those terms. The contrast with the situation of AFA and the flight attendants unions, in which representation is more dispersed and no individual union has anywhere near the resources of ALPA, is clear.

Carrier-Based Coalitions

Coalition Activity at Pan Am

Through 1987 and 1988, the Joint Labor Council, a coalition of unions representing workers at Pan American World Airways, was very active. This coalition is worth examining in some detail because it illustrates nicely many of the dynamics of airline union coalitions, especially ones that arise in response to the problems of financially troubled carriers.

Background and Chronology

Pan Am had been beset by financial woes since at least 1974, when it first began to seek and receive concessions from its workers. Its merger with National Airlines in 1980 added little to the company besides debt (*Wall Street Journal*, Sept. 23, 1984, F-25). Pan Am lost money in almost every year during the 1980s, sold off most of its valuable assets, and engaged in multiple rounds of concession bargaining with its unions. Pan Am's unions had a history of engaging in coalitions, dating back to the 1940s. The Joint Labor Council was active throughout the 1980s and included all five of Pan Am's major unions: ALPA, FEIA, IUFA, the TWU, and the IBT. At the beginning of 1987, the TWU exited from the coalition, for reasons that will be explained below.

The following is a chronology of events at Pan Am:[5]

January 1987—The Joint Labor Council, already minus the TWU, retains Rothschild, Inc., to act as its financial adviser in any takeover of Pan Am or any acquisition by the carrier.

February 1987—Labor Council leaders meet with Pan Am chairman C. Edward Acker, to whom they offer a concession package in exchange for increased equity and protection in the event of a merger or takeover. A total of $600 million in concessions are offered in exchange for the unions receiving seven of fifteen board seats, stock, and a change in top management. The offer is rejected. The reason for obtaining the services of Rothschild, as now explicitly stated, is to approach potential buyers.

March 1987—ALPA agrees to a settlement on several matters, including a two-tier wage structure. The settlement is only an interim measure and discussions over concessions continue with all unions. The TWU rejects the idea that it must provide concessions in order for the company to survive. A letter is issued to all Pan Am unions stating the company's profit goals and the cost reductions ($180 million per year for three years) it needs to survive and compete. The letter also outlines a suggested distribution of these reductions among Pan Am's unions (ranging from $55 million per year for ALPA to $25 million per year for FEIA).

October 1987—The Joint Labor Council considers a plan by Kirk Kerkorian to buy Pan Am. It would require a higher level of concessions than demanded by the present management and involve spinning off some of the more profitable parts of the company, including the shuttle. The potential deal eventually falls through.

December 1987—A purchase offer by Thomas Pritzker, a major owner of Braniff, receives some support from Pan Am management. The deal, which would result in a merger of the two carriers, is contingent on the unions agreeing to deliver cost savings of at least $200 million per year in exchange for partial ownership of the company. A "letter of encouragement" had been sent to Pritzker by the Joint Labor Council in November. The letter proclaimed confidence in the ability of Pan Am's unions to provide the $200 million in concessions in exchange for a viable buyout offer, a sound business plan, and new management acceptable to the council. The TWU, which opposes the Braniff merger, objects to the Joint Labor Council appearing to commit the union to any concessions and refuses to discuss the possibility until the council unions have acted first. The Pan Am board establishes a stringent timetable for the unions to agree to the stipulated concessions. The timetable is not met and the deal with Braniff collapses. At the same time, the IBT engages the services of the Tower Financial Corp. to continue to pursue a hostile takeover bid.

January 1988—The Pan Am Board of Directors, led by William T. Coleman, initially strikes a deal with ALPA, and then with FEIA and IUFA, to receive some $180 million in concessions while removing CEO Acker and other top managers. Acker is replaced by Thomas Plaskett. The pilots and flight engineers settle on concessionary contracts, while the flight attendants reach a tentative agreement.

February 1988—The IBT's contract expires. Despite numerous threats to strike and attempts to seek support from other Pan Am unions, a strike does not occur. The carrier imposes its final offer on the IBT.

June 1988—The Pan Am Board threatens to sell off company assets if the remaining unions do not agree to concessions. IUFA's tentative agreement was rejected by its membership and the TWU has continued to resist concessions. Joint Council leaders meet to discuss once again searching for a buyer for the airline.

August 1988—The IBT threatens a strike if Pan Am's Latin American routes or its maintenance facilities are sold off and claims to have support from other unions at Pan Am for such an action. TWU members reject a tentative settlement.

November 1988—IUFA members ratify a concession agreement.

February 1989—An interest arbitration decision is rendered regarding the TWU's contract. The arbitrator decides largely in favor of Pan Am.

The activities of the Joint Labor Council unions during 1987–88 included holding regular meetings, developing a plan for restructuring the operations of the carrier, agreeing on the provision of concessions and approximate shares of the concessionary burden, retaining and sharing the cost of financial advisers, and aggressively pursuing buyers for Pan Am. The council's ability to strategize, carry out actions, and be viewed as a credible entity by external parties were all achievements not to be lightly dismissed. Moreover, the council succeeded in uprooting Pan Am's management. The dire nature of the carrier's problems and shared antipathy toward Pan Am's top managers provided all the glue needed to bind the unions in the Joint Council together. Nevertheless, in the aftermath of these efforts, Pan Am continued to limp along on the shakiest of financial footing. The very considerable sacrifices that workers made via the dealings of the Joint Labor Council were incapable of resolving the carrier's fundamental problems. Additionally, the coalition was hampered by its inability to incorporate and unify all five unions at Pan Am. Even among its four members, limits to solidarity and the taking of unilateral actions were evident.

Joint Labor Council–TWU Relations

Shortly after the TWU's departure from the coalition, Margaret Brennan, president of IUFA and chairperson of the Joint Labor Council, diplomatically attempted to account for the absence of the TWU in terms of its "'different procedures to get approval from its membership for the move'" (*New York Times*, Jan. 15, 1987, D-2). Although Joint Council members made few public comments about the TWU's defection, the TWU, and especially John Kerrigan, the director of its Air Transport Division, had a great deal to say. The issues involved in this case—discrepant definitions of the problems, equity concerns regarding the concession burdens borne by each union, philosophical and tactical differences with respect to labor's involvement in the management and ownership of firms, and personal antagonisms between union leaders—all have surfaced elsewhere and strained inter-union relations.

In opposition to the Joint Labor Council, the TWU took the positions that concessions were not necessarily called for, that even if concessions were in order they should come from those bargaining units at Pan Am whose contracts were not competitive with the rest of the industry, that continual reopening of contracts on the basis of the latest profit-loss figures must cease, and perhaps most important, that the unions should not attempt to trade concessions for control of the company (*TWU Express*, Feb. 1987, 5; July–Aug. 1987, 9).

The Joint Labor Council's actions demonstrated a belief in the necessity of making further concessions to the carrier and a willingness to do so—under the right conditions. These conditions included a change of management and/or greater labor ownership and control. Without denying the seriousness of Pan Am's financial plight, the TWU maintained that council members were purposely overstating the problems of the carrier, with the effect of further undermining its standing in financial circles (*New York Times*, Oct. 18, 1987, D-4). Kerrigan characterized the Joint Labor Council's position as follows:

> We must point out that the end result of both the Company and Union Coalition proposals are the same. A three year agreement covering contract reductions producing $540 million savings. What the company must give and who will control the company in exchange is the basic dispute between Pan Am and the Labor Coalition (*TWU Express*, July–Aug. 1987, 9).

For its part, the TWU maintained that "our current labor contracts at Pan Am are competitively favorable to Pan Am. Very frankly, if they can't compete with these agreements then they should fold up rather than bring everyone else down" (*TWU Express*, July–Aug. 1987, 9).

Disagreement over whether to render concessions was compounded, and likely surpassed, by concerns about equity of sacrifice. During its 1985 negotiations with the carrier, the TWU had agreed to a number of substantial "productivity adjustments," including expansion of part-time employment and cross-utilization of workers. Kerrigan saw the issue as follows:

> "Most of these adjustments were contingent on Pan Am accomplishing the same adjustments with its other employee bargaining groups." Two years have passed and, "Pan Am has failed to meet these commitments" (*TWU Express*, May 1987, 2).

> Some of the other Pan Am groups have refused to bite the bullet or admit that they are part of the Pan Am problem (*TWU Express*, July–Aug. 1987, 9).

The carrier's proposal had the TWU delivering $35 million per year in concessions, an amount equal to that asked of the Teamsters and second only to the $58 million per year sought from the pilots (*TWU Express*, July–Aug. 1987, 9).

The TWU's own account of why it did not join the coalition emphasized the clash over the proper role of unions vis-à-vis the ownership and control of carriers (*TWU Express*, July–Aug. 1988, 3). Kerrigan argued that the same tactics employed by the Joint Labor Council had led to disastrous results at Frontier, Republic, and Eastern (*TWU Express*, Feb. 1987, 5). Kerrigan's view was, quite simply, that "we don't believe the union belongs in running the company" (*Daily Labor Report*, Dec. 23, 1987, A-11).

The divergence in philosophy and strategy between the TWU and the Joint Labor Council unions was fundamental, but Kerrigan's harshest criticisms of the Council were reserved for its tactics in toppling Acker, Pan Am's CEO, and its vice-chairman, Martin Shugrue. Kerrigan blasted the agreement struck with the board of directors in January 1988 as "'an infamous, shameful deal'" and declared that "'I have repeatedly stated that we do not propose to trade concessions for management heads'" (*New York Times*, Jan. 13, 1988, D-3). Kerrigan also voiced concern that an ominous precedent had been set and that the board's actions had "'only whetted the Coalition's lust for power and added to Pan Am's long range problems'" (*TWU Express*, Jan. 1988, 5).[6]

Although the TWU remained apart from the Joint Labor Council, underlying interdependence dictated that both parties would have an effect on each other. The Joint Labor Council's effectiveness depended critically on its ability to be a credible representative of organized labor at Pan Am in its dealings with Pan Am management, the board of directors, and potential buyers. The absence of the TWU (the largest union at the carrier) from its fold limited what the council could promise to deliver. On one occasion at least, a representative of the Joint Labor Council, lawyer Michael Connery, apparently presumed to speak on behalf of the TWU in telling the board of directors that the council was confident it could get the TWU to go along with concession agreements made by the council (*TWU Express*, Jan. 1988, 5).

The TWU's searing response to this perceived infringement on its autonomy was predictable, but, in fact, the union's bargaining activities were already highly constrained by council decisions. Hence, proposals made to Pan Am by the TWU during contract negotiations in 1988 were rejected on the grounds that they "did not strictly adhere to the concepts agreed to by the company and the Pan Am Labor Coalition including wage reductions" (*TWU Express*, May 1988, 3).

When the TWU's contract dispute with Pan Am was finally settled via an interest arbitration decision in early 1989, which held largely in favor of the carrier, the arbitrator indicated that the prior concessions of Joint Labor Council member unions had been a significant consideration in the decision. Mike Bakalo, vice president of TWU International, was quoted as stating that the concessionary contracts of the other unions "'put our negotiating committee into a damage control mode right from the start'" (*TWU Express*, Feb. 1989, 2). The TWU did gain by staying apart from the coalition to the extent that its concessions of $20.8 million per year were the lowest total for any of the unions at Pan Am, substantially below management's original proposal, and did not entail direct wage cuts (*TWU Express*, Feb. 1989, 2).

When the Joint Labor Council scaled back its activities following the settlements in 1988 and (at least temporarily) shelved its quest for new ownership, the TWU resumed participation in the coalition.

Intra-Coalition Processes

Although relations with the TWU were a central dynamic in the Joint Labor Council's processes, several aspects of its internal workings also deserve note. First, Earl Johnsted, the chair of the ALPA MEC at Pan Am and one of the prime movers behind the coalition, was killed in a plane crash in September 1987 (*New York Times*, Oct. 18, 1987, D-4). ALPA's participation in the coalition was likely affected by this tragic event, in the direction of a less prominent and committed role. The structural emphasis of this analysis should not obscure the fact that individuals carry out the boundary-spanning activities of unions and that changes in personnel stand to affect inter-union relations.

The issue of equity of sacrifice also surfaced within the coalition. Despite initial agreement to go along with the pilots and flight engineers in delivering concessions to the company in exchange for new management, almost a year elapsed before IUFA flight attendants ratified any concessions. The major reason for the delay was that the flight attendants felt the contributions required of them did not adequately take into account their much lower salaries. IUFA's situation underscores the fact that commitments made to other unions and management in a coalition setting may still require the ratification of members and such consent may not be readily forthcoming.

Another notable feature of the workings of the Joint Labor Council was the role of the Teamsters. William Genoese, director of the IBT Airline Division, tended to inspire comment from other union officers, both praise and criticism. One interviewee referred to Genoese as having "a different agenda," and another indicated that his union attempted to circumvent Genoese by dealing with other IBT officers. The IBT was especially eager to oust Pan Am's managers and to find new owners for the carrier. Even after Acker's removal as CEO, Genoese continued to maintain that "the company's troubles . . . [were] due solely to gross mismanagement" (*Daily Labor Report*, Aug. 19, 1988, A-2). The IBT also repeatedly threatened to strike, both prior to and following management's unilateral implementation of contract terms for Teamster office and clerical workers in February 1988.

Although the IBT actively sought the aid of other unions at Pan Am, as well as at the national union level, support for a strike against Pan Am was not forthcoming and an IBT walkout did not occur (*Daily Labor Report*, Feb. 19, 1988, A-12; *International Teamster*, April 1988, 20). Thus, there are strong hints that the IBT's inclusion within the coalition was problematic. Whatever the correctness of the IBT's positions, they tended to be more extreme than those held by other coalition members. Furthermore, collaboration to alter the course of the carrier did not entitle the IBT to support in a strike against Pan Am, in large measure because a successful strike would have contradicted the overarching aim of keeping the carrier afloat.

Lastly, it is important to recognize that it was the pilots who settled first and that their settlement prompted the other unions at Pan Am to come to terms. Moreover, it was reported that William Coleman's agreement to have Acker removed came in a meeting with the pilots (*New York Times*, Jan. 19, 1988, D-2). Hence, while acting within the framework of the position the Joint Labor Council had developed, unilateral actions by the pilots were instrumental in producing the eventual outcomes.

Summary

The case of the Joint Labor Council at Pan Am illustrates a number of significant points. First, the coalition became activated in the face of a serious common problem—the possible demise of the carrier because of its financial problems. Environmental opportunities and threats have been shown to be important in fostering coalitions among social movement organizations generally (Staggenborg 1986: 375). The ability of the Joint Labor Council unions to reach agreement was facilitated by their shared disdain for Pan Am's management but, even more so, by the need to be credible in dealing with external parties, particularly prospective buyers. Earlier airline union coalitions at Frontier, Republic, and TWA were formed under similar circumstances and involved unions in many of the same activities undertaken at Pan Am.

Second, Pan Am's unions confronted a number of serious obstacles to unity. Concerns over unequal sacrifice, discrepant definitions of the problems, differences in philosophy and preferred strategies, and personal antagonisms were all evident. Kirsten R. Wever's (1988: 10–11) account of Western Airlines and Beverly Smaby et al.'s (1988: 7, 10) description of the pre-1987 experience at Eastern Airlines show that many of the same obstacles to unity have been played out in other settings.

Third, it is not coincidental that the TWU, the largest union at Pan Am and representing mechanics, was the union that chose to exit from the council and proceed on its own course. Similarly, it is not surprising that the actions of ALPA brought matters to a head. Although IUFA and the IBT were hardly bit players, neither was in a position either to remain aloof from the coalition or to exert a controlling influence over events. This aspect of the scenario at Pan Am has also been seen elsewhere, such as at Frontier and Republic Airlines in 1984–85. At both of these carriers, the IAM remained apart from or left coalitions and refused to join in offering concession packages, while the pilots played the role of settling first and establishing the tone for concessions by other unions (*Daily Labor Report*, Sept. 5, 1985, A7-9; *Business Week*, April 9, 1984, 33).

Occurrences of this sort are entirely consistent with the theoretical argument that the resources and power of potential parties to a coalition (particularly the extent to which these vary) are key determinants of coalition formation and process (Bacharach and Lawler 1980: 5; Lawler and Bacharach 1983: 97). More powerful actors are often able to dominate coalitions, engage in unilateral actions that affect other coalition members, or avoid entering into coalitions altogether.

Finally, the experience of the Joint Labor Council demonstrates that the activities of labor coalitions can substantially affect corporate and labor relations outcomes. Yet, to a considerable extent, the coalition's influence was centered on the issue of granting or withholding concessions, rather than on an affirmative strategy to implement a labor agenda. The magnitude of the carrier's problems, which impelled coalescence, also dictated that union efforts to resolve them could go only so far. To the extent that labor coalitions are born of crisis, their prospects for decisive victories are already greatly diminished.

The coalition at United Airlines differed in that it undertook a more proactive attempt to shape events at that carrier and its formation was preceded by a period of fairly intense conflict between two of United's unions.

Coalition at United Airlines

The three major unions representing workers at United Airlines are ALPA, AFA, and the IAM (District 141). In April 1987, in the aftermath of their 1985 strike and amid mounting concern about the direction in which the company was being taken, the ALPA MEC at United initiated an employee buyout of the carrier (*New York Times*, April 6, 1987, D1-4). John Peterpaul, IAM International vice president and Airline Division head, immediately voiced objections to the idea, saying that the IAM did not intend to negotiate concessions for its members and that he had "'difficulty'" with the seven-year moratorium on strikes proposed by ALPA in conjunction with the buyout plan (*Daily Labor Report*, April 16, 1987, A8–9). Although they had devised the buyout plan unilaterally, the pilots were interested in eventually involving the other employee groups at United. Rick Dubinsky, chair of the ALPA MEC at United, optimistically appraised the positions of the other unions in mid-1987 as follows:

> IAM has historically not supported ESOP's. It has yet to take an active role in our initiative, although it has indicated that the door is open to reconsideration. . . . [AFA] is currently monitoring what is happening. AFA's attitude toward ESOP's, however, is very positive. . . . As we gain momentum, I believe you will see AFA assume a more active role (in *Air Line Pilot*, June 1987, 26).

Dubinsky also noted that a buyout agreement would necessarily have certain repercussions for inter-union relations: "Lender(s) who are going to give us several billion dollars will require a no-strike clause to protect their investment. . . . Additionally, it is almost certain that the lenders will also require a no-sympathy strike clause, which is not that uncommon in the airline industry (*Air Line Pilot*, June 1987, 28).

Mild opposition turned to outright conflict when the IAM signed an agreement in November 1987 that included several so-called protective covenants (*Daily Labor Report*, Nov. 27, 1987, A-12). In general terms, the provisions incorporated in the IAM contract gave the union a number of options in the event of a takeover or buyout, including renegotiation of its contract and participation in any ESOP on terms favorable to the IAM. An officer from the United Airlines (UAL) MEC indicated in an interview that the IAM's signing of this pact was considered a "sell-out of ALPA" and that communication between the two unions ceased entirely at that point.

Whatever the intent, the practical effect of the agreement between UAL and the IAM was to make it impossible for ALPA to obtain financing for its bid. The IAM's Peterpaul continued to maintain that a buyout was "not necessary" and "would further exacerbate the airline's financial leverage problems" (*TWU Express*, May 1988, 18). Peterpaul also indicated in an April 6, 1988, letter to ALPA's Dubinsky that "'based on the current facts, we cannot provide any assurance or assistance that may be required by lenders who are considering financing your proposed buy-out'" (*TWU Express*, April 1988, 18).

ALPA filed suit against the UAL Corporation in May 1988, charging that the anti-takeover measures in the IAM contract were illegal. By May 1989, the courts had ruled in favor of ALPA, declaring one of the main protective provisions invalid (*Daily Labor Report*, May 17, 1989, A10–11).

Clearing this hurdle did not immediately advance the pilots' plan, however. It was the appearance of several takeover specialists (notably Marvin Davis) expressing interest in making their own bids for United that injected new life into the buyout initiative. In late August 1989, Davis actively sought the support of the IAM for his takeover attempt. IAM financial adviser Brian Freeman was quoted as saying, "'They will have to deal with us. Whoever wants control has to deal with the Machinists'" (*New York Times*, Sept. 3, 1989, 28). Confronted with the prospect of a hostile takeover, UAL management became markedly more receptive to the pilots' plan. In September 1989, the UAL Board of Directors approved a buyout proposal that would have given workers a 75 percent share in the company (*Daily Labor Report*, Sept. 18, 1989, A-7).

At this juncture, the pilots and a group of nonunion employees were the only workers who had committed to the buyout (the latter group at management's discretion). ALPA and UAL management were still eager to broaden the base of participation (which can also be read as spreading the purchase cost more thinly), and a new contract was held out as an inducement for AFA, which had been engaged in protracted, fruitless negotiations with the carrier (*Daily Labor Report*, Sept. 15, 1989, A-14).

In October 1989, AFA agreed to join with ALPA in the buyout, but the IAM announced that it still would not participate in the plan. Moreover, it launched an aggressive campaign to defeat the purchase. Peterpaul claimed that the buyout would violate several provisions of the Employee Retirement Income Security Act (ERISA) and, in a letter to Labor Secretary Elizabeth Dole, characterized the plan as "egregious and abuses both the government and employees" (*Daily Labor Report*, Oct. 13, 1989, A-10). Similar objections were raised with the Treasury Department and the Security and Exchange Commission. Despite repudiation of such clauses by the courts, Peterpaul wrote that "I urge every IAM airline district to attempt to negotiate protective covenant provisions in their next contract" (*Machinist*, Nov. 1989, 9). Finally, branding UAL president and chairman Stephen Wolf as "greedy and irresponsible" for his sanctioning of the buyout, Peterpaul called for Wolf's resignation (*Daily Labor Report*, Oct. 18, 1989, A-6).

For a number of reasons, the Machinists' opposition being prominent among them, financing for the deal reached in September collapsed. Consequently, the UAL Board announced on October 23, 1989, that it had ceased negotiations with the Airline Acquisition Corp., the official name of the pilot-led coalition. Not easily deterred, Dubinsky responded to these developments by affirming that "we remain committed to pursuing our goal of majority employee ownership of United Airlines" (*Daily Labor Report*, Oct. 25, 1989, A-12).

The first inkling that the IAM was rethinking its position came shortly after the failed deal, when Peterpaul stated that "'we might have to participate in majority ownership through an ESOP even though we don't want to'" (*Daily Labor Report*, Nov. 1, 1989, A-7). Given the intensity of the IAM-ALPA conflict, it is little short of amazing that by January 24, 1990, the two unions, along with AFA, were making a joint buyout proposal to the UAL Board. In a letter to the board signed by Peterpaul, Dubinsky, and the president of the United AFA MEC, V. Diane Robertson, it was stated that the unions had "reached an historic written agreement in principle as to the key economic ingredients that would form the foundation of the acquisition" (*Daily Labor Report*, Jan. 26, 1990, A-16). These "ingredients" included formation of the United Employee Acquisition Corp., accord on the manner in which ownership would be allocated among the different groups of workers, and agreement on five-year concessionary contracts. In March 1990, the three unions agreed to align themselves with an investor group seeking to use a proxy battle to remove the current board of directors. On April 6, 1990, the buyout bid of the three unions was accepted in principle by the UAL Board (*New York Times*, April 9, 1990, D-1).

Subsequent events once again derailed the plan, however. Although tentative financial support had been lined up from five banks, an October 1990 deadline for finalizing the arrangements could not be met. Rather than the concern in financial circles over the lack of support by all the employee groups that had undermined the previous plan, the depressed state of the economy, the hesitancy of troubled financial institutions, and the potential implications of the impending Gulf War for air travel conspired to scuttle the 1990 buyout effort. For their part, the unions continued to espouse the goal of purchasing the carrier and asserted that their new-found unity would be an asset when contract talks (suspended during the buyout negotiations) resumed (*Machinist,* Nov. 1990, 9). It would take four more years for the buyout to (apparently) come to fruition (*New York Times,* Oct. 23, 1993, A-1).

What had changed to bring United's unions into collaboration on the buyout? Accounts offered by the principals are not terribly satisfying. ALPA's Dubinsky was quoted as explaining that "'we found that there were really no differences. . . . What we found was that over the months and the years there had been insufficient communication'" (*New York Times,* April 9, 1990, D-1). Similarly, regarding the potentially difficult issue of determining ownership shares, IAM adviser Brian Freeman implied that it was resolved rather easily, being treated as a matter of "'pure economics'" (*New York Times,* April 9, 1990, D-4). One alternative explanation, entirely speculative, is that higher officers within the IAM pressured Peterpaul to alter his stance, perhaps in response to urging from ALPA International and as reciprocation for its support in the Eastern strike. Whether or not there was prodding from above, the eventual coming together of the unions at United again reflects the themes of interdependence and power that run throughout this book. The basic explanation for the turnabout is that the unions were fundamentally interdependent and that it became evident over time that they would be unable to bring about their preferred outcomes unilaterally.

All indications are that the pilots originally conceived their buyout strategy in isolation and had given very little thought to potential problems in involving other unions at United in the process. As a relatively large pilot group (some seven thousand) with substantial resources and the determined leadership of Dubinsky, the United pilots were able to advance the takeover plan reasonably far on their own. By themselves, however, the pilots were unable to bring their plan to fruition, necessitating intensified efforts over time to line up the support of other unions for the bid and the eventual accommodation with the IAM.

The IAM, far and away the largest union at United (representing about twenty-three thousand workers) and with leaders at both the district and national levels generally opposed to employee ownership schemes,[7] also held considerable power in this situation. The IAM was able to use its leverage to thwart the pilots' designs for more than two years. AFA, which came to support the buyout plan only reluctantly, was to a certain extent caught in the middle of the ALPA-IAM struggle. Although it leaned toward ALPA because of the established relationship between the two unions, its support was not a foregone conclusion, and AFA's numbers (about thirteen thousand) made its ultimate decision consequential.

By late 1989, it had become evident to ALPA that, even with the obstacle of the IAM-UAL protective covenants removed through legal means, IAM support for the buyout was critical. The IAM, although it was able to use its power to obstruct the buyout, was not able to advance any positive program to ensure that the traditional bargaining role it desired would remain viable. After management lent its support to the pilots' bid and AFA joined the effort, the IAM was left isolated in its opposition and unable to exert control over the process. At that point, inclusion became the more attractive option for the IAM.

In the context of what increasingly came to be defined as the shared problem of mismanagement and of the fundamental interdependence of the unions at United, substantial differences in philosophy and strategy were put aside (though not necessarily eliminated) and a union coalition centering on the buyout of United Airlines was formed. Joining forces appears to have ultimately resulted in the unions realizing their objective, whereas disunity had effectively stymied the buyout effort. Thus, under the right circumstances, even fairly intense prior conflicts do not pose an insurmountable obstacle to unified action. Yet coalescing occurred only after the two most powerful unions had tested the efficacy of unilateral action and found it wanting.

Discussion

The foregoing case studies of airline union coalitions say a good deal about the circumstances under which unions collaborate, the potential impact of joint effort, and, even more so, the process of working together. Thinking realistically about how airline unions work together necessarily involves consideration of a variety of obstacles to cooperation. Collaboration is far less common in practice than general endorsement of the value of labor solidarity by union leaders and the potential benefits of joint action would imply. In large part, the obstacles to cooperation are rooted in the same interdependencies that account for the presence of inter-union ties.

Airline union coalitions are most often formed when unions representing workers at the same carrier are confronted with a serious common threat involving the viability of that carrier and the continued employment of their members. The labor coalition at Pan Am clearly illustrates this tendency, while the United case involved a more proactive strategy to deal with a longer-term threat. The activities in which coalitions of this kind typically engage (e.g., concession bargaining, searching for new ownership, proposing business plans) place a premium on maintaining a united front in dealing with management or potential investors. In contrast, the Coalition of Flight Attendant Unions is based on common interests arising from representation of the same craft. Focused on political and regulatory activity, the relatively similar resources of coalition members are aggregated into a more effective political voice. For other crafts with less dispersed representation, political and regulatory activity remain within the province of national unions and/or the AFL-CIO.

The coalitions examined here each had an impact. From the removal of a carrier's management, to the negotiation of concession packages, to the apparent purchase of one of the world's largest airlines, to the passage of legislation, the outcomes produced by inter-union collaboration were unlikely to have occurred in its absence. Furthermore, the efficacy of broadening the coalitions (e.g., the addition of AFA to the Coalition of Flight Attendant Unions, the IAM joining in the United buyout) was apparent. Yet none of the coalitions enjoyed unqualified success. Working together gives unions more leverage in dealing with carriers, makes labor more credible in financial circles, lends political clout to unions, and so forth, but it by no means guarantees preferred outcomes. Indeed, it is precisely because coalition formation is often reserved for dire circumstances that the prospects for decisively shaping outcomes tend to be dim from the outset.

More than anything else, the case studies point to some of the difficulties airline unions encounter in working together. Concern with maintaining organizational autonomy, unequal resources and status, competition, craft identification, differences in strategy and tactics, interpersonal conflicts, and divisive actions by employers all make the benefits of joint action more difficult to attain.

Airline unions, like other organizations, prefer not to be constrained by needing to gain the approval of other unions to act or otherwise be bound by their choices. More than other relations, participation in a coalition requires a considerable sacrifice of autonomy. For ALPA, the prospect of being co-opted by participation in the pilot dialogues was reason enough to nip any movement toward coalition formation in the bud. The organizational interests of ALPA were simply not served by any arrangement that might require it to consult with other pilots unions, take closer account of their needs, or reach a consensus before acting. Although AFA chose to join the Coalition of Flight Attendant Unions, it was also concerned about how participation would affect its ability to act quickly and to pursue goals (e.g., professional certification) not fully shared by other coalition partners.

The manner in which concern for maintaining autonomy expresses itself is closely intertwined with the power dynamics between unions. Some unions, because of their superior bargaining power, political wherewithal, financial resources, or strong national union backing, are in a better position to assert their autonomy by remaining apart from coalitions, controlling the activities of coalitions, or taking unilateral actions that affect other coalition members. ALPA's decision to curtail the pilot dialogues and its insistence on affiliation as the price for drawing on its resources and legitimacy were premised on its dominant position among pilot unions. Joining with other pilot groups was simply not essential to ALPA's effectiveness. Although AFA might have been inclined to take a similar stance with respect to the Coalition of Flight Attendant Unions, doing so would have meant losing a useful vehicle for advancing flight attendants' interests. Both the Pan Am and United coalitions featured instances in which relatively powerful unions either remained apart from coalitions (e.g., the TWU's withdrawal from the Joint Labor Council, the IAM's steadfast opposition to the United buyout) or took unilateral actions that affected other coalition members (e.g., ALPA's agreement with the Pan Am Board of Directors).

The differing power positions of unions resonated in the statements of the union officers interviewed. One respondent of a pilots union, for example, declared that "we don't look a whole lot for support. We figure if we can't do it ourselves, we don't deserve to get it." An officer of a mechanics union sounded much the same theme: "Mainly, we're the hub here. We turn to ourselves." The different status of the more powerful unions is evident even when concessions are in the offing. As one respondent in a pilots union said, "Very often we get pushed to the front [in concession bargaining] . . . We're the most important group."

Far from empty bravado, these statements speak to a substantial imbalance in the capacities of airline unions that was also generally acknowledged by officers of less powerful unions. For example, an officer from a small union representing communications personnel stated that "the pilots are aloof. They don't need anyone." The ability to reciprocate support adequately was an underlying issue in a number of comments. One officer of a flight attendants union, for instance, suggested that "there's nothing we can do for the pilots, so there's no need for them to do anything for us. . . . They don't need to go through the hassles of cooperating." Not having to reciprocate, rather than being unable to do so, was the concern of one officer of a pilots union, who referred to the desirability of being in a position where one does "not have to pay back debts."

The point is not that pilots and mechanics unions have no need for cooperation and support (particularly with one another). The increased prevalence of coalitions itself suggests that a "go-it-alone" strategy has become less viable for all airline unions. However, the fact that there is often disparity in the need of unions for support and their ability to contribute to joint efforts makes working together far more complicated.

The Coalition of Flight Attendant Unions has been shaped by the relative similarity of its members. The similarity of the member unions allows for identification of common goals, sustained involvement, and relatively equal participation. Yet, although craft identification is important as a basis for relations with unions representing the same category of workers, it tends to obscure the significance of relations with unions representing other crafts, especially on the part of more "elite" or "skilled" job groups. Additionally, although competitive tensions were not significant in undermining the coalitions examined here, competition remains a potential source of division among unions with overlapping jurisdictions.

Not surprisingly, airline unions often disagree on strategies, tactics, and other matters. These disputes reflect both differences in philosophy and clashes of organizational interests rooted in the differing circumstances of unions. Disagreements regarding the nature of carriers' problems, their need for concessions, and the desirability of employee ownership or other forms of participation in management were quite evident in the Pan Am and United cases. Likewise, perceived inequity in contract outcomes, particularly in the context of concession bargaining, has been a source of contention in a number of settings, including at Pan Am (e.g., IUFA, TWU). Although bargaining outcome interdependence in the airline industry is usually greatest for unions representing the same craft, resource scarcity in the form of a carrier's need for concessions and the political needs of union leaders to demonstrate that members' sacrifices are warranted, make equity in settlements an abiding concern. Substantive differences are often compounded by interpersonal antagonisms or power struggles between union leaders. Although these conflicts clearly make it more difficult to identify common goals and to work together, airline unions have also displayed a facility for surmounting antagonisms when circumstances require doing so. The accommodation between the IAM and ALPA at United is a graphic, but not the only, example.

Carriers are hardly indifferent to whether the unions they deal with are united and cooperate with one another. Consequently, the possibility that carriers will take actions to promote division is quite real. Some ways in which such division might be fostered include encouraging affiliated bargaining units to form their own independent unions (as it was alleged that American Airlines did in the 1950s), playing unions off against each other in bargaining, fostering perceptions of inequity in bargaining outcomes, and demanding or refusing to modify no-strike clauses. The manner in which UAL's management played both sides to its own advantage in the IAM-ALPA conflict, by first negotiating protective covenants with the IAM and later, when threatened with a hostile takeover, joining forces with ALPA, demonstrates one way in which carriers can affect inter-union relations. Appealing though it may be to attribute a lack of unity to a carrier's machinations, this is only one potential obstacle among many and one that also requires some participation by the unions themselves.

Conclusion

Airline unions were engaged in several coalitions in the late 1980s. Serious shared problems and the need to pool limited resources provided the basic incentives for the formation of these coalitions. The processes of coalitions are affected by issues of organizational autonomy, the unequal resources and status of unions, craft identification, disputes over strategy and tactics, perceived inequity in bargaining outcomes, interpersonal conflicts, and divisive actions by carriers. Airline union coalitions affect corporate, legislative, and labor relations outcomes, but the formidable problems that prompt coalitions to be formed often do not lend themselves to unequivocal victories.

The events at Eastern Airlines in the late 1980s clearly support this view. A serious threat to the unions at Eastern, and arguably to all airline unions, led to coalition activity and an attempt to mobilize the support of all of airline labor. Yet the magnitude of the problems at Eastern also blunted the impact of those extraordinary efforts. This is the subject of the following chapter.

Chapter 8

Mobilizing the Airline Union Network:
The Struggle at Eastern Airlines

Without question, events at Eastern Airlines provided the single most important focus for inter-union activity in the airline industry during the late 1980s. The handling of the carrier and its workers by Frank Lorenzo and Texas Air Corporation presented airline unions with a threat of enormous magnitude. For many, the issues at stake were no less fundamental than whether workers could stop a firm in which they had invested years of their labor from being dismantled for the benefit of others; whether workers would be made to foot the bill for leveraged buyouts; and whether meaningful union representation and collective bargaining would survive in the face of a quest for unilateral managerial control.

The Eastern conflict is notable for the potentially far-reaching ramifications it was said to have. The message was consistently conveyed that the Eastern struggle was one of broad concern to all of labor. Hence, former IAM president William Winpisinger declared that "unyielding efforts by the carrier and Texas Air management to destroy its union workforce have made this struggle one of major concern to our union and of national significance for all of labor" (*Machinist*, March 1989, 3).

Teamster members were counseled likewise: "The Eastern workers fight is everyone's fight. If Lorenzo prevails, union leaders feel that other airlines will also try to destroy the unions on their property. It will be a tremendous setback for the entire labor movement" (*International Teamster*, May 1989, 11).

Fused with the compelling concerns underlying the strike was the person of Frank Lorenzo, who came to symbolize corporate America at its ugliest and provided a tangible common enemy against which to rally.[1] Faced with

serious threat and a clear villain, airline unions responded with an unprecedented degree of inter-union support and joint effort. In this respect, the
events at Eastern constituted a special situation that made evident the capacities, not often tapped under more benign circumstances, of airline unions for
mutual support. At the same time, there were clear limits to the solidarity
achieved, rooted in enduring obstacles to inter-union cooperation and the
nature of the airline union network itself.

A dizzying series of moves and countermoves by Eastern and its unions
unfolded over the approximately five-year period between the takeover of
Eastern by Lorenzo in 1986 and its ultimate demise at the beginning of 1991.
The following chronology summarizes these events, emphasizing actions
that directly involved or had consequences for Eastern's unions.[2]

February 1986—Eastern Airlines agrees to be sold to Texas Air Corporation.

July 1986—Eastern goes to court to have the pilots' contract, signed shortly
before the sale, declared invalid. ALPA is ultimately upheld by the courts in 1989.

August 1986—The IAM makes a buyout offer for Eastern, but the bid is dismissed
by the EAL Board.

October 1986—IAM District 100, TWU Local 553, and the ALPA Eastern MEC
form the Eastern Airlines Employee Coalition Acquisition Corporation. Their
counteroffers (to the not-yet-finalized Texas Air purchase) to buy the company
are unsuccessful.

April 1987—Preliminary discussions on the development of a joint strategy for
dealing with Lorenzo begin between Mary Jane Barry, president of TWU Local
553, and Industrial Union Department staff.

July 1987—The IUD's Jobs with Justice campaign is initiated with a rally in
Miami. This campaign organizes rallies in numerous cities through 1988, with the
Eastern situation being one major focus.

February 1988—A scheme to transfer the Eastern shuttle to Texas Air is announced.
The unions go to court to have the plan enjoined, and in July 1988, Texas Air
decides to drop the idea.

A concerted "Stop Lorenzo" campaign on the part of the unions at Eastern is
announced. The unions issue a call for a DOT investigation of the operations of
Texas Air. The unions also form APEAL (Abused Passengers and Employees
Against Lorenzo).

March 1988—With union encouragement, a Citizen's Commission of Inquiry
into Texas Air Corp. is formed and hears testimony.

The IAM, followed by ALPA and TWU, petitions the National Mediation Board
to issue a finding that Eastern and Continental constitute a single carrier for labor
relations purposes. Hearings on the matter take place in May 1988, but a decision
is never rendered.

The unions go to court to block Eastern from leasing aircraft to nonunion Orion
Air for the purpose of training replacement pilots to be used in the case of a strike.

May 1988—Texas Air files suit against Eastern unions under the Racketeer Influenced and Corrupt Organizations (RICO) statute, charging them with using extortionate means to gain control of Eastern.

July 1988—Eastern's unions and company officers meet at DOT headquarters with former Secretary of Labor William Brock and produce a joint agreement to ensure safe operations at Eastern.

August 1988—A temporary restraining order is obtained by Eastern's unions to stop the carrier from laying off workers in connection with a plan to terminate service to a number of cities, including its Kansas City hub. The courts ultimately allow Eastern to curtail service and four thousand workers lose their jobs.

October 1988—Eastern's unions meet with Carl Icahn regarding a possible buyout offer. No offer is made.

Donald Trump agrees to buy the Eastern shuttle. The unions contest the sale in the courts, but Eastern is upheld in December 1988 and the sale is completed in May 1989.

November 1988—Eastern's unions push for a second and more comprehensive investigation of whether Texas Air management is fit to operate an airline. The previous DOT investigation had focused on potential safety problems posed by labor-management conflict and had largely ignored the issue of Texas Air's business practices. Because of continuing asset sales and layoffs, the unions also withdraw from the Master Safety Council established under the July 1988 agreement with the DOT.

February 1989—The IAM and Eastern are released from mediation by the National Mediation Board after sixteen months of fruitless negotiations. This begins a thirty-day cooling-off period.

The AFL-CIO Strategic Approaches Committee meets to discuss the Eastern situation. A Fairness at Eastern Committee is established and activities to mobilize support for the IAM are begun.

The AFL-CIO Executive Council pledges support to Eastern unions. TWU Local 553 passes a resolution holding that it will respect IAM picket lines in the event of a strike.

The National Mediation Board recommends the establishment of a Presidential Emergency Board, a move the AFL-CIO has also been calling for.

March 1989—President George Bush decides not to appoint an emergency board.

Numerous air and rail carriers obtain temporary restraining orders to block sympathy strikes.

A strike by the IAM begins on March 4. ALPA and the TWU engage in sympathy strikes. The vast majority of members from all three unions refuse to cross picket lines.

Eastern claims in court that the pilots are conducting an illegal primary strike. The court refuses to issue an injunction against ALPA and in April decides in ALPA's favor.

A legislative campaign to compel the appointment of an emergency board continues.

A Fairness at Eastern Fund is established by the AFL-CIO to channel strike funds to the Eastern unions.

Eastern files for bankruptcy under Chapter 11 on March 10.

A creditors' committee is formed that includes representatives from the IAM and ALPA.

Flight attendants at Continental Airlines launch a brief and ineffective strike.

April 1989—An investor group led by Peter Ueberroth makes an offer for Eastern. The offer has the support of the unions and apparently goes through, but the deal ultimately collapses.

Texas Air announces that Eastern will be shrunk rather than sold.

May 1989—Several other potential buyers surface, including William Howard and Joseph Ritchie. None of the prospective buyers succeeds in gaining bankruptcy court backing for his offer, despite union support and offers of even more extreme concessions.

June 1989—The bankruptcy court orders ALPA and Eastern to meet and negotiate for the first time since the beginning of the strike.

July 1989—Talks take place with all three unions and Eastern, but no progress is made and negotiations cease.

Eastern receives the first of numerous extensions for filing a reorganization plan.

August 1989—A substantial number of pilots offer to return to work following an August 6 statement by Jack Bavis, chairman of the ALPA MEC at Eastern, that an end to the sympathy strike might be best.

An AFL-CIO sponsored "Journey for Justice" starts out in Miami. The journey includes rallies and demonstrations in support of the Eastern strikers in major East Coast cities, ending with a rally in Washington, D.C., in early September.

Eastern pilots ask for a nationwide job action by ALPA pilots and guarantees that Eastern pilots transferring to other carriers will be eligible to maintain their seniority. The ALPA Executive Council rejects both requests.

The ALPA Executive Board votes to continue payment of strike benefits for the time being and to poll members again on whether strike benefits should be maintained.

September 1989—Jack Bavis is "recalled." He is replaced by Skip Copeland, considered to be more in favor of sustaining the strike.

Union efforts become increasingly focused on the political arena, particularly legislation to have a bipartisan commission appointed to review the events at Eastern.

October 1989—ALPA and the IAM file suit against Texas Air under the RICO statute.

ALPA announces that members have voted to continue paying assessments to finance strike benefits for Eastern pilots.

November 1989—On November 21, President Bush vetoes legislation that would have established a bipartisan commission to recommend a settlement to the Eastern strike.

Members of the ALPA MEC at Eastern end their sympathy strike on November 22. The TWU ends its sympathy strike a day later. The strike by the IAM continues.

January 1990—The ALPA Executive Board votes to continue strike benefits for Eastern pilots through February. Despite the end of the sympathy strikes, few, if any, pilots and flight attendants are rehired.

March 1990—Congress fails to obtain the two-thirds majority necessary for an override of the presidential veto of legislation for the creation of a bipartisan commission.

The court-appointed examiner finds that Texas Air had improperly conducted thirteen of fifteen transactions with its subsidiary Eastern, costing Eastern several hundred million dollars.

April 1990—Eastern loses the support of its unsecured creditors for its recovery plan. Creditors press for appointment of a trustee to run the airline.

On April 18, the bankruptcy court removes control of Eastern from Frank Lorenzo. Martin Shugrue is appointed as trustee to run Eastern.

July 1990—Eastern and nine of its managers are named in an indictment charging that vital aircraft repairs were routinely ignored and safety records falsified during the period from July 1985 to October 1989.

August 1990—A federal court rules that union pilots have the right to replace persons who were trainees when the sympathy strike was called off in November 1989. Eastern appeals the decision.

Frank Lorenzo announces on August 9 that he is stepping down as CEO of Continental Airline Holdings, Inc., and selling his stock shares to the Scandinavian airline SAS.

The bankruptcy court grants Eastern's request to cut pilots' wages and benefits temporarily by 20 percent.

January 1991—Eastern Airlines ceases operations permanently on January 18. The strike by the IAM is officially concluded.

Inter-union relations played a prominent role in the Eastern Airlines conflict. Support activities among the affiliates of particular national unions, joint action by Eastern's unions, leadership from the AFL-CIO, and attempts to elicit a broader union response were all significant pieces of the Eastern story.

Support Activity within ALPA

Fairly intensive support activities took place among the affiliates of all three of the major unions representing workers at Eastern—the IAM, the TWU, and ALPA. The experience of the Eastern pilots in drawing on ALPA International and individual MECs for support is of particular interest. The events highlight both a genuine impulse toward solidarity and abiding differences within ALPA that were exacerbated by the difficult choices forced on the union in the strike.

Especially in the early weeks of the IAM strike, the refusal of ALPA pilots to cross the Machinists' picket lines was critical to the success achieved in curtailing the carrier's operations. Some 96 percent of Eastern's pilots refused to cross IAM picket lines at the outset of the strike (*Air Line Pilot*, Summer 1989, 6), and their sympathy strike remained strong for a number of months. Impressive financial support for the Eastern strikers from within ALPA was clearly instrumental in buttressing this solidarity. Eastern pilots were voted strike benefits of $2400 per month. Interest-free loans were made available by ALPA to replace the last paycheck owed to pilots (but were denied them because Eastern filed for bankruptcy), as were guaranteed loans of up to $2,000 (*Air Line Pilot*, April 1989, 28). The ALPA Executive Board extended its merger policy in cases of plane or route sales to EAL pilots, allowing them to maintain their seniority if they were transferred in conjunction with asset sales. The board also resolved to develop a plan for implementing the ALPA "first right of hire" policy (which would give displaced Eastern pilots preferential hiring status with other carriers) if Eastern went out of business (*Air Line Pilot*, April 1989, 29).

Individually, ALPA MECs contributed to the strike effort in a variety of ways. The MECs joined the Eastern pilots on picket lines and in rallies, negotiated with their carriers to hire Eastern pilots, arranged rides home for stranded strikers, wrote letters of support, and provided strike training and coordination.

This impressive support was not easily arranged, however, and it clearly had its limits. The decentralized character of ALPA, the sharp focus of the MECs on the affairs of their "own" carriers, and divisions between MECs representing pilots at "have" and "have-not" carriers all affected the degree of support available to the Eastern pilots. This influence could be seen in difficulties encountered by ALPA International in selling the notion that the Eastern conflict affected all pilots, orchestrating ALPA-wide job actions, in protecting the seniority of displaced Eastern pilots, and in financing strike activities.

The message that the events at Eastern posed a serious problem for all MECs appeared not to get through within ALPA, despite considerable efforts to convey this notion. Statements of ALPA International officers throughout the strike were replete with references to the vital stake all ALPA units had in the outcome of the struggle at Eastern. At least as far back as the spring of 1988, the International was disseminating information to MECs for distribution to pilots to "ensure that pilots become aware that the outcome [of events at Eastern] would affect all of them and not just Eastern employees" (*Air Line Pilot*, April 1988, 31). Following the onset of the strike, ALPA president Duffy asserted that "this is indeed the time that we must stand together, for we are not warring only with Lorenzo, but with all the carriers that stand to gain mightily should he win (*Air Line Pilot*, Summer 1989, 1).

Despite consistent articulation of this theme, however, Roger Hall, first vice president of ALPA, publicly lamented the prevalence of the attitude that "'it won't happen to me'" (*Air Line Pilot*, Summer 1989, 25). Shortly before the end of the sympathy strike and after almost a year of struggle, ALPA secretary Schulte opined that "'some people [within ALPA] have not yet realized why we should support the strike and that it affects everyone in the industry'" (*Air Line Pilot*, December 1989, A-17).

Limits to solidarity within ALPA were also manifested more concretely. ALPA International requested that pilots at all carriers engage in a rule-book slowdown on March 8, 1989, to place pressure on government officials to appoint an emergency board. Despite claims by ALPA that 60 percent of pilots had participated in the slowdown and that the action would continue, little disruption of service was reported and the strategy quietly slipped into oblivion (*New York Times*, March 8, 1989, B-5). Having failed to execute a work slowdown to any effect at a point when pro-strike fervor was presumably at its zenith, it was not surprising that an August 1989 request from the Eastern MEC to conduct a vote among all ALPA members concerning their support for a nationwide suspension of service was dismissed by the ALPA Executive Board (*Daily Labor Report*, Aug. 7, 1989, A-5).[3] The bottom line is that the ability of ALPA to generate a nationwide job action under any circumstances remains, at best, unproven. The Eastern experience failed to render this capacity any less suspect.

The thorny issue of seniority also entered into the Eastern strike. That former Eastern pilots might, under a number of different scenarios, find themselves working for other carriers raised questions about how they would be fit into those carriers' seniority schemes. Even the relatively modest ALPA resolution to implement a policy allowing Eastern pilots who transferred to other carriers in connection with asset sales to retain their seniority met with opposition. It was to those who balked at this arrangement that ALPA president Duffy addressed the following statement:

> A willingness to share that seniority to ward off a bad situation that would eventually harm all of us is not only the moral way to operate—even though it may impinge on one's own advancement—it is also an important check of our association's character. Conversely, a move up that results from Eastern equipment sales or transfer to "our" company is a move up off the backs of the striking pilots. To profit thereby is a serious breach of faith (*Air Line Pilot*, Summer 1989, 2).

Once again, stronger demands eventually emanated from the Eastern MEC, which sought the right to maintain its members' seniority under any circumstances, when they obtained employment at other carriers. Although adoption of such a measure was arguably consistent with the message being expounded that the Eastern pilots were fighting a battle on behalf of all pilots, the sacrifices the measure would have required of individual pilots made it politically untenable. The demand was denied by the ALPA Executive Board (*New York Times*, Aug. 21, 1989, D-1).

Lastly, there was the matter of finances. As noted above, strike benefits were substantial for the ALPA strikers. Paying for those benefits and for myriad legal and legislative activities (the bill already approached $70 million by September 1989) (*New York Times*, Sept. 13, 1989, D-1) posed serious difficulties. On top of the 2.35 percent of their salaries regularly paid in dues, ALPA pilots were assessed an additional 3.5 percent to finance the strike (*Air Line Pilot*, May 1989, 8). Even at the outset of the strike, enthusiasm for the extra levy was not rampant. Hence, only about 57 percent of the pilots actually voted in favor of giving strike benefits to the Eastern strikers (*Air Line Pilot*, Summer 1989, 24).[4] Commenting on the provision of strike benefits, chair of the Eastern MEC, Jack Bavis, noted: "The backing of our fellow pilots will prove to be a critical element in maintaining our action against Eastern. It is a sure sign that our entire union is willing to take extraordinary measures to win this battle" (*Daily Labor Report*, March 15, 1989, A-13).

Backing for the pilots proved difficult to sustain over the course of the strike. Increasingly, pilots were late in remitting the assessment or stopped paying it altogether (*New York Times*, Sept. 13, D-1). Although a second vote in October 1989 resulted in the continuation of strike benefits, a clear message was conveyed to the Eastern MEC that if the legislative efforts to have a bipartisan committee appointed to review the strike failed, the strike would have to be terminated (*New York Times*, Nov. 23, 1989, D-5). The legislative initiative came to naught, and the sympathy strike (but not immediately payments to strikers) was ended. These experiences raise questions as to whether even a union with the resources of ALPA can afford to underwrite strikes at such a high level of benefits and use the financing mechanisms it employed in its last several strikes. Ironically, it may have been because of the financial drain on ALPA and the impact that having a depleted major contingency fund had on negotiations at other carriers (*New York Times*, Sept. 13, 1989, D-1, 5) that the interdependence of the MECs was most fully grasped.

Pilots at Eastern, then, were able to draw upon considerable support from other MECs and ALPA International as a whole. Limits to unity and support within ALPA could be discerned early in the strike, however, and became increasingly evident as the conflict wore on. Characteristic tensions within ALPA, including the carrier-specific outlook of the MECs, disputes over the use of funds, and contention over matters of seniority, were all brought to the surface by the Eastern strike. The impetus toward unity that circumstances at Eastern provided was not sufficient to surmount these long-standing conflicts rooted in the organization of ALPA.

Solidarity and Schism among Eastern's Unions

As the foregoing chronology indicates, joint action and inter-union support among the unions representing workers at Eastern were extensive, occurring on the picket lines, in the halls of Congress, before regulatory bodies, in the courts, in dealings with prospective investors, and at rallies. Yet, although the activities of the union coalition at Eastern clearly surpassed those of the coalitions at Pan Am and United, the three coalitions were also similar. These commonalities concern both the circumstances under which joint action arose and the processes of these coalitions.

Like other carrier-based coalitions, the Eastern coalition developed in a situation of serious threat to the unions and their members. As elsewhere, formal initiation of the coalition occurred with the launching of efforts to effect a buyout or otherwise change the ownership of the carrier. The shared enmity toward top management, which was significant in drawing unions together in the other coalitions, was vividly present at Eastern. More distinctive features of the context for the emergence of the Eastern coalition were the long history of attacks upon unions by Texas Air's management, the unambiguous intent of Eastern's management to break the carrier's unions, and the major strategic advantage afforded Texas Air because it controlled two major carriers (Eastern and Continental) simultaneously.

The process of working together at Eastern Airlines was also shaped by some of the same factors affecting other airline union coalitions. These included a history of intense conflicts and a perception of inequity in contract outcomes, management efforts to divide and conquer, differences in preferred strategies and tactics, interpersonal antagonisms, attempts to assert autonomy, and a lack of parity in the resources and status of coalition members. Yet, despite these obstacles, it was still possible to engineer lengthy sympathy strikes and an unprecedented level of joint activity.

The solidarity that emerged among the unions at Eastern was not forged overnight. By all accounts, serious divisions and tensions had existed for some time among these unions (Bernstein 1990: 60; Smaby et al. 1988: 7, 10; *New York Times*, Nov. 6, 1988, 86). The unions had weathered numerous financial crises at the carrier going back to the 1970s and had had representatives on the Eastern Board of Directors in 1984–85. The unions had become engaged in buyout negotiations in late 1986 and, starting in early 1987, had begun working together with the Industrial Union Department under the aegis of the Jobs with Justice campaign. Thus, the unions at Eastern had been working together quite intensely, albeit not without friction, for some time before the strike in March 1989.

Even more so than at Pan Am, parity in settlements was a contentious matter at Eastern. On several occasions, including in the 1986 negotiations that led to the sale of Eastern to Lorenzo, the pilots and flight attendants rendered concessions that were not matched by the IAM (Smaby et al. 1988: 25). Most prestrike analyses of the situation at Eastern made prominent reference to the equality of sacrifice issue, pointing to the pilots' resentment of the greater concession burden they had borne and their belief that it was the unwillingness of Charles Bryan, IAM District 100 general chairman, to accept similar sacrifices that had allowed the carrier to fall into the hands of Frank Lorenzo (*New York Times*, Nov. 6, 1988, 82). Although inclined to attribute tensions between the IAM and ALPA to management efforts to cultivate them, an ALPA publication nonetheless acknowledged the seriousness of the schism: "Lorenzo's managements have been adept at encouraging and exploiting the fractures between employee groups and within individual crafts. At Eastern, those fractures cut deep enough that one couldn't blame a reasonable man for betting that a near-unanimous inter-union job action could ever have been successfully launched" (*Air Line Pilot*, Summer 1989, 14).

Facing an imminent strike, Lorenzo attempted to capitalize on the enmity between the pilots and machinists by sending all ALPA members a videotape describing a contract offer and appealing for their support in an IAM strike. As described by pilots, the video implied that Lorenzo was willing to cut a deal in exchange for their support in a strike by the machinists.

More subtle was a concerted attempt by Lorenzo and Eastern management after the strikes had begun to minimize the impact of the IAM and TWU job actions and to focus entirely on ALPA. This action played to some pilots' sense of themselves as elite and sought to diminish the importance of the unity among Eastern workers.

Eastern spokesman Robin Matell accused ALPA of "'clubbing management'" through its support of the IAM and asserted that "'[the IAM] is not what's causing us to reduce the operation as drastically as we have. . . . It's the pilots. They are not coming to work, and they can't stay on picket lines under the guise of supporting I.A.M. when they are trying to use a sympathy strike to obtain their own economic objectives'" (*New York Times*, March 7, 1989, A-1). Similarly, in announcing Eastern's flight into bankruptcy proceedings, Frank Lorenzo declared that the filing was "brought about by the shutdown of the company brought about by the pilots union" (*Daily Labor Report*, March 10, 1989, A-13).

To be sure, such statements were in large part a matter of legal posturing, since the carrier was pleading its case in court to have the ALPA strike enjoined on the basis that it was an illegal primary strike (*Daily Labor Report*, April 13, 1989, E-1). Yet the statements also had the effect of invalidating the unions' solidarity, an effect unwittingly reinforced by numerous commentators (including many sympathetic to labor) who focused almost exclusively on the pilots' sympathy strike.

Even if the pilots' support of the IAM strike is not the only story, it nonetheless requires explanation. Given the history of the relationship between ALPA and the IAM at Eastern (and throughout the industry), bitterness over unequal sacrifices rendered, management efforts to divide and conquer, and personal animosity between union leaders (to say that Bavis and Bryan did not get along is a gross understatement), the situation was indeed one in which the "reasonable man" could have expected another outcome. An understanding of the decision by the ALPA MEC at Eastern to support the IAM is aided not only by several prospective and retrospective accounts of the decision-making process but also by documents from legal proceedings in which Eastern sought to have ALPA's sympathy strike enjoined. In these proceedings, the precise issue before the court was the pilots' motives for engaging in the strike.

It is clear that the decision to conduct a sympathy strike was reached after ALPA considered its own interests and, not to any great extent, out of concern for the IAM. As Rick Chapman, secretary-treasurer of the ALPA MEC at Eastern, put it about two weeks before the strike, "'Whatever decision is made, . . . it will be made because it's in the pilots' best interests'" (*Daily Labor Report*, Feb. 23, 1989, A-14).

In their own negotiations, which were still in progress at the time of the IAM strike, the pilots had proposed that if the carrier would guarantee to end asset sales, outline a viable business plan, and make Texas Air a party to any agreement reached, a settlement containing concessions could be reached (*New York Times*, Feb. 23, 1989, D-1; *Air Line Pilot*, Summer 1989, 3). Eastern rejected these demands. Although it was never explicitly stated that ALPA would have crossed the IAM's picket lines if management had acceded to its demands and a new contract was in place (*Daily Labor Report*, April 13, 1989, E-4), there was certainly strong speculation to that effect (*New York Times*, Feb. 23, 1989, D-2). One mitigating factor was that many ALPA representatives believed that management would fail to honor any agreement reached. As district court judge Edward B. Davis noted in his decision regarding the legality of the ALPA sympathy strike, "The pilots' overwhelming distrust of the Lorenzo management group, whether founded or not, is the keynote of this labor dispute" (*Daily Labor Report*, April 13, 1989, E-4).

Faced with continued dismantling of the carrier, an inability to obtain credible contractual job protection, and mindful of the history at Continental Airlines, where an unsupported IAM strike was followed by a failed ALPA strike, pilots increasingly came to the view that it was preferable to confront Eastern then and together, rather than later and alone. Some of the numerous considerations involved in reaching the decision to launch a sympathy strike are enumerated in the following retrospective account: "They compared the risks of facilitating Lorenzo's attack on IAM with the risks of shutting down Eastern Airlines. They reviewed the progress of alternative strategies pursued for the previous three years, and they considered trade union principles. Most importantly, they consulted the membership" (*Air Line Pilot*, Summer 1989, 6).

ALPA's varied motives were also the prime rationale for the court's ruling that the sympathy strike should not be enjoined. Despite agreeing with plaintiff Eastern that there was evidence in support of the view that ALPA's sympathy strike "was a mere pretext for its own self-help," the court concluded that

> the totality of the evidence in this case shows that ALPA and its Master Executive Council instructed pilots to join the IAM strike for a multiplicity of reasons. . . . including failure to secure a fence agreement, safety concerns, dislike for EASTERN Chairman Frank Lorenzo, and general long-term concern for the survival of EASTERN. Additional evidence bolsters the showing that ALPA instructed its pilots to engage in a sympathy strike out of a perceived need for the two employee groups to work together for their mutual benefit (*Daily Labor Report*, April 13, 1989, E-3, 4).

Thus, although ALPA's support of the IAM strike was hardly a spontaneous expression of principles of trade union solidarity, the unions at Eastern were able to discern their fundamental interdependence, to subordinate numerous conflicts, and to act in accordance with their shared interests. The pilots realized that they faced the same problems as the IAM, that whatever happened to the IAM would have direct implications for their own fate, and that a pooling of resources and efforts would offer the best chance of effecting change at Eastern. From this perspective, the issue of whose interests were being pursued becomes irrelevant. Rather, the point is that the unions shared a broad range of common interests and were able to recognize them. Forging unity does not require selflessness so much as the capacity to see the larger picture and to be imaginative in finding common interests, while minimizing clashes of particular interests.

Nor does ALPA's largely utilitarian approach to rendering support in the Eastern strike mean that the importance of sentiments of solidarity should be dismissed. To the contrary, beliefs and values holding that it is "right" and "good" for unions and union members to support one another facilitate attempts to find common ground, encourage the provision of support in situations in which the calculation of self-interest leaves room for discretion, offer a broader rationale for incurring the sacrifices associated with rendering support, help draw in other unions more distant from the particular issues at hand, and, in general, animate labor struggles by imbuing them with larger meaning. If such considerations had relatively little impact on the Eastern MEC's decision, they appear to have had more to do with the rank-and-file's persistence in sustaining the sympathy strikes and with the support received from other unions far removed from the airline industry and Eastern.

Some of the power dynamics evident in the processes of other union coalitions were also manifested at Eastern. As at United, a powerful union initially attempted to arrange a buyout of the carrier and, failing to do so on its own, then joined with other unions in this effort. In the case of Eastern, however, it was the IAM that had the greatest enthusiasm for a buyout strategy and that made the initial foray (*New York Times*, Oct. 4, 1986, 33).

Despite working together, ALPA and the IAM continued to assert their autonomy by pursuing their own strategies and seeking to exert control over events. Aaron Bernstein (1990: 174) suggests that when the focus of the conflict moved from the picket line to the search for prospective buyers, Bavis was no longer required to play second fiddle to his long-time rival Bryan and readily assumed a dominant role in the proceedings: "Bavis reveled in his new strength. He was the one sitting at the table, negotiating with Ueberroth."

The chaotic process of locating and negotiating with prospective buyers for Eastern, then, was greatly affected by prior antagonisms and the desire of both the IAM and ALPA to play the leading role. Bernstein (1990: 175) sums up the situation well: "The result was a contest for control. Virtually every union power center struck out in search of different buyers."

Broader issues in the relationship between pilots and flight attendants unions were also manifested in the process of working as a coalition. In December 1987, Bavis came out in support of Eastern management's decision to suspend four TWU flight attendants. The flight attendants had walked off an Eastern plane that had been sitting on a runway in Denver for more than an hour in fifteen-degree temperature because the pilot had refused to have the plane de-iced again. The incident followed on the heels of a Continental Airlines crash under virtually identical weather conditions. Bavis took the position that only the pilot has the authority to decide whether or not a flight should take off (*TWU Express*, January 1988, 10–11). Workflow interdependence and hierarchical relations between pilots and flight attendants on the job tend to generate disputes between workers that become sources of tension between unions. Shared disdain for management and the beginnings of joint efforts among the unions at Eastern did not alter this fact or lessen the pilots' inclination to side with the company in upholding their authority.

Exclusion of the TWU from the creditors committee established by the Federal Bankruptcy Court can reasonably be viewed as a manifestation of the TWU's lower status within the coalition. Whether the other unions fought to have Local 553 included on the committee is unclear, but the omission was particularly galling in that Mary Grace Jones, an employee of the Eastern Human Resources Department, was given a seat on the committee to represent nonunion workers at Eastern (*New York Times* March 23, 1989, D-5). Ed Cleary, president of the New York State AFL-CIO, was prompted to remark that

> we have three AFL-CIO unions at Eastern with a vital stake in the proceedings, and two of them, quite properly, were put on the creditors' panel. I am disturbed that the flight attendant unit—the only predominantly female group of Eastern workers—was not allowed a seat on the committee (as quoted in *Daily Labor Report*, March 28, 1989, A-13).

Finally, and again characteristically, it was ALPA that made the move to end its sympathy strike, with the TWU following suit the next day. The notion that the flight attendants at Eastern had limited ability to effect outcomes and a lesser status within the coalition only goes so far, however. TWU Local 553 was extremely active, played an important part in initiating and carrying out the imaginative prestrike campaign against Lorenzo, announced its intention to support IAM picket lines early, while ALPA was still sitting on the fence, and received the majority of the funds coming through the AFL-CIO. Local 553 officers and members displayed considerable energy, imagination, and militancy. What the union lacked, like other flight attendants unions, was financial resources, sufficient power to command the attention of employers and government, and, perhaps, the full respect of other, largely male, unions.

The AFL-CIO and the Eastern Strike

A prominent feature of the Eastern conflict was the heavy involvement of the AFL-CIO at both the national and state and city levels. The AFL-CIO Executive Council issued a statement in February 1988 denouncing Lorenzo and supporting a broad union campaign against him (*TWU Express*, April 1988, 7). Most of the activity prior to 1989, however, was coordinated by the semi-autonomous Industrial Union Department. The federation as a whole became more closely involved as the strike loomed near. The major role played by the AFL-CIO in the Eastern strike is quite clear; the consequences of that involvement are far less so.

The Industrial Union Department was brought into the Eastern picture by Mary Jane Barry, president of TWU Local 553, in early 1987. Barry and the IUD organized a brainstorming meeting of Eastern's unions on strategies for dealing with Lorenzo. The initial rally kicking off the IUD-sponsored Jobs with Justice program took place in Miami in July 1987. This was the first of a series of rallies throughout the country during 1987–88 that highlighted the struggle at Eastern (and many other issues) and linked the Eastern unions to the broader labor movement in a concrete way.

Despite differences over strategy (particularly whether or not political efforts should be emphasized), the Eastern unions, with IUD assistance, waged an energetic campaign against Lorenzo well into 1988. The experience thereby gained was invaluable in developing the capacity of Eastern's unions to work together. One interview respondent suggested that a suit filed by Texas Air under the RICO statute in mid-1988 may have slowed the campaign's momentum. More certainly, rivalry between AFL-CIO bodies and the Jobs with Justice network surfaced. As "ownership" of the Eastern struggle became a contested matter and the onset of the strike approached, the IUD was nudged out of the picture and had relatively little direct involvement in the strike.

In February 1989, the AFL-CIO Strategic Approaches Committee met to discuss the Eastern situation and began the process of mobilizing support. The AFL-CIO Executive Council called on all affiliated unions and state and local bodies to lend the "'fullest possible support'" to the Eastern workers (*Daily Labor Report*, Feb. 22, 1989, A-8). Especially in the early months of the strike, most coordination occurred within the AFL-CIO. As one interview respondent put it, the strike was being led "at the highest levels of the labor movement." ALPA president Henry Duffy underscored this point: "[The] AFL-CIO has singled out this strike and involved itself to an exceptional degree. Through the federation's 'Fairness at Eastern' campaign, unions in virtually every state of the country are actively supporting the IAM strike" (*Air Line Pilot*, May 1989, 2).

This "exceptional" involvement on the part of the AFL-CIO included establishing a sizable Fairness at Eastern Fund to aid strikers from all three unions, lobbying heavily, initiating a boycott against Eastern and Continental, sponsoring the Journey for Justice caravan, and, via pledges from affiliates, providing access to funds that could have been used for a buyout. Activity was also intense at the state and local levels, where AFL-CIO bodies organized numerous rallies, bolstered picket lines, and operated food banks, among a variety of other support activities (*AFL-CIO News*, numerous issues).

What were the consequences of the role played by the AFL-CIO at Eastern? To be sure, the unusual extent of AFL-CIO engagement brought numerous benefits. The AFL-CIO provided access to resources that the three unions could not have commanded on their own. The Fairness at Eastern Fund amassed well over a million dollars, much of it through relatively large donations by affiliates (*AFL-CIO News*, June 24, 1989, 1). Some $50 million in loan guarantees were solicited from affiliated national unions (*AFL-CIO News*, June 10, 1989, 1). Legislative staff from the AFL-CIO constituted another important resource that would not have been so plentiful otherwise.

The AFL-CIO was also instrumental in broadening support for the strike. Its characterization of the Eastern struggle as "a battle that would engage the entire labor movement" (*AFL-CIO News*, March 18, 1989, 4) had some merit. Support came from many quarters of the labor movement and was in no way restricted to unions with a direct interest in the airline industry. Wide-ranging support was important in a material sense, but also because it lent legitimacy to the struggle, demonstrating that it was something more than a conventional "labor dispute." In linking its prestige to the strike, the AFL-CIO also increased the visibility of the struggle.

Lastly, the involvement of the AFL-CIO probably affected relations among the unions at Eastern for the better. The AFL-CIO's presence committed the unions to a joint stance from which they could not readily extricate themselves and probably helped in smoothing over conflicts.

Some questioned whether the AFL-CIO's role in the Eastern strike was truly an asset. Kim Moody was among those who found much to criticize in the AFL-CIO's handling of the strike: "The AFL-CIO leadership has displayed its customary paralysis at moments of crisis. . . . The most the AFL-CIO has done, however, is to set up a solidarity fund (1989: 14).

Paul J. Baicich, an IAM member, gave more credit to the AFL-CIO's contribution in fund-raising and picketing but was no less scathing in his appraisal of its role in the strike:

> Unfortunately, the AFL-CIO's participation too often served as a drag on the strike. In the face of an all-out attack against labor, not limited to this strike, the near-timid AFL-CIO response was foolhardy if not suicidal. Too many proposed audacious activities were undercut by the AFL-CIO for fear of "losing public sympathy." . . . The mere thought of actions resulting in civil disobedience or arrests had the AFL-CIO in near-apoplexy (1990: 11).

To what extent are such charges valid? The AFL-CIO's predilection toward political action weighed in favor of emphasizing legislative solutions, thereby increasing concern about doing anything that might alienate potential political allies. The AFL-CIO is also very conscious of its public image and clearly sought to maintain favorable public opinion of the Eastern strikers, again, possibly militating against more strident actions. Likewise, leading a strike "at the highest levels of the labor movement" necessarily limits the influence and involvement of local unionists and the rank and file. Fundamentally, it can be questioned whether the AFL-CIO, with its reliance on achieving broad consensus among affiliates, a structure oriented toward political activity, and a necessarily broad agenda in which numerous issues compete for attention, is equipped to spearhead a sustained,[5] militant struggle. Its capacity to mobilize resources was demonstrated impressively in the Eastern strike, but its ability to engage in an ongoing campaign that was innovative and fully involved members was far less evident.

Even if the AFL-CIO's presence contributed to overly cautious strategies and measures, which then affected how available support was used, there is still the question of whether this approach fundamentally shaped the character of the conflict or merely amplified tendencies already present within the national unions. There is little reason to believe that ALPA and the IAM would have pursued very different strategies in the absence of AFL-CIO guidance, since both unions placed great emphasis on the buyout attempts and legislative activity, strategies that inevitably restricted militancy and rendered the struggle more distant from members. Likewise, if the AFL-CIO is often hampered by internal politics and lacking in both adequate structural mechanisms and the will to engage in all-out conflict, many national unions are similarly afflicted. Thus, Moody, although taking aim at the AFL-CIO, ultimately locates the problem in the business unionist ideology he feels is predominant within the American labor movement:

> This is not a question of "sell-outs" by the leaders of ALPA's Eastern unit, IAM District 100, and the TWU's air transport division, or "betrayals" at the hands of the AFL-CIO brass. It is a deeper malady—the failure of business unionism. For the business unionist a strike is just a strike, not some disruptive crusade

that upsets political allies or "responsible" employers currently under union contract. . . . Solidarity is at best a matter of fund-raising, strongly worded resolutions, and photo-picketing by high officials (1990: 10, 13).

The reality of the Eastern struggle was too complex to frame within a simple business unionism/social unionism dichotomy. The actions of the AFL-CIO and Eastern unions, if they evidenced business unionism, certainly pushed at the bounds of that concept. Further, recalling the lack of enthusiasm within ALPA for a nationwide slowdown early in the strike, it was not simply that national unions resisted intensifying the conflict and thereby stifled the boundless militancy of members. External parties, particularly the courts and federal government, also played a role in curtailing militant actions (see the following section). Nevertheless, to the degree that union leaders at all levels can accurately be characterized as adhering to an orientation that emphasizes narrowly construed economic issues, focuses on the gains of individual unions, obscures the commonality of all workers, and ignores the labor movement's historic role in transforming society, fundamental constraints are placed on labor solidarity and its uses.

Breadth of the Eastern Conflict

One of the most significant features of the struggle at Eastern was the unusually far-reaching ramifications claimed for the strike and the issues underlying it. If an injury to Eastern's unions truly was an injury to all airline unions (and maybe the labor movement in general), then there were grounds for expecting that the strike would engender unusually widespread and intense support. To a considerable extent, this is what happened. Almost all of the airline unions studied engaged in contact related to the Eastern strike, usually with more than one of the Eastern unions.[6] The coalition at Eastern was extraordinarily active. The AFL-CIO succeeded in making the Eastern struggle one that reached beyond the confines of the airline industry to engage a sizable portion of the U.S. labor movement. In several instances, support was even provided by unions in other countries.[7] In short, the Eastern unions were at the center of a relatively dense support network. Yet the depth and breadth of that support were limited in some basic ways. In particular, several attempts to extend the conflict to other air and rail carriers failed. However much the Eastern unions were engaged in a battle on behalf of all airline labor, that fight remained largely on their own turf.

ALPA's failure to orchestrate a slowdown throughout the industry has already been mentioned. Suffering much the same fate as the ineffectual rule-book slowdown by ALPA was an attempted strike by flight attendants (represented by UFA) at Continental. The intent of the walkout was ambiguous and several quoted statements of union leaders denied a connection to the Eastern strike (*New York Times* March 21, 1989, D-1). UFA was then in the process of affiliating with the IAM, however. In light of this fact and statements of interview respondents linking the two strikes, it is fair to conclude that an attempt to widen the offensive against Texas Air was at least one of the ends contemplated. In any event, UFA was not successful in persuading large numbers of flight attendants to strike and the action faded quickly.

In the realm of measures proposed that never got beyond the drawing board, William Genoese, director of the Teamsters' Airline Division, threatened a sympathy strike against Pan Am. Mindful that Pan Am provided the main competition for the Eastern shuttle (still part of Eastern at the time), Genoese reasoned that "one of the targets would be the shuttle of Pan American. . . . Therefore we could tie up the Northeast corridor of the United States" (*New York Times*, March 19,1989, 22). Genoese also suggested that an employee buyout could be arranged that would combine both Eastern and Pan Am.

It is difficult to discern the extent to which the IBT's threatened sympathy strike constituted a serious attempt to join the Eastern conflict versus a maneuver to put pressure on Pan Am to alter the imposed contract terms under which the Teamsters' bargaining unit was working. Despite Genoese's claims that Pan Am's other unions would probably provide support, nothing further came of the proposal.

A more serious threat to widen the Eastern conflict came when the IAM warned that it was prepared to set up picket lines at other air and rail carriers where it had members. By disrupting transportation on the East Coast, this strategy was intended to politicize the conflict and exert pressure on the Bush administration to appoint an emergency board.[8] The credibility of this threat rested in part on the fact that, in contrast to the Taft-Hartley Act, the Railway Labor Act does not prohibit the use of secondary[9] pressure. Further, a recent (1987) Supreme Court decision in the *Burlington Northern* case had reaffirmed the right of workers to engage in such action (Guerrieri 1988: 250–51). Had the IAM's plan been carried out, it would have been the first time that an airline union had resorted to secondary pressure (*New York Times*, March 16, 1989, B-8).

Just before the strike began, a number of air and rail carriers flocked to the courts to have secondary picketing and/or sympathy strikes enjoined. In one case, the district court in Minneapolis issued a temporary restraining order against IAM District 143 at the behest of Northwest Airlines. Judge Paul A. Magnuson indicated that his decision was based on the public's interest in continuing commerce and on a balance of harm test that weighed "'very strongly'" in favor of the carrier (*Daily Labor Report*, March 3, 1989, A12). Guy Cook, general chairman of IAM District 143, labeled the judge's action, "'another nail in the coffin of working people'" and decried the fact that it contradicted the Supreme Court's ruling in *Burlington Northern* (*Daily Labor Report*, March 3, 1989, A12–13).

In a second case, a group of carriers, including United, Piedmont, and TWA, was represented by the Airline Industrial Relations Conference. Acknowledging *Burlington Northern*, the judge in this case, John H. Pratt, nonetheless issued a temporary restraining order, based largely on the holding that the interpretation of the Machinists' no-strike provisions was a minor dispute to be submitted to arbitration (*Daily Labor Report*, March 20, 1989, E1–2). Stating that "'we're in effect going to cut the baby in half,'" Judge Pratt devised a scheme whereby the IAM would be allowed its statutory right to set up secondary pickets at other carriers but workers at those carriers could still be disciplined or discharged for refusing to cross picket lines (*Daily Labor Report*, March 6, 1989, A9–10). Whatever its intent, the ruling had the effect of undercutting the right to engage in secondary pressure, while ostensibly maintaining that right, and pitting the interests of workers at different carriers against one another.

The injunctions, after considerable delay, were upheld by the court of appeals. In early 1990, the Supreme Court declined to review lower court rulings barring the IAM from setting up picket lines at several commuter railroads. The railroad cases are distinguishable from the airline cases noted above because no-strike provisions were absent from the relevant contracts, but the courts nonetheless used the same rationale that the dispute needed to go to arbitration (*Daily Labor Report*, Jan. 17, 1990, A4–5). If, as the railroad unions argued in their brief to the Supreme Court, the court decisions surrounding the Eastern strike have effectively instituted "an across-the-board proscription on sympathy strikes in the railroad and airline industries, regardless of the terms of the applicable labor agreements" (*Daily Labor Report*, Jan. 17, 1990, A-5), then legal constraints have become a much more significant obstacle to cooperation among airline unions.

Although the courts played the central role in containing the strike, the Bush administration and its allies in the legislative branch also got into the act. Following his unprecedented decision not to accept the NMB's recommendation to appoint an emergency board, and in the context of threatened secondary action, President Bush declared: "We cannot allow an *isolated labor-management dispute* to disrupt the Nation's entire transportation system. . . . If secondary boycotts threaten to disrupt essential transportation services, I will submit, and urge that Congress promptly enact, legislation making it unlawful to use secondary picketing and boycotts against neutral carriers (*Daily Labor Report*, March 6, 1989, A-12; emphasis mine).

Definition of the Eastern conflict as conventional and limited marked the Bush administration's discourse on the matter. Its willingness to usurp legislatively workers' statutory rights under the Railway Labor Act was eagerly backed by the likes of Senator Orrin Hatch, who saw an opportunity to dispose of the threat of broadened strikes for good (*Daily Labor Report*, March 6, 1989, A-12).

Although the Bush administration needed little prodding to ignore the urgent concerns of labor in the Eastern strike, its actions also reflected a broader agenda. The strike occurred early in the Bush presidency and following the embarrassing rejection of John Tower as secretary of defense. The quoted comments of an administration aide (unfortunately, but understandably, unnamed) were quite revealing: "There's a sense here that the issues go beyond the narrow labor issues. The issue is whether the Bush Administration is going to govern the country or are we going to be pushed around by Congressional Democrats and left-wing unions" (*New York Times*, March 8, 1989, B-5).

The existence of a close personnel nexus between Texas Air and the White House was also undoubtedly relevant. Using a well-worn corridor, some thirty individuals had moved in one direction or the other between the Reagan and Bush administrations and Texas Air Corporation (*Air Line Pilot*, March 1990, 6–7).

Hence, although support for the Eastern strikers came from many quarters of the labor movement, the actions of the courts and the Bush administration helped to ensure that the conflict was contained within the conventional limits of a struggle between a single firm and its workers. The courts and Bush administration both defined the situation as such and then took steps to prevent workers at other rail and air carriers from bringing that definition into question by their respect for the Eastern workers' pickets. The objective of the planned sympathy actions was simply to force the hand of the Bush administration to appoint an emergency board—as provided for by law. That this thoroughly modest aim was shunted aside so readily by the Bush administration and led to threats to further limit workers' right to strike speaks volumes about the current state of the U.S. political economy and the marginal position of labor within it.

Discussion

The events surrounding the Eastern Airlines conflict marked a significant departure from "business as usual" for airline labor. The compelling issues underlying this struggle elicited an inter-union response unprecedented in the history of the U.S. airline industry. Support came from within national unions, from other unions in the airline industry, and from the labor movement as a whole. It cut across the domains of craft and carrier and other interdependencies that generally form the contours of inter-union relations. The unions at Eastern formed a coalition, worked closely together in contesting Lorenzo, surmounted numerous obstacles to unity, and sustained lengthy sympathy strikes. The AFL-CIO played a major and unusually central role in planning strike strategy and mobilizing support for the Eastern strikers.

Yet there were clear bounds to the solidarity that was achieved. Support within ALPA was limited by the parochialism of the MECs and divisive seniority and financial issues. The coalition of unions at Eastern, an uneasy alliance throughout, manifested less than equal status for all coalition members and struggles for control. The capacity of the AFL-CIO and national union headquarters to lead a sustained, militant struggle was not demonstrated. Early threats to extend the struggle to other air and rail carriers never materialized. Relatively quickly, the Eastern struggle receded in importance for most other unions.

An injury to the workers at Eastern, though unpalatable and to be avoided if possible, was regarded as something less than an injury to all. The negative consequences for other airline unions of a defeat at Eastern were neither so certain nor so immediate as to compel them to share fully in "ownership" of the struggle. In an industry lacking a substantial tradition of inter-union support and where labor is segmented into relatively narrow parcels for purposes of representation, it is perhaps only surprising that the support went as far as it did.

To some extent, it is inevitable that claims of broad significance intended to rally support will inflate the importance of a conflict and outstrip the support that is ultimately forthcoming. Nor can it be said with any certainty that wider and more intense inter-union support would have produced markedly different outcomes. A more militant campaign extended to other air and rail carriers would have provoked responses from other parties and kept the strike from languishing, but there is no guarantee at all that it would have generated outcomes more favorable to Eastern's workers. Certainly, the strategic advantages enjoyed by Lorenzo, including simultaneous operation of Continental, government and judicial support, the shelter of Chapter 11, and the prolonged forbearance of creditors, rendered the prospects for a decisive union victory dim from the outset.

With the benefit of hindsight, we know that life goes on in the airline industry following the Eastern strike and that some other carriers (and presumably their employees) have been aided by the departure of Eastern from the industry. Given the persistent overcapacity and financial woes of the industry, it is also easy to imagine that Eastern eventually would have succumbed to bankruptcy regardless of the outcome of the strike. Yet the stakes in the Eastern strike really were high for airline labor. Had Lorenzo prevailed and successfully operated an effectively (or actually) nonunion Eastern, the impact on the industry and airline unions would have been enormous. At the very least, it would have greatly increased the downward pressure on wages and encouraged even more aggressive labor relations strategies on the part of other carriers. Conversely, had the unions produced a clear-cut victory, the Eastern strike would have been regarded as a distinct turning point in the fortunes of American labor.

The actual outcome was far more ambiguous. With the removal of control of Eastern from Lorenzo by the bankruptcy court, his subsequent departure from Continental, the grounding of Eastern, and the strong message sent to other carriers, there was a basis for claiming a heavily qualified labor "victory." If the impact of the Eastern conflict seems mild in retrospect (and that is surely the viewpoint of an academic observer and not a former Eastern employee looking for work), that is because the worst-case scenario for labor was averted. It is also because we have yet to see whether the lessons learned from the Eastern experience have appreciably improved the capacity of airline labor for large-scale mobilization.

Predictably, perhaps, some of the most optimistic assessments of the struggle and life after Lorenzo came from the IAM. Members were told that "the brave Eastern strikers, with the help of a newly solidified labor movement, beat Frank Lorenzo. Every would-be Lorenzo in corporate America is re-evaluating their corporate strategy" (*Machinist*, Sept. 1990, 3).

IAM President Kourpias also pointed to the beneficial effects of the strike for future inter-union relations: "We will continue to use the one positive aspect of the Eastern struggle—the renewed and strengthened solidarity of AFL-CIO unions to work together to rebuild the lives of the Eastern strikers and their families and to prevent this from ever happening again" (*Machinist*, Feb. 1991, 4).

Other evaluations of the outcomes of the strike reflect greater ambivalence. TWU president George Leitz, for example, wrote that "now that the war is over—unfortunately with no winners—[the unions] are walking away with their pride and dignity intact" (*TWU Express*, Feb. 1991, 6). The director of the TWU Airline Division, John Kerrigan, was even less sanguine: "Some are saying that this is a victory for Labor over Lorenzo. If it is, the cost to employees was extremely great, while Lorenzo walked away much richer than he came in" (*TWU Express*, Jan. 1991, 9).

One of the more eloquent commentaries on the strike came from Captain Don Huckabee, a former Eastern pilot. Huckabee's words capture well the mixed legacy of the strike:

> Even the mention of a Real Eastern pilot, or being in the presence of one, evoked for most other ALPA pilots a feeling of discomfort, a slight embarrassment, an awkward situation in which one did not quite know whether to express sympathy, outrage, or politely ignore the obviously painful situation, much as one is made uncomfortable around those afflicted with a terminal illness, or the unsuccessful conclusion of a war, à la Vietnam. . . . "One day longer!!!" Labor must never gloat over this small satisfaction, but the otherwise empty victory has an enduring legacy: Workers in America will suffer many indignities when necessary, but once they have collectively determined that "enough is enough," then the same spirit of independence exemplified by our country's founders will exert itself and tyranny will be resisted. . . . The Real Eastern pilots were thrust accidentally into a classic labor confrontation. Monetary reward was never an issue here. At stake were such abstract issues as the right of representation; the preservation of dignity . . . and perhaps the most important of all, the realization that they had a duty toward their predecessors and followers (*Air Line Pilot*, March 1991, 10, 15, 17).

Conclusion

It is more than merely putting a favorable "spin" on events to claim that those who follow the Eastern strikers will find both inspiration and instruction in their efforts. Eastern's unions did indeed fight the good fight against enormous odds, and airline labor joined in that struggle as it had never done before. Relationships formed out of the strike and experience gained offer hope for the future of inter-union activity in the airline industry. Yet future efforts will have to account for the difficulties in sustaining support, the lack of adequate mechanisms for coordinating large-scale struggles, and parochialism rooted in union structure and ideology.

Airline unions have no shortage of issues around which to coalesce. Although one interview respondent offered the view that Eastern "is a one of a kind situation [because] we're dealing with a maniac," that assessment will likely prove overly hopeful. The Eastern experience provides ample repudiation of Lorenzo's scorched earth labor relations policy and is sufficient to make those who would follow the same path take pause. Yet the continuing turmoil in the airline industry and the altered character of its labor relations suggest that other major confrontations may lie ahead. It will be in the response to such threats or opportunities that the true significance of the Eastern conflict will become known.

Conclusion

The principal aim of this book has been to draw attention to the topic of inter-union relations and to demonstrate the viability of one coherent, theoretically informed approach to analyzing those relations. Inter-union relations provide a powerful lens for examining the labor movement, labor solidarity, and the ability of unions to shape events that affect workers' lives. That airline labor has been at the center of the swirling winds of change in U.S. labor relations and corporate structure, while lacking an established tradition of inter-union solidarity, makes it an especially interesting and instructive case. In this chapter, I conclude by summarizing the book's major conclusions and implications with respect to inter-union relations generally and to the specific circumstances of airline labor.

Inter-Union Relations

Generalizations regarding inter-union relations drawn from this work are necessarily provisional until empirical studies are done of unions in other industries. However, the analyses presented here point to several major, if tentative, conclusions regarding the connectedness of inter-union and labor-management relations, the role of interdependence in explaining inter-union ties, and efforts to improve inter-union relations.

Connectedness of Inter-Union and Labor-Management Relations

This book places relations between unions on center stage. In so doing, it runs counter to most industrial relations works that treat inter-union relations as, at best, an issue peripheral to the main concern of labor-management relations. The essential point, however, is that inter-union relations and labor-management relations are integrally linked. *Inter-union relations both reflect and shape labor-management relations.* The intertwining of the two is especially evident in the effects of representational structure, shared threats, and bargaining power differences on inter-union relations and the impact of inter-union cooperation on labor relations outcomes.

The formal structure of union representation in an industry is perhaps the most basic point of connection between inter-union and labor relations. This alignment of unions, workers, and employers defines the organizational boundaries across which inter-union relations may occur and heavily shapes the interests unions bring to bear in their dealings with one another. In this study, the relatively decentralized nature of the airline union network was accounted for by the decentralization of the industry's bargaining structure. When carrier-level unions have considerable control over the key activity of bargaining, they are relevant to other unions and communicate with them. Discussions of the relative advantages and disadvantages of narrower and more inclusive forms of labor organization (i.e., craft versus industrial union-ism) most often center on the consequences of homogeneity and heterogene-ity for the internal workings of unions and less often recognize the implica-tions for inter-union relations. *But, to the extent that less inclusive forms of organization are utilized, interdependencies that might otherwise be incor-porated within unions become the bases for potential ties between unions.*

The interpenetration of labor relations and inter-union relations is also apparent insofar as the common problems unions confront and their need to combine forces often stem from employer actions. Mergers, bankruptcy filings, concession demands, and the use of permanent replacements are only a few examples of employer actions that pose threats to unions and may prompt them to work together. In general, *the presence of labor-management conflict places a premium on inter-union support, provides a common enemy to rally against, and may promote greater cohesion among unions than would be present under more benign circumstances.* The ability of employers to undermine labor solidarity by playing unions off against one another and fostering perceptions of inequity is another facet of the same theme.

The interplay between labor-management and inter-union relations is also found in the connection between the bargaining power of unions and the character of their ties with other unions. *Unions that are better able to influence and obtain favorable terms from employers also enjoy a position of power in dealing with other unions.* Bargaining power is a critical resource for unions. Yet, like other valued resources and capacities, bargaining power is not equally distributed. That the support of some unions is consequently more valuable contributes to an imbalance in relations whereby relatively powerful unions are able either to remain aloof or to call the shots in their dealings with other unions. The labor movement is not monolithic. Even within the same industry, unions are diverse in a number of important respects, including their size, bargaining power, political clout, financial resources, and status. These inequalities provide the structural basis for the stratification and power dynamics among unions.

The relationship between labor-management and inter-union relations also runs in the other direction. *Supportive inter-union relations stand to affect labor relations outcomes in workers' favor.* This impact can occur in numerous ways, including by keeping unions from being pitted against one another in bargaining, by allowing funds and other resources to be pooled, by imposing higher costs on employers in strikes, by increasing the visibility and legitimacy of conflicts, by sharing successful strategies, by joining together in employee buyouts, by presenting a united voice in the political arena, by not splitting the pro-union vote in representation elections through competitive contests, and by dealing directly with workplace problems between members. Just as power is often best reflected in the absence of overt conflict because the powerful are able to dissuade challenges (Lukes 1974), the efficacy of labor solidarity may sometimes be manifested in decisions by employers and others not to take unions on. The case examples in this study showed that by working together unions can make a difference, but that this edge does not necessarily produce optimal outcomes. *To the extent that labor solidarity is viewed as a tactic reserved for the most severe circumstances, the prospects for producing decisive victories are clearly diminished.*

Interdependence and Inter-Union Relations

Relations between unions are structured. That is, they exhibit a coherent pattern and are based on relatively enduring grounds. Inter-union ties are not established for reasons so historically specific or idiosyncratic as to defy generalization. Nor is the structuring of labor solely a matter of formal national union and federation affiliations. Instead, relations between unions draw much of their essence from their interdependence. *A basic explanation for why unions establish relations with one another is that their actions and outcomes affect one another in various ways.* Unions compete, draw on each other for resources and support, have overlapping organizational affiliations, confront shared problems, are linked through the work process, influence one another's bargaining outcomes, and operate in the same domains. Inter-union links established in response to these interdependencies help unions deal with uncertainty, obtain resources, and shape important outcomes, but they also reinforce the extent to which their fates are intertwined.

The concept of interdependence provides a key to understanding the quality of relations between unions, as well as their presence or absence. *Inter-union relations differ in their intensity, instrumentality, collectiveness, reciprocity, formality, and balance of cooperation and conflict, depending on the particular type(s) of interdependence that is (are) present.* Relations between unions representing the same craft tend to reflect a combination of conflict and collective action; between unions that differ in their resources and capacities, a combination of instrumentality, lack of reciprocation, and conflict; between unions linked by common problems, intensity, and collective action; and between unions linked by organizational affiliation, formality.

Yet, if most of this book's arguments are in line with the essentially utilitarian thrust of organizational theory (Turk 1985), there are clearly limits to that view. One obvious point is that unions do not maintain the same ties with all the other unions with which they are interdependent. For example, although numerous prospective sources of support may be available, a union is more likely to cultivate a smaller number of reliable allies. Within the broad parameters of interdependence, choices about particular inter-union relations undoubtedly reflect such specific factors as the personal ties between union officers and the history of relations between the unions.

Inter-union relations are also shaped by the organizational characteristics of unions. It is important to consider the means and opportunity to engage in relations, not only the pressures to do so. The relevance of shared beliefs and values should not be dismissed. If consensus on this level is not a prerequisite for inter-union contact, it nonetheless affects how unions work together and their ability to achieve desired ends.

Norms of solidarity and the collective ethos of the labor movement create a context for inter-union relations that is different from that for most other interorganizational relations. Union officers necessarily consider the interests of their own members first. Often they conclude that the price is too high and the benefits too remote to justify solidaristic actions on behalf of other workers. Valuing solidarity does not change this, but it impels unionists to take a broader view of the potential impact of another union's defeat (that an injury to others may in fact be an injury to us as well), it imbues struggles with larger meaning by making them "causes" worthy of support, and it tilts the balance toward involvement when the calculation of organizational self-interest leaves room for discretion.

Practical Implications

This is not a "how-to" book. Yet there are several broad implications in this study for improving relations between unions. *Sustained relations between unions will usually require substantial interdependence. It is not enough simply to invoke notions of labor solidarity and participation in the labor movement. The nexus between unions in terms of activities and concerns must be stronger.* Efforts to engender cooperation thus have to be realistic in identifying the interests of individual unions and finding ways to further those interests jointly. At the same time, the interdependence of unions and the possibilities for joint efforts are often more extensive than is realized. The structural emphasis of this study and the willingness to assume that perceptions of interdependence are at least partially rooted in objective circumstances should not obscure the practical import of widening union officers' perceptions of interdependence.

Interdependence can result in conflict as readily as cooperation. *The ability of unions to work together to produce positive outcomes is affected by a number of factors. These include the identification of unions with particular crafts or employers, the desire to assert autonomy, inequality in resources and capacities, competition, perceived inequity in bargaining outcomes, disagreement over strategies and tactics, legal obstacles, divisive actions of employers, and the absence of sentiments of solidarity.*

This study has emphasized that *cooperative efforts by unions have to take account of the variety in unions, particularly their unequal abilities to contribute resources and meaningful support. That differences in resources and capacities across unions tend to coincide with differences in craft, national union affiliation, the status of members' work, and sometimes gender compounds the effect of these differences on inter-union relations.* There are no easy ways to promote cooperation under these circumstances. But the fact that many of the threats facing unions are shared equally, to the extent this is recognized, places a premium on joint activity and lessens the importance of these distinctions. If a company goes out of business, all of its unions and their members are out of luck, regardless of how much bargaining power each had previously. Speaking with a single voice and being inclusive are especially important to the success of certain tactics, such as attempting an employee buyout or engaging in political action. Use of these tactics may facilitate participation by less elite unions on a more equal basis. Additionally, less powerful unions often make subtle contributions. These include providing useful information or adding legitimacy to the actions of other unions by showing that these actions are undertaken for causes worthy of wide support.

Although the unions discussed in this study were able to submerge their conflicts in several situations, other evidence suggests the importance of having a track record in dealing with one another over a period of time. *Close working relationships need time to develop and cannot simply be summoned into existence when a crisis occurs.* Even when support is available, finding ways to sustain that support throughout the increasingly lengthy struggles in which unions find themselves is a major concern. Maintaining funds for inter-union support and other joint activities, rotating support responsibilities, sustaining plentiful communication and involvement at the rank-and-file level, and creating realistic expectations at the outset of conflicts could all help in this regard.

A more general problem is how to move toward institutionalizing solidarity and cooperation. *Where they are lacking, unions need to develop organizational mechanisms and understandings that support inter-union solidar-*

ity. National union headquarters and the AFL-CIO obviously play major roles as organizational mechanisms for furthering solidarity. Yet more flexible mechanisms, capable of focusing intently on particular struggles, engaging in militant tactics when necessary, and staying involved for the long haul, would be desirable. The Jobs with Justice program provides one encouraging model. The potential for such mechanisms to be viewed as threats to existing entities is very real, however.

Unions need to have a reasonably firm basis for expecting or not expecting support under particular circumstances. Clearly, the past experiences of unions have a great deal to do with their expectations of support and their willingness to provide it to other unions. The provision of aid in one instance, or the failure to provide it, thus has longer-term implications.

What kinds of struggles, if any, should appropriately be led at the highest levels of the labor movement and/or widened to include direct action by other unions? Beyond the legal constraints, there are both benefits (e.g., greater resources, publicity, legitimation) and costs (e.g., loss of control, remoteness from rank and file, wider risk) associated with higher-level coordination and broadening of inter-union support. If the extreme degree of "tight coupling" presupposed by a literal reading of the slogan "An injury to one is an injury to all" is both unattainable and undesirable, then there is a need for principles that articulate an alternative, "practical solidarity." For example, rather than wait on dubious allies in Congress and the executive branch to pass legislation banning the permanent replacement of strikers, unions might reach agreement among themselves that when faced with permanent replacement, they can count on a specified, substantial level of support.

A final practical implication of this study is that *supportive inter-union relations render the formal structure of union representation more flexible.* Within a craft-based bargaining structure, unions stand to gain the advantages of broader forms of organization, while retaining the benefits of relative homogeneity, autonomy, and smaller size. Yet the possibilities in this regard are clearly limited. At some point, high interdependence or asymmetrical dependence becomes incompatible with informal arrangements and exerts pressure for changes in formal structure, such as mergers or other forms of incorporation.

Airline Labor

What about inter-union relations in the airline industry specifically? Conclusions emerge from this study regarding the changing status of the relations among airline unions, the distinctive features of the airline industry as a context for inter-union relations, and future prospects for airline labor solidarity.

Changing Status of Relations among Airline Unions

Against the backdrop of a reputation for indifferent, if not antagonistic, inter-union relations and a history that tended to validate that image, *relations among airline unions showed signs of becoming more cohesive and strategically important in the late 1980s.* Airline unions have responded to their increased interdependence since deregulation by forging closer ties. To be sure, substantial cooperation and inter-union support are still far from the norm. A rhetoric of solidarity was not prominent among the airline union officers interviewed for this study, and only a minority felt that inter-union relations, in their current state, are highly instrumental in achieving union goals. For many airline unions, communication, if it occurs at all, is infrequent or routine. Even when airline unions are able to form meaningful coalitions and support one another in struggles, these efforts are often marred by differences over strategy and tactics, failure to align all the relevant unions, and an inability to produce decisive, positive outcomes.

On the brighter side, airline union coalitions have become more common and have been employed to considerable effect, if not to produce unequivocal "victories." Union officers cited numerous instances in which they worked together, shared information, and supported one another. Although by no means willing to bet the union hall on it, airline union officers tend to see other airline unions as prospective allies, ready to offer at least mild support. The Eastern Airlines struggle, featuring as it did lengthy sympathy strikes and far-reaching support activities, saw airline union solidarity reach unprecedented heights.

The current state of airline labor, then, represents a departure from indifference and antagonism in the direction of greater awareness and occasional displays of genuine solidarity. The significance of developments in the late 1980s, however, depends on the extent to which they point to distinctive features of the airline industry as a context for inter-union relations and to trends likely to extend into the future.

U.S. Airline Industry as a Context for Inter-Union Relations

Inter-industry comparisons are required to demonstrate convincingly distinctive aspects of the relations among airline unions. Nevertheless, in light of the model of inter-union relations developed here, *several features of the airline industry and its labor relations appear particularly important in determining the character of airline union relations. These features are the decentralized, craft-based representation structure; the relatively extreme degree of differentiation in the resources and capacities of unions, particularly across crafts; the substantial identification of employees with "their" carriers, reinforced in a number of cases by union structure and seniority provisions; the substantial variation in the extent to which representation of crafts is concentrated within the same national unions; a history of industry regulation during which strike support was not a critical consideration; a*

current environment that is volatile and replete with threat; and a produc-
tion process that employs a wide variety of "skilled" and "less skilled" labor
and brings in-flight crew into the closest working relationships.

In response to these circumstances, relations are found primarily among unions representing either workers in the same craft or employed by the same carrier. The decentralized industry bargaining structure is matched by a relatively decentralized network of communication in which carrier-level unions, and not only national union headquarters, are active. Imbalances among unions in resources and capacities, stemming from the characteristics of the craft represented and its position in the production process, as well as their national union affiliations, have a pervasive effect on airline union relations. The fabled aloofness of pilot unions, which has a partial basis in fact, is best understood as a reflection of their power relative to that of many other airline unions, rather than of something peculiar to pilots or ALPA. Similarly, the actions of the mechanics unions, particularly the IAM, in contending with ALPA and often pursuing a relatively autonomous course, reflect the presence of their relatively strong bargaining power and substantial organizational resources. The imbalance in the typical relationship between pilots and flight attendants unions can be understood within the same framework, although issues of workflow interdependence, status, gender, and prior affiliations complicate matters.

The identification of airline employees with their carriers has a number of ramifications for inter-union relations. On the one hand, it is one (of many) factors encouraging airline unions to pursue employee ownership or otherwise assume a larger role in the management of carriers, leading to joint activity by unions. On the other hand, and especially for ALPA and AFA MECs, it reinforces a parochial, carrier-centered outlook and makes concerted activity by the affiliates of these unions problematic. That the representation of flight attendants is dispersed across numerous unions, while most pilot groups are represented by affiliates of ALPA (representation of mechanics is dominated by the IAM, but to a lesser extent than ALPA dominates among pilots), is also of consequence for inter-union relations. Relations between flight attendants unions are marked by both competition and coalition formation, while the pilots unions are coordinated largely within the ALPA International, which is able to insist that other pilots unions affiliate if they want to share in its resources.

The history of the airline industry and its formerly extensive regulation continues to be relevant to inter-union relations. The absence of a tradition of labor solidarity in the industry can be traced, in part, to prior circumstances in which carriers were largely protected from failure and strikes led to a cessation of operations, affording airline unions the luxury of going it alone. Current circumstances, of course, are far less benign.

In the turmoil and threat of the airline industry since deregulation, the permanent replacement of strikers, failing carriers, merger mania, and a host of other ills have increased the need of unions for support and cooperation. The increased interdependence arising from these circumstances has been a major impetus for closer relations among airline unions. Thus, coalitions of airline unions have primarily been responses to the threats posed by financially troubled carriers. The Eastern conflict produced a broad mobilization of support that extended beyond the usual domains of craft and carrier. To some degree, the serious and shared nature of many of the industry's problems has a leveling effect on unions, since powerful unions stand to be affected no less than other unions and the problems are too large for any one union to resolve by itself. Insofar as relations among airlines are driven by crises, however, cooperation tends to be sporadic and vulnerable to changing circumstances.

Future of Inter-Union Relations in the Airline Industry

What implications do the experiences of airline labor in the late 1980s hold for the 1990s and beyond? Judging from the experiences of airline unions in working with one another and the likelihood that they will remain or become even more interdependent, *there is reason to believe that inter-union dealings will continue at least at their current level and perhaps intensify.* This does not mean that relations will necessarily be cooperative or that the many obstacles to achieving solidarity have been surmounted.

Some circumstances have already changed. For a host of financial and political reasons, the mega-mergers of the 1980s are not likely to occur again in the near future. Frank Lorenzo has exited the airline industry scene (albeit, like the proverbial bad penny, perhaps only temporarily) (*New York Times*, April 30, 1993, C-3). The devastation of Eastern Airlines stands as a warning to carriers contemplating permanent replacement of their workers. A Democratic administration, professing concern for the airline industry and its workers, has come into office.

At the same time, the airline industry remains in a state of flux. Carriers teeter on the edge of bankruptcy (or fall into it), engage in self-defeating fare wars, and relentlessly press unions for concessions. Even following the Eastern experience, few union officers would be sanguine about the prospects of facing permanent replacement in a strike. Moreover, the difficulties of carriers are increasingly defined as problems of the industry as a whole. If merger activity has abated, the restructuring of the industry presses on in the form of "globalization." International travel constitutes an increasingly important part of the airline business, interlining arrangements and other operational alliances between carriers are now rife, and the infusion of capital from other nations is of growing importance to the financial health of domestic carriers.

The bottom line is that airline unions will continue to affect one another profoundly by their activities and outcomes. Indeed, there are indications that the spheres of interdependence may be expanding. Growing consensus that the problems of carriers are endemic to the industry and may require public policy measures (*New York Times*, March 22, 1993, 1) suggests a broadening of the shared problems that unions face and of the potential base for inter-union activity. Even more so, globalization portends widened interdependence, extending to unions representing airline workers in other countries. The intertwining of operations and finances across nations makes unions in other countries far more relevant, such as when a strike occurs at one of a pair of interlined carriers. Attempts by airline unions to limit foreign operations in domestic markets also speak to a growing interdependence, although inter-union conflicts are likely in this area.

Although most of what can be glimpsed on the horizon suggests a continuation or intensification of inter-union activity, legal impediments to inter-union support in strikes are likely to become more severe as carriers seek to counter union solidarity with the aid of an accommodating federal judiciary. Given the continued pressure on unions to render concessions, and indeed to produce large-scale concession packages with other unions to save carriers from bankruptcy, perceptions of inequity will loom large as a continuing obstacle to cooperation. This scenario unfolded most recently at Northwest Airlines. Unions there formed a coalition to deal with the carrier regarding its debt problem, but the initial unity dissolved and two groups of unions went their own ways in negotiating with the carrier (*New York Times*, July 8, 1993, C-1; Rachleef 1993).

Do the increase in interdependence and inter-union activity have any implications for the future structure of representation in the airline industry? Moody (1987b: 8–9) has advanced a fairly sweeping argument for revamping the industry's craft form of organization:

> Craft unionism is an anachronism in a jet-age industry that is going through a drastic restructuring. . . . If they are to deal with their changed industry, the airline unions will have to adopt both innovative strategies and many of the practices of industrial unionism, bargaining together on an industry-wide basis for all categories of workers.

Certainly, when unions are being whipsawed and concessions rendered to carriers are frittered away in fare wars, the need for mechanisms to achieve greater coordination in bargaining is real. *Short of actual consolidation of the bargaining structure through industry-level bargaining by craft or multi-union bargaining, the increased exchange of bargaining-related information (including carrier demands, contract language, and tactics), provision of support to unions on strike or facing a strike, and meetings to agree on uniform negotiation aims are looser but more readily attainable forms of inter-union coordination in bargaining.*

Coordination of bargaining is presumably most easily accomplished among affiliates of the same national union. ALPA's Collective Bargaining Committee, with its mission of investigating the possibilities for coordinated bargaining across carriers by ALPA MECs, reflects increased thinking along these lines, although, as yet, little change in practice. Additionally, and largely because of the insistence of failing carriers that all of their unions agree on overall concession packages, loose forms of multi-union bargaining have occurred at a number of those carriers.

Given the entrenchment of the decentralized, craft-based bargaining structure in the industry and that airline management has little incentive to alter a set of arrangements that (in contrast to earlier years) works in its favor (Cappelli 1985), it is not surprising that Moody's recommendation has not been widely embraced or even discussed. The role of the National Mediation Board in airline negotiations—specifically, its ability to determine the duration of the negotiation process—also tends to blunt the impact of coordinated bargaining efforts. In contrast to occasional multi-union bargaining at individual airlines, disparity in the financial health of carriers since deregulation has been a major force undermining any impetus toward coordination of bargaining across carriers. Yet, as almost all carriers continue to languish, the prospects for some form of closer coordination in bargaining across carriers may improve. Certainly, the largest carriers would like to see other carriers moved out of Chapter 11 status and more similar cost structures imposed on them.

The structure of union representation in the airline industry has also been affected by corporate consolidation. Fewer unions now represent the airline workers at the major carriers, although in cases where mergers have transpired, the bargaining units have increased in size. Beyond consolidation generated by corporate restructuring, there has been little organizational realignment among airline unions. One intriguing exception is the affiliation of the Union of Flight Attendants at Continental Airlines with the IAM in 1990 (culminating a process that had begun in 1984). If ever there was a case of an airline union being located at an outpost in hostile territory, under siege, and without the necessary resources to engage in combat, this was it. Whether the UFA-IAM affiliation turns out to be an anomaly or a harbinger of future events remains to be seen. Supportive, mutually beneficial inter-union relations offer an attractive alternative to the loss of autonomy and identity associated with formal organizational affiliation. Yet, especially when there is major disparity in the resources and capacities of unions, pressures for incorporation within the same organization exist.

Final Thoughts

Where do we go from here? From an academic perspective, any renewed interest in the structure of the labor movement that this book might encourage among industrial relations scholars would be a welcome development. Without suggesting a proliferation of studies of inter-union relations in other industries, research on the relations in industries with different representation structures and environmental pressures than those characterizing the airline industry, and across industries, would be especially valuable for gaining perspective on this work. More generally, industrial relations researchers can gain from paying more attention to the social embeddedness of individuals and organizations—the essential insight of network concepts. Strike outcomes, organizing and representation election outcomes, the diffusion of labor relations strategies, labor political action, employer organization, and pattern bargaining are only a few of the industrial relations topics for which a network perspective promises fresh insights. For organizational researchers, renewing old acquaintances (e.g., Sayles and Strauss 1967 [1953]) with organizational studies of unions would provide one corrective for a pronounced tendency to use "organization" as a euphemism for "large, Fortune 500 corporation." Unions have a number of interesting and distinctive characteristics that are useful in examining generalizations based on other organizations. The possibilities for integrating organizational and industrial relations scholarship are numerous (e.g., Bacharach, Seeber, and Walsh, forthcoming).

Finally, this book underscores the critical importance to the labor movement of developing solid and supportive inter-union relations. Inter-union cooperation is one essential prong in any larger strategy to revitalize the American labor movement. It is part of the practice of unionism at its best, not merely a tactic to be trotted out when unions are in trouble. Ultimately, it comes down to this: If unions cannot depend on their members and one another, then what else is there? The realization that the labor movement is not monolithic and that the many and diverse organizations that make it up have differing interests and circumstances is important if the prospects for labor solidarity are to be realistically appraised. But that unions start at different points is less important than that they move in the same direction and share common the destination of a more just and democratic society.

Afterword

An editor's request: "Gee, there's so much interesting stuff going on in the airline industry right now. Why don't you update the proof and mention some of these things?" An author's anguished reply: "Sure, and if I work diligently, I just might be able to avoid authoring this book posthumously!"

In fact, much has happened in the airline industry following the events that I have described here. Northwest's unions concluded negotiations for a substantial ownership share in the carrier. United's unions appear to have gone even further in this direction. Flight attendants at American Airlines courageously and quite successfully struck. A presidential commission has deliberated on the problems of the airline industry and put forth some thoroughly modest proposals for change. The industry's most infamous former owner has petitioned the DOT to start a new airline with the utterly incongruous moniker "Friendship Air."

One can no more write a book on the airline industry that remains fully up to date than keep long in sight a jet taking off from a runway. Yet recent events serve only to underscore the relevance of inter-union relations for airline unions and the industry. The financial woes of carriers and the industry continue, placing unions in the position of negotiating together with carriers to trade concessions for ownership shares. That this occurred at both Northwest and United with less than total labor unity (or even inclusion in the case of flight attendants at United) reflects many of the same issues discussed throughout this book. The industry's continued movement toward employee ownership can only heighten the importance and delicacy of inter-union relations, as unions deal with each other in new settings and attempt to influence the course taken by carriers. However tepid the proposals of the presidential commission, the existence of such a body reflects the systemic nature of the industry's problems and the continuing relevance of political forces, both of which call for a unified and effective labor political voice. And if a certain former owner returns to the industry to weave his magic once again....

The November 1993 strike by flight attendants at American Airlines could be interpreted as an indication that inter-union support in strikes is less critical than I have maintained or that flight attendants are at less of a disadvantage with respect to bargaining power than I have suggested. Certainly, strategic timing, careful preparation, and skillful use of public relations enabled the union to conduct a very effective strike. Whether claims that the flight attendants preferred to have the pilots continue flying (so as to impose greater cost on the carrier) were accurate or merely a case of putting the best face on a lack of support, it is unlikely that the strike would have been joined by American's other unions. Further, the ability to conduct the strike so effectively rested on both the brief duration that was planned for it and the apparent disbelief on the part of American's management that the union could actually convince the majority of its members to strike. This is far from the first time that a flight attendants union has displayed considerable ingenuity and militancy. But the fact that they were on their own and had to rely on some exceptional circumstances is telling. Structurally, the position of flight attendants unions (and not only flight attendants unions) is such that they have difficulty obtaining the support they need from other unions and in exerting influence over inter-union activities. The inspiring events at American were not inconsistent with that.

Appendix 1

Survey of Inter-Union Relations

Below is the survey instrument used in this study. Bracketed items were tailored to the particular respondent, and the instrument was modified slightly to make it more appropriate for national union respondents.

This survey is intended to gather information regarding your union's contacts with other unions that also represent airline workers. It is *not* expected that you will take the time to complete the survey in writing, but I do hope that we will be able to discuss these issues in a telephone interview. If the meaning of any question is not clear or if the response choices that have been provided are not adequate to describe your union's experience, please do not hesitate to point this out.

First, a few questions regarding [union] itself:

1. How many workers does [union] represent at [carrier]? What is the total number of workers that [union] represents?

2. About how many full-time officers and staff does [union] have?

3. In your bargaining with [carrier(s)], which of the following describes the role of the inter/national union? (indicate as many as apply)
   (a) inter/national participates in formulation of bargaining strategy (b) inter/national has substantial influence over bargaining demands and strategy (c) inter/national must approve agreements (d) inter/national representative actively participates in most negotiations (e) inter/national representative is head of negotiating committee

4. Which of the following activities has [union] engaged in during the past two years (since early 1987)? (indicate as many as apply)

(a) organizing (b) bargaining (c) litigation against a carrier (d) presentation of a case or testimony before a regulatory agency (e.g., NMB, FAA) (e) political action on an issue of craft or industrywide concern

5. How long has the current [president/secretary-treasurer/general chairman/MEC chairman] held that position? Held any elected office in [union]?

Questions 6 through 21 relate to your union's contacts or relationships with the other unions listed on the last page of this survey (excluding the [union] Inter/national). For each of these questions you can simply give me the name(s) or corresponding number(s) of the union(s), *if any*, which apply. Unless otherwise stated, the questions refer to [union]'s relationships with these other unions *during the past two years* (roughly early 1987 to the present).

6. With which of the unions listed has [union] had any *direct communication or contact* (e.g., letters, telephone calls, meetings, etc.) during the past two years?

6a. With which of these unions has *communication or contact generally occurred at least once a month* during the past two years?

6b. With which of these unions has *communication or contact occurred no more than once or twice a year* during the past two years?

7. In addition to those unions already mentioned in answering question 6, for which of the unions listed do you currently *know of or have on file the name* of some particular officer or staff person who could be contacted if the need arose?

8. From which of the unions listed would you currently *expect at least mild support* (any helpful action) if requested?

8a. On what do you base your expectations of support?

9. With which of the unions listed has [union] received from or exchanged *information* (e.g., regarding carriers, bargaining outcomes, industry issues, etc.) during the past two years?

9a. Can you provide an *example* of a type of information that was received from or exchanged with one of the unions listed?

9b. To which of the unions listed would you tend to *turn first for information about settlements or contract language for your craft/job group* elsewhere in the industry? *Information about [carrier]*?

10. With which of the unions listed has [union] received from or exchanged *resources other than information* (e.g., funds, use of facilities, training materials, etc.) during the past two years?

10a. Can you provide an *example* of a type of resource received from or exchanged with one of the unions listed?

11. Which of the unions listed do you think *provided substantial support* (took action that made a real difference in helping [union] achieve its goals) in recent years?

11a. Can you provide an *example* of an instance in which [union] received substantial support from one of the listed unions?

11b. *If no substantial support was received,* did [union] seek any support in recent years?

11c. To which of the unions listed would you tend to *turn first for support in a strike situation?*

12. With which of the unions listed has [union] maintained *written or oral agreement(s)* (e.g., regarding jurisdiction, strike support, membership transfer, etc.) during the past two years?

12a. Can you provide an *example* of a written or oral agreement that [union] maintains with one of the listed unions?

13. At which of the unions listed do you have *personal friends* (as opposed to simply acquaintances) among the officers or staff?

13a. Are these personal friends generally people that you *met in the course of your work* with [union] *or* are they people that you *originally met elsewhere?*

14. With which of the unions listed has [union] carried out some form of *joint action* (worked together to achieve a common goal, such as in joint lobbying, joint legal action, forming a coalition, etc.) during the past two years?

14a. Can you provide an *example* of a joint action undertaken with one or more of the other unions listed?

14b. *If any joint action involved a coalition,* which of the other unions listed belonged to the coalition and what was the issue(s) around which the coalition acted?

15. With which of the unions listed did [union] have contact during the past two years through *joint attendance* at a meeting or other event sponsored by a *state labor federation, central labor council, or other labor coordinating body?*

16. With which of the other [union] [type of unit] listed did contact over the past two years occur *primarily through meetings or events sponsored by the [union] International or one of its divisions* (e.g., conventions, officer meetings, training sessions, etc.), rather than directly?

17. With which of the unions listed has *contact become more intense* (required considerably more time and attention than previously) during the past two years?

17a. With which of the unions listed did the *first communication or contact* occur within the past two years?

18. With which of the unions listed [has/did] [union][had/have] *contact or communication related to the Eastern strike* of 1989?

18a. With which of the unions listed was *all or nearly all of the contact or communication* that occurred during the past two years related to the Eastern strike?

18b. Can you provide an *example* of contact or communication with one of the unions listed that was related to the Eastern strike?

19. With which of the unions listed is [union] *interdependent* (in the sense that [union] is likely to be affected by what these other unions do or by what happens to these other unions)?

20. Which of the unions listed is, at least some of the time, a *competitor* with [union] (e.g., for new members, size of settlements, etc.)?

21. With which of the unions listed did [union] *have some type of disagreement or dispute* (e.g., concerning jurisdictions, merging of seniority lists, tactics, etc.) during the past two years?

21a. Can you provide an *example* of an issue over which there was a disagreement or dispute with another of the unions listed?

The remaining questions refer to your union's overall experience dealing with other airline unions.

22. How does the *amount of contact* [union] has with other unions that represent airline workers *compare* to the amount of contact it has with other unions that *do not* represent airline workers?
    (a) almost all contact is with airline unions (b) more contact with airline unions (c) about an equal amount of contact with both (d) more contact with unions not representing airline workers (e) almost all contact is with unions not representing airline workers

23. Overall, *how important* are the ties that [union] has with other unions representing airline workers in terms of [union]'s ability to get its job done?
    (a) not important at all (b) somewhat important (c) quite important (d) very important

24. Can you point to one or two relationships with other airline unions that you regard as the *most important* to [union]? Which one(s)? Why?

25. Based on your experience, which of the following would you say are *major obstacles* to more cooperative relations between unions in the airline industry?
    (a) lack of sufficient common interests across crafts/job groups
    (b) lack of sufficient common interests across carriers
    (c) lack of membership support for inter-union cooperation
    (d) lack of sufficient staff and resources to devote to inter-union contact
    (e) experience of lack of support in the past
    (f) competition between unions

(g) interpersonal conflicts between leaders

(h) political and ideological differences between leaders

(i) basic disagreements over strategy and tactics

(j) efforts by carriers to pit unions against one another

(k) inequitable contract settlements

(l) broad judicial interpretation of no-strike clauses as covering sympathy strikes

(m) lack of sufficient support from inter/national unions

(n) concern with maintaining autonomy of individual unions (e.g., not becoming dependent on or tied up with other unions)

(o) inequality in bargaining power across unions

(p) differences in AFL-CIO affiliation status across unions

(q) other major obstacle _____

25a. Can you cite an *example* of a situation in which one of these obstacles was present, negating an opportunity for cooperation?

26. Which of the following do you regard as a *serious problem or threat* to [union]? (indicate as many as apply)

(a) carrier at which members are employed is financially troubled

(b) carrier demands for givebacks

(c) subcontracting of bargaining unit work

(d) merger or acquisition of carrier

(e) lack of statutory or regulatory protection in mergers (LPPs)

(f) creation or purchase of a nonunion subsidiary by carrier

(g) disinvestment in carrier or sale of assets

(h) mismanagement of carrier

(i) existence of nonunion or largely nonunion carriers in the industry

(j) spread of concessions across carriers

(k) inability to wield sufficient bargaining power

(l) permanent replacement in strike situations

(m) inadequate recognition of professional status of members

(n) carriers not sufficiently concerned with safety

(o) government not sufficiently concerned with safety

(p) imposition of random drug testing

(q) absence of economic regulation of the airline industry

(r) granting to foreign carriers increased access to domestic market (cabotage)

(s) other problem or threat _____

27. Where on the following scale would you locate the views of [union] leaders concerning *employee ownership*?

1 2 3 4 5 6

Employee ownership
is a viable and
attractive option

Employee ownership
is not a viable and
attractive option

28. Where on the following scale would you locate the views of [union] leaders concerning *labor-management cooperation?*

1   2   3   4   5   6

Cooperative efforts   Cooperative efforts
should be actively   *should not be* pursued
pursued

Thank you very much for your help

These are the unions I am referring to in my questions:

1. APA (American—pilots)
2. FEIA, AMERICAN AIRLINES CHAPTER (flight engineers)
3. APFA (American—flight attendants)
4. TWU, LOCAL 513 (American—mechanics, etc.)
5. UFA, LOCAL 1 (Continental—flight attendants)
6. ALPA, DELTA MEC (pilots)
7. PAFCA (Delta—dispatchers)
8. ALPA, EASTERN MEC (pilots)
9. TWU, LOCAL 553 (Eastern—flight attendants)
10. IAM, DISTRICT LODGE 100 (Eastern—mechanics, etc.)
11. ALPA, NORTHWEST MEC (pilots)
12. IAM, DISTRICT LODGE 143 (Northwest—mechanics, etc.)
13. IBT, LOCAL 2747 (Northwest—flight attendants)
14. TWU, LOCAL 528 (Northwest—radio/telecommunications)
15. TWU, LOCAL 540 (American/Pan Am/Northwest/Piedmont/TWA/United/U.S. Air—dispatchers,meteorologists)
16. ALPA, PAN AM MEC (pilots)
17. FEIA, PAN AM CHAPTER (flight engineers)
18. TWU, LOCAL 504 (Pan Am—mechanics, etc.)
19. IBT, LOCAL 732 (Pan Am—passenger service)
20. IUFA (Pan Am—flight attendants)
21. ALPA, TWA MEC (pilots)
22. IFFA (TWA—flight attendants)
23. IAM, DISTRICT LODGE 142 (TWA—mechanics, etc.)
24. ALPA, UNITED MEC (pilots)
25. AFA, UNITED MEC (flight attendants)
26. IAM, DISTRICT LODGE 141 (United/U.S. Air—mechanics, etc.)
27. ALPA, U.S. AIR MEC (pilots)
28. AFA, U.S. AIR MEC (flight attendants)
29. IBT, LOCAL 2707 (U.S. Air—passenger service)
30. ALPA, INTERNATIONAL
31. FEIA, INTERNATIONAL
32. AFA, NATIONAL
33. IAM, AIRLINE DIVISION

34. TWU, AIR TRANSPORT DIVISION
35. IBT, AIRLINE DIVISION
36. ALEA, NATIONAL
37. TCU, INTERNATIONAL

Appendix 2

Categories Used in Constructing Interdependence Measures

Resource Dependence

High Bargaining Power Unions (Represent pilots or mechanics—carrier-level unions only.)

APA, TWU Local 513, Delta MEC (ALPA), Eastern MEC (ALPA), IAM District 100, Northwest MEC (ALPA), IAM District 143, Pan Am MEC (ALPA), TWU Local 504, TWA MEC (ALPA), IAM District 142, United MEC (ALPA), IAM District 141, U.S. Air MEC (ALPA), IBT Local 2707

Substantial Political Capacity (Assesed in terms of number of Washington representatives employed, PAC expenditures, and location of union head-quarters. Only inter/national-level and independent unions are included in this measure.)

ALPA, IBT, IAM, TCU

Common Problem Interdependence

Financially Troubled Carriers (Carriers that had low ROEs and cash flow, high debt/equity ratios, high debt/capital ratios in 1987.)

Continental, Eastern, Pan Am, TWA

Eastern Airlines (Unions representing workers at Eastern.)

IAM District 100, ALPA Eastern MEC, TWU Local 553, ALPA International, IAM International, TWU International

Bargaining Outcome Interdependence

Competing Carriers (Carriers that overlapped the most in service to major domestic and foreign markets. Overlap was defined as both carriers having carried 1 million or more passengers in a market in December 1987. The two carriers that overlapped the most with a given carrier were considered its "prime competitors" unless there was a tie, in which case more than two carriers were so designated.)

American—Delta, United
Continental—United, Eastern, Northwest
Delta—American, Eastern
Eastern—Delta, U.S. Air, Pan Am
Northwest—United, Continental
Pan Am—Delta, Eastern
TWA —American, Delta, Pan Am, United
United—American, Continental
U.S. Air—Delta, Eastern

Appendix 3

Explanation of Analyses

Multiple Regression/Quadratic Assignment Procedure

This procedure was developed to allow regression analyses and significance testing to be undertaken with dyadic, relational data (Krackhardt 1988). The analysis of such data is complicated by the problem of network autocorrelation, which renders questionable the normal assumption in regression of independent observations on the dependent variable (Lincoln 1984; Doreian, Teuter, and Wang 1984). The clearest form of potential nonindependence in dyadic data stems from the fact that the same actors are included in multiple dyads (all the cells within the same rows and columns of an adjacency matrix) and hence in multiple observations of the dependent variable.

The quadratic assignment procedure (QAP) (Hubert and Baker 1978; Baker and Hubert 1981; MacEvoy and Freeman 1987) is used to compare the similarity of two matrices of relational data. In essence, QAP indexes the probability that the similarity between two matrices can be explained as a random permutation of the rows and columns of either matrix. The lower that probability, the more likely it is that the two matrices are in fact similar. In its permutation variant, QAP entails first computing the Pearson correlation between two matrices, then holding one matrix constant and randomly permuting the rows and columns of the second matrix. By permuting rows and columns rather than individual cells, the dependence within rows and columns is built into the significance test. An empirical distribution of correlations over some number of random permutation trials is thereby generated and the observed correlation prior to any permutations is compared to the values in this distribution. The p-value is the proportion of correlations in the permutation trials that are equal to or greater than the observed correlation. The minimum p-value that can be attained is equal to $1/k$, where k is the number of permutation trials.

Although QAP is limited to comparisons of two matrices, Krackhardt (1988) has shown that it can nonetheless be used in a multiple regression framework. This is accomplished by, for each regressor and for the dependent variable, partialling out the influence of all other regressors and then using QAP to compare the two matrices of residuals. Thus, QAP, in conjunction with OLS regression, can be used to conduct valid tests of significance for multiple regression models predicting dyadic ties in a network. A FORTRAN program written by Krackhardt (MRQAP6) produced the regression results reported in chapter 5.

One additional concern is that the dependent variables in this study are dichotomous. When applied to dichotomous dependent variables, OLS regression can produce biased coefficient estimates without known distributional properties (Aldrich and Nelson 1984: 13, 30). Since multiple regression (MR)/QAP does not rely on the distributional properties of estimated standard errors in its significance tests, however, and estimation of the precise magnitude of effects is not critical to the purposes of this study, the limitations of OLS regression in handling dichotomous dependent variables do not preclude its usage here.

As a check on the performance of MR/QAP, its results were compared with logistic regression (SAS LOGIST procedure) results. For the eight models estimated in chapter 5, there was agreement between the two procedures on the statistical significance (that is, both procedures found the variable to be either significant or nonsignificant) of 82 percent (98 of 120) of the estimated coefficients. Of the twenty-two discrepancies, sixteen (73 percent) were cases in which the logistic regression analysis found a variable to be significant while MR/QAP did not. Overall, this comparison suggests that both procedures produce roughly similar results but that MR/QAP is somewhat more conservative in this case.

Convergence of Iterated Correlations (CONCOR)

CONCOR (Breiger, Boorman, and Arabie 1975; Arabie, Boorman, and Levitt 1978; Knoke and Kuklinski 1982) is a widely used algorithm that systematically detects network structure by identifying groups of structurally equivalent (or approximately so) actors and describing relations among those actors and with other actors. Structural equivalence is assessed in terms of the similarity in the relational profiles of two network actors. Regardless of whether two actors maintain direct ties with one another, they will be considered structurally equivalent and assigned to the same network position if they maintain similar ties to other network actors.

Assuming that multiple relations are being analyzed, CONCOR operates on a stacked $k(n \times n)$ matrix, with k equal to the number of different relations examined and n the number of actors in the network. An initial set of correlations between pairs of columns (indicating similarity between two actors in their pattern of ties with other network actors) is computed and these correlations are then recorrelated in iterative fashion until all correlations converge to +1.0 or -1.0 (or very close to that). Actors that are negatively correlated are assigned to different positions, and those that are positively correlated are assigned to the same position. The process is then repeated within positions to produce successive bi-partitions up to a desired level of fineness in depicting network structure. After actors have been grouped into positions based on their structural equivalence, the matrices for each type of relation are permuted to group together actors within the same position. The matrices of densities within and across positions for each kind of tie are computed. Image matrices reduce these block density matrices to dichotomous representations of network structure by taking on a value of 1 when cell density is equal to or greater than the mean value for that relation and 0 otherwise. UCINET 3.0 (MacEvoy and Freeman 1987) was used to perform the blockmodeling described in chapter 6.

Notes

Chapter 2

1. This is not to say that an organizational perspective is the only useful vantage point. Social historians (Gutman 1977; Montgomery 1979), for example, have made a persuasive case for attending to the lives, emergent protests, and community ties of workers. Focusing on unions may obscure the cohesion and cleavage among workers at the rank-and-file level. Similarly, an organizational perspective tends to overlook broader issues pertaining to the segmentation of the U.S. working class (Gordon, Edwards, and Reich 1982). Nevertheless, much can still be learned about the labor movement by examining unions and their relations, particularly given the relatively fine-grained, industry-specific focus of this study.

2. Although the focus here is on interdependence as a basis for establishing inter-union ties, it is important to realize that interdependence both promotes and is reinforced by relations among organizations. Mark S. Mizruchi (1987: 212) has made this point succinctly: "When two firms are interdependent, they are likely to establish relations with one another. At the same time, once relations are established, the interdependence relation is solidified."

3. The line between the intra- and interorganizational is often quite blurry. While relations between locals affiliated with the same national union might be considered intra-organizational, the geographic separation and relative autonomy of many locals (especially vis-à-vis one another, as opposed to the national headquarters) suggest that their organizational boundaries are usually sufficiently distinct (Lincoln 1982: 27) to justify the treatment of relations among locals as an interorganizational phenomenon.

4. Since this analysis is being pursued at the organizational level and focuses on general rather than particularistic factors, personal friendships between union officers and the unique history of relations between particular unions are not considered. This does not reflect a judgment that they are unimportant, however.

5. Mizruchi (1990: 19) has argued that despite regular usage, the concept of solidarity (cohesion) remains ill defined. A subjective view of solidarity, emphasizing

shared values, a sense of mutual responsibility, and group identification, is the most common. A more objective approach, focusing on actual social relations and similarity of behavior, is also found in the literature. Michael Hechter (1987: 18), for example, defines solidarity in terms of the average proportion of each group member's private resources that are actually contributed to collective ends. My own view is that although it is cohesive behavior that ultimately "matters," removing feeling and thinking from the concept of solidarity distorts and unnecessarily limits that concept.

6. Discussions of bargaining structure (e.g., Kochan 1980) typically focus on the degree of inclusiveness of units in terms of occupational groupings and the degree of centralization in terms of corporate structure. The organizational issue of whether separate bargaining units are represented by the same union, unions affiliated with the same national union, or unions not affiliated with each other in any way tends to be ignored. That bargaining unit boundaries and union organizational boundaries need not coincide is quite relevant to inter-union relations, however. I use the term "structure of union representation" to incorporate this organizational dimension along with the other aspects of bargaining structure.

The topic of bargaining structure invites consideration of inter-union relations, but the industrial relations literature has never gone very far in that direction. The concepts of "pattern bargaining" or a "unit of direct impact" (Weber 1961) point to an intertwining of bargaining outcomes, but I am not aware of any attempts to specify underlying inter-union mechanisms (e.g., exchanges of contract information). Similarly, there has been implicit theorizing regarding the probable effects of bargaining structure on inter-union relations, such as when a craft-based structure or "bargaining unit proliferation" are presumed to encourage jurisdictional disputes and wage "leap-frogging" (Kochan 1980; Schwarz and Koziara 1992), but the discussion goes little farther than that.

7. Examining inter-union relations necessitates a departure from the norm in most industrial relations research of considering individual (however large the "N") unions, firms, or bargaining units as units of analysis. Because *relationships* are the objects of inquiry, the basic unit of analysis is the dyad or union pair. Between any two unions, a specified tie may or may not be present.

The issue of which unions establish which ties with one another is fundamental to this study and can be usefully addressed by examining multiple union pairs. Even a relatively small number of unions results in numerous potential pairings. Information about both parties to a relationship can be used to explain why a particular link was established. A dyadic analysis does not reach several important issues, however. Examining pairs of unions obscures any larger groupings (e.g., coalitions) acting in concert. Additionally, knowledge of multiple dyadic ties does not tell us how those links fit together into a larger pattern. A given relationship can have very different meanings depending on the broader system of relations in which it is embedded. Hence, this study considers "action-sets" (coalitions and federations) and networks, as well as dyads.

8. Although this device is helpful for analytical purposes, as an empirical matter, pairs of unions, and even more so whole networks, are likely to be interdependent in multiple ways.

9. That is, to return the same kind of resources or support. Other forms of reciprocation, however, such as accepting the suggestions or leadership of elite

unions and occasionally providing useful information, may be both possible and expected.

10. This is not to deny the difficulty of engendering collective action, even when there appear to be strong common interests. However, free-riding and the imperceptible effects of contributions, which rational choice theorists (Olson 1965; Hechter 1987) take to be major impediments to collective action, may not be controlling factors here. First, available theory and empirical evidence throw doubt upon rational choice as the sole basis for collective action (Knoke 1990: 37). Second, Mancur Olson (1965: 34–36) suggests that actors are more apt to contribute to collective action (albeit still not to the optimal extent) when the numbers involved are small. In the case of unions responding to common problems, often only a relatively small number of unions will be involved, since the *direct* impact of problems is apt to fall upon unions representing workers of particular employers or crafts. Third, unions have many incentives to adopt an influential and visible role in collective efforts to deal with common problems. By staying on the sidelines in the face of a threat, a union does not simply allow other unions to incur the cost of producing some known collective good. The outcomes of joint efforts to deal with problems are highly uncertain, and the choices that are made could easily disadvantage a union that exerts no influence over the process. Furthermore, as leaders of political organizations, union officers have a keen interest in demonstrating to their members that their unions played a significant role in producing any positive outcomes.

11. A number of writers (Litwack and Hylton 1962; Klonglan et al. 1976; Pfeffer and Salancik 1978) have argued for the importance of perceptions of interdependence in accounting for interorganizational relations. Yet the causal status of perceptions of interdependence is murky. Do perceptions lead to the establishment of ties, follow from them, or mutually reinforce one another? Insofar as most studies have been cross-sectional and used only one type of indicator (perceptual or "objective") of interdependence, empirical work has not been very helpful in sorting these issues out. One exception, a longitudinal study by Andrew H. Van de Ven and Gordon Walker (1984), provided support for the notion that perceptions of interdependence and established ties mutually reinforce one another. The argument, then, is that the causal status of perceived interdependence is debatable in a cross-sectional study. This general problem is compounded in the present study because respondents were reporting on their ties over the previous two years, while their perceptions of interdependence were elicited at the time of the interview. It is only by assuming that their perceptions of interdependence were constant over the entire study period that perceived interdependence could be regarded as a cause of the ties reported. In light of these conceptual and methodological problems, I focus on interdependence as a structural phenomenon, rather than as a matter of perception.

Chapter 3

1. Counting all locals and other relevant subunits, the number of unions representing these workers was much larger than thirty-seven. Of the subunits selected for inclusion in this study, all either had primary responsibility for bargaining or were the largest subunit representing a group of workers.

2. An extreme example in terms of variation in size is TWU Local 528, with a total membership of ten radio and teletype operators at Northwest Airlines, and IAM

District 141, with some thirty-three thousand members at United Airlines, U.S. Air, and elsewhere. Although one is a local and the other an intermediate body, both are the primary units representing their members in bargaining. Even at the same organizational level and within the same union, there is significant variation in size (e.g., TWU Local 540 has 560 members, whereas TWU Local 513 has 4,500 members). The term "status" refers here to the type of work performed (e.g., "skilled" versus "unskilled," white versus blue collar).

3. Union membership figures are typically less than precise. The estimates cited in this chapter come from the reports of union officers, checked against the figures in Gifford 1990.

4. The newly minted (as of 1990) Department of Transportation Trades is another industrial and trade department of the AFL-CIO relevant to airline unions, but it did not exist during the period on which this study focuses.

5. These are the dates when the National Mediation Board (NMB) considered the carriers to be operationally merged (U.S. NMB, *Determinations of the National Mediation Board*, vols. 14–16).

6. The strikes examined are those listed in the *Annual Report of the National Mediation Board* for fiscal years 1969–86. Evidence concerning the operational status of struck carriers was drawn from a variety of sources, occasionally the NMB's annual reports but more often the *Daily Labor Report*, the *New York Times*, and union publications. The large proportion of cases for which no evidence could be found is troublesome, but there is no reason to believe that strikes in which the carrier continued to operate were less likely to be reported in the sources used. Indeed, the reverse seems more plausible. In any event, the contrast between before and after 1979 appears sufficiently dramatic to withstand the limitations of the data.

7. In a 1989 decision (*IFFA v. TWA*) stemming from the TWA flight attendants strike of 1986, the Supreme Court held that "crossovers" (workers already employed at the carrier at the time of the strike who crossed picket lines at some point during it) were entitled to keep their positions despite the greater seniority of many of the flight attendants who sought reinstatement when the strike was called off (*Daily Labor Report*, March 1, 1989, D1–12). An earlier appeals court decision arising from the 1985 ALPA strike at United (*ALPA v. United*) held that the carrier did not have to hire some five hundred pilot trainees who had been recruited as strikebreakers, but then elected to honor ALPA's picket lines (*Daily Labor Report*, Oct. 14, 1986, A5–6). Both decisions effectively strengthen the hand of carriers in strikes, as they increase the incentive for both trainees and current employees to cross picket lines.

8. For 1987 data supporting this generalization, see *Standard & Poor's Industry Survey* (July 1989), A46–47 (for returns on equity and debt/capital ratio); ALPA, *Negotiator's Factbook of Selected Economic and Financial Statistics* 1988, 67–68, 74–75) (for cash flow and debt/equity ratio).

9. Texas Air Corporation was renamed Continental Airline Holdings, Inc., in 1990. Since Texas Air was the relevant entity throughout most of the study period, it is referred to here.

Chapter 4

1. These data come from U.S. NMB, *Determinations of the National Mediation Board*, vols. 5–13. The time frame examined (1970–86) is somewhat arbitrary. The

intent, however, was to look at a reasonably long period and one that leads directly into the years on which this study focuses.

2. The IBT had not yet reaffiliated with the AFL-CIO during the period to which these figures pertain. Of the very few raids among affiliates, most involved cases of the raided union disclaiming interest in continuing to represent the unit.

3. The status of AFA's strike action was disputed; the carrier claimed it was an illegal strike taken in pursuit of AFA's own bargaining objectives (the flight attendants were in mediation at the time of the IAM strike).

4. The other areas included the effects on working hours and employment of the introduction of jet aircraft, air safety problems, the Landrum-Griffin Act, and the rapid expansion of the IBT in air freight (*AFL-CIO News*, Sept. 26, 1959, 2).

Chapter 5

1. Western, Piedmont, and Flying Tiger, although major carriers during the study period, were excluded because they had either merged or were in the process of doing so at the time data were being gathered.

2. In this context, an "independent" is a union that is affiliated with neither the AFL-CIO nor a larger inter/national union.

3. There are several reasons for excluding relations between national union headquarters and their affiliated locals or intermediate bodies. First, the vertical authority dimension to these relations potentially makes them qualitatively different from the other relations considered. If any a priori distinction between intra- and inter-union relations is to be maintained, this seems to be the clearest line of demarcation. Second, the same individuals sometimes occupy roles within both subunits and the national union, making it difficult to separate the two. Third, there was concern that respondents might be reluctant to comment on relations between national headquarters and particular subunits, thereby jeopardizing their participation in the study.

4. This figure represents the number of ordered pairs formed by the thirty-three unions N(N-1) (reflexive relations were not considered), minus those ordered pairs resulting from the pairings of national unions and their subunits (for which data were not collected). Specifically, 33(33–1) = 1,056 – 32 = 1,024.

5. It is difficult to decide whether to symmetrize relational data to make the reports of dyadic partners consistent. Because some relations are inherently symmetrical and the data are intended to reflect as fully as possible actual inter-union relations, inherently symmetrical relations were symmetrized. Symmetrizing by intersection (A_{ij} and $A_{ji}=1$ only if both A_{ij} and $A_{ji}=1$) rather than by union (A_{ij} and $A_{ji}=1$ if either A_{ij} or $A_{ji}=1$) results in a more conservative estimate of the prevalence of symmetrical relations but increases confidence in the accuracy of the data. This procedure was deviated from in the case of the relationship "belonged to the same coalition," because multiple reports were available to verify coalition membership, and with regard to the relationship "had contact related to the Eastern strike," because the pattern of discrepancies suggested systematic underreporting by one of the unions that was a principal to the strike. The union method of symmetrizing was used in that case.

6. Measures of interdependence used by other researchers (e.g., Van de Ven and Walker 1984; Morrissey, Hall, and Lindsey 1982) are not readily adapted to the case of airline unions and fail to capture multiple forms of interdependence. Thus, new

measures were devised for this study. These indicators of interdependence are context-specific, rather than general, and positional, rather than perceptual. Positional measures of interdependence identify unions likely to impinge upon each other in specified ways by virtue of their joint characteristics (e.g., overlap in craft represented, relative bargaining power). The difference is between, for example, asking respondents which other unions they depend on for resources (a perceptual measure) versus using knowledge about the distribution of resources and capacities among unions to identify probable lines of resource dependence (a positional measure). The perceptual approach is likely to yield more impressive correlations, but at a steep price. Use of the same method to measure interdependence and the presence/absence of inter-union relations in the context of a cross-sectional study leaves the reason for any observed association and the direction of causality open to serious question. Does perceived interdependence precede, follow, or, as is most likely, reciprocally reinforce actual inter-union ties? The positional approach avoids these quandaries and emphasizes the structural bases of interdependence.

7. There are a few exceptions to the expectation of positive relationships. One concerns the measure of ideological (or at least tactical) consensus (EMPLOWN). Because it is operationalized as a difference score, a larger value indicates less consensus. Hence, a negative relationship is hypothesized for this variable, except when predicting conflict. Having the same AFL-CIO affiliation (AFLSTAT) and having represented a bargaining unit for a longer period of time (LEGITMCY) are expected to have a negative relationship with conflict.

8. A hierarchical clustering procedure (SAS VARCLUS) was used to identify dependent variables that were relatively distinct. In a four-cluster solution, DIRCOMM, JOINTACT, KEYTIE, and DISPUTE were placed in separate clusters. "Received substantial support from" and "most important tie" were combined to form KEYTIE because they were located within the same cluster and doing so provided more variation than if the variables were analyzed separately.

9. The estimates for common national union affiliation (NATIONAL) and common problem interdependence related to events at Eastern Airlines (EALPROB) were not treated as statistically significant because their negative signs were contrary to expectations and one-tailed tests were employed. Why might such counterintuitive results appear? For national union affiliation, the most plausible explanation is that the national union as a whole, and not particular other affiliates, was considered the locus of any joint action that occurred. The negative relationship between common problem interdependence related to Eastern and joint action is more puzzling considering the evidence of abundant joint action by the Eastern unions themselves and at the level of the AFL-CIO (see chap. 9). Yet, for individual airline unions, it may ultimately be more accurate to describe their involvement in the struggle as "helping out" than as joint action around a threat regarded as a shared problem.

10. Contrary to expectations, the sign for LEGITMCY is positive. This implies that conflicts were more likely to occur when greater domain consensus was present (that is, the unions had represented workers in their jurisdiction for a longer period of time). Insofar as ALPA units have been in existence the longest, this finding might be interpreted as indicating that ALPA was involved in a disproportionate share of conflicts. When a variable indicating pilot unions was included (post-hoc) in the model, however, it was not significant, and it did not appreciably change the effect of

LEGITMCY. The negative relationship for common problem interdependence related to events at Eastern Airlines (EALPROB) also was not predicted. Certainly, there was conflict among the Eastern unions themselves. Other unions apparently avoided disputes with them, however, and focused on support activities.

11. Caution is required here because contact related to the Eastern strike was embedded within the larger set of ties from which prevailing lines of inter-union relations were inferred. Longitudinal data, allowing a comparison of ties before and during the strike, would be required to demonstrate compellingly unique aspects of the Eastern strike. However, this limitation should favor the finding that contact related to the strike did not differ from the prevailing pattern, but I find the opposite.

Chapter 6

1. There is no clear standard for designating a network "high" or "low" in density. One point of reference is provided by Edward O. Laumann and David Knoke (1989). They found a density of .30 for routine communications and .17–.19 for confidential communications among organizations located within common national policy domains (health and energy). Laumann and Knoke (1989: 45) suggested that their results were "comparable to those found for more homogenous, functionally interdependent groups of organizations." Certainly, densities of close to 1.0 would be expected only in very small, cohesive groups and not in most real-world networks. Indeed, it is the essence of networks that not every actor needs to be directly connected to every other actor to maintain access to information, resources, and so forth. From this standpoint, which ties are established is far more important than how many.

2. These figures and all of the analyses in this chapter include the thirty-two dyads made up of national union headquarters and their subunits. Insofar as data were not collected for these pairings (see chap. 5) and because it would be impossible to perform a network-level analysis otherwise, assumptions were made. The specific assumptions were that national unions and their subunits had direct communication/ contact; received from or exchanged information with each other; engaged in joint action; expected at least mild support from one another; perceived mutual interdependence; received from or exchanged resources other than information (for example, per capita payments from locals to nationals and national provision of organizers and strike funds to locals); and maintained written/oral agreements (e.g., charter, union constitution). An asymmetrical tie was assumed to exist between nationals and their subunits in terms of the relations "would turn to first in a strike situation or for information," "most important tie," and "received substantial support from." No tie between national unions and their subunits was assumed with respect to perceptions of competition, and the presence of a disagreement or dispute. Making a realistic assumption about the latter relation was perhaps the most difficult. Although there undoubtedly is conflict between national unions and their subunits, it is not clear that conflict exists in the majority of cases, which is what the assumptions had to capture. It is because of these additional dyads that the densities in table 6-1 do not equal the means for the same variables reported in table 5-1.

3. Additional evidence in this regard was provided by respondents' ratings of the overall importance of inter-union relations to their union's ability to "get its job done." Thirty-nine percent of respondents indicated that ties with other airline unions were "very important" or "quite important" in this respect. The largest

number (48 percent) of respondents, however, gave the lukewarm "somewhat important" response (the remaining 13 percent of respondents classified their ties with other unions as "not important at all").

4. Chi-square with 1 df = 7.028, p < .01. The number of citations is greater than thirty-three because a few respondents named more than a single most important relation.

5. Note that the term "centralization" as employed in network analyses differs from the more familiar conception of centralization as the extent to which decision-making authority is concentrated at the top level of an organization. A network could be highly centralized in relational terms but the ties center on an actor who does not occupy a formal position of authority or who has less authority than others. The observation that middle managers often have more control over information flows than top managers is consistent with this view.

6. Centrality is most meaningful with respect to networks based on ties involving actual communication, rather than perceptions or expectations. Additionally, centrality measures are more readily applied to symmetrical than to asymmetrical relations. Hence, the relations examined all involve actual contact and two of them are symmetrical ties.

7. The specific position assignments made by CONCOR are the following: APA, the FEIA chapters at Pan Am and American, ALEA, and TWU Locals 504, 513, and 540 (position 1); AFA National, AFA MECs at U.S. Air and United, APFA, UFA, IUFA, IFFA, and IBT Local 2747 (position 2); ALPA International, IAM International, IAM District 100, ALPA MECs at Eastern, United, Delta, Pan Am, U.S. Air, Northwest, and TWA (position 3); IAM Districts 141 and 142, TWU International, TWU Local 528, IBT Locals 2707 and 732, TCU, and PAFCA (position 4).

8. The size, range of activity, political activity, and degree of concern regarding the lack of sufficient bargaining power for individual unions were obtained through the survey (specifically questions 1, 4, and 26k) (see appendix 1). Unions representing only a single craft were treated as craft unions. High bargaining power/political capacity unions are noted in appendix 2.

9. The measures of similarity used in the MDS procedure are the initial correlations generated by CONCOR (correlations between the columns of the stacked, unpermuted matrices indicating the extent of similarity across unions in their pattern of ties with other unions). The form of MDS used is MINISSA, a nonmetric algorithm that combines the rank image and monotone regression methods in successive stages of the computations (MacEvoy and Freeman 1987: 109; Kruskal and Wish 1978: 81). Although the stress (1) value for the two-dimensional solution (.24991) is relatively high, I decided to focus on this solution because it best allows for the desired visual representation.

10. In assessing correspondence between formal and informal structuring, two criteria that can be used are whether all units of a national union are included within the same network position and whether all units of a national union are the only occupants of a network position. The latter is the stronger criterion and is met only in the case of AFA when the network is partitioned into a larger number of groups.

11. To illustrate the interpretation of block densities, the figure of 0.024 in the first cell of the first row for the relation "would turn to first in a strike" indicates that only one out of the forty-two ordered pairs formed by the seven position 1 unions was

linked by this relation. In fact, position 1 unions were more likely to turn first in a strike to unions in any of the other positions, particularly position 4. Hence, the figure of 0.089 in the fourth cell in row 1 indicates that five out of the fifty-six dyads formed by position 1 and position 4 unions were linked by this relationship.

12. For example, the first cell in the first row of the image matrix for the relation "would turn to first in a strike" has a value of 0 because 0.024 is less than the overall density for this relation (0.066), while the fourth cell in the first row of the image matrix has a value of 1 because 0.089 is greater than the overall density for this tie. Thus, position 1 unions showed a relatively high propensity to turn to position 4 unions in the event of a strike, a tendency the first cell in the fourth row of the image matrix indicates was not generally reciprocated.

13. Consistent with organizational theory, this study emphasizes lack of parity in resources and capacities as a factor creating distinctions among unions and affecting their relational patterns. In the case of flight attendants, however, limited bargaining power co-exists with a largely female membership and modest occupational status (the false but prevalent image of flight attendants as airborne waitresses, rather than as workers with important safety and public relations skills). References to gender and job status differences by the union officers interviewed were infrequent (although they were not explicitly asked about these things either). One exception was the observation of an officer of a flight attendants union that "lack of respect for each other's jobs" impedes relations. She also likened the pilot–flight attendant relationship to "a doctor–nurse relationship." Within the parameters of this study, it is not possible to unravel these factors fully and it is sufficient to realize that they compound one another.

Chapter 7

1. By "coalition," I am referring to groups of three or more unions that interact with one another, that meet at least some of the time, that are centered on some purpose or goal, whose member unions conceive of and represent themselves as being part of a collective entity (which is usually given a name), and, most important, that engage in decision making and action on behalf of the entire group (Stevenson, Pierce, and Porter 1985).

2. Another House bill (H.R. 14), dubbed the "Flight Attendant Duty Time Act," was passed in 1991 (Daily Labor Report, Aug. 2, 1991, A3). Both the House and Senate passed duty time legislation as part of larger transportation appropriation bills in 1992. Facing a likely presidential veto, the duty time provisions were dropped from the bills during the House-Senate conference on them (Dailr Labor Report, Sept. 28, 1992, A12). The legislation was reintroduced in 1993. In the face of continued legislative pressure, the FAA announced in March 1993 that it would propose flight attendant duty time regulations (Daily Labor Report, March 30, 1993, A7). The proposed regulations fall somewhat short of the standards contained in the prior bills, allowing carriers considerably more flexibility in scheduling and basing the hour counts on scheduled, rather than actual, hours.

3. The "relative" aspect of the equality of flight attendant unions must be emphasized. Certainly, AFA has more members and greater capacity for political action than the other coalition partners. Indeed, the tensions surrounding AFA's involvement in the coalition result largely from its being "first among equals." Still, there is a

marked contrast between AFA's position relative to other flight attendant groups and ALPA's position relative to other pilot groups. The consequences of this difference are made clearer in the following section.

4. The seven points of agreement were as follows:

1. Encourage and assist Texas Air pilots in achieving their "legitimate status in the industry."

2. Endorse the concept of an "industry user group" to address safety and air traffic control issues.

3. Call for the release of Aviation Trust Fund monies.

4. Deplore the chaos created by mergers and financial manipulation.

5. Oppose cabotage.

6. Recognize the problems and aspirations of regional airline pilots.

7. Continue the dialogue between pilots and controllers.

It is not clear to what extent action on these matters was contemplated and whether any such action would be left to individual unions or conducted jointly. The impression is that this was primarily a statement of common concerns.

5. This chronology is based on facts reported in the *New York Times, Air Line Pilot, Daily Labor Report,* and the *TWU Express.*

6. More personal issues may have been at stake for Kerrigan as well. Kerrigan and Martin Shugrue were said to have been close friends, stemming from a time in which Shugrue's father, a policeman, helped prevent strikebreakers from interfering in a strike Kerrigan was leading (*New York Times,* Jan. 18, 1988, D-2).

7. An officer of IAM District 141 stated in an interview that "we don't believe that we should own the company" and that "our role is to bargain. . . . We only want a fair piece of the action." The IAM International has also generally taken a dim view of employee ownership (Eastern Airlines is an exception).

Chapter 8

1. Personalizing the conflict was a conscious strategy on the part of the unions at Eastern. In Frank Lorenzo, the unions found an all-too-obliging villain. I refer at several points in this chapter to the unions' struggle with Lorenzo (rather than with Texas Air Corporation, for example) because that is how the situation was presented (and to a considerable extent seen) by the unions. In truth, I think that personalizing the conflict was a double-edged sword that made it easier to mobilize support but that also foreclosed any options short of his removal.

2. This chronolgy is based on articles from the following sources: the *New York Times, Air Line Pilot, IUD Digest, AFL-CIO News, Daily Labor Report, TWU Express,* and the *Machinist.*

3. This is not to say that support for this measure was completely lacking within ALPA. The United and Northwest MECs were reportedly the strongest advocates of a suspension of service in support of the Eastern strikers (*New York Times,* Aug. 7, 1989, D6).

4. This figure is inferred from the following facts: 76 percent of those who returned their ballots voted to be assessed for strike benefits; however, only three-quarters of those eligible to vote returned their ballots (*Air Line Pilot,* May 1989, 8).

5. The issue of the duration of support is an important one. Interviewing union officers just a few months after the strike had begun, it was often apparent that

intervening matters had claimed most of their attention and energies. Failure to produce the "quick knock-out" hoped for, followed by the ups and downs of a seemingly endless series of potential deals never finalized, led to a dissipation of support for the strike over a fairly short period.

6. Also recall the regression results from chapter 5, which showed that the best predictor of contact related to the Eastern strike was a pattern of ties in which each airline union was linked to each Eastern union (which is how common problem interdependence related to the Eastern strike was operationalized).

7. International labor support was not a central aspect of the Eastern strike, but several instances can be noted. "Stop Lorenzo" logos appeared at several places along the Berlin Wall, suggesting that the struggle at Eastern had come to symbolize worldwide efforts to contend with union-busting employers (*Machinist*, Oct. 1989, 9). Unions affiliated with the International Metalworkers Federation and the International Transport Workers Federation sent letters to President Bush urging his intervention in the strike. Unions representing workers at SAS, which held a 10 percent stake in Texas Air, pressured SAS (apparently to no avail) to use its influence to help resolve the strike (*ITF News*, Sept. 1989, 19). ITF affiliates also played a role in coordinating consumer boycotts in their nations against Eastern and Continental. Lastly, the ITF-affiliated Bermuda Industrial Union picketed Eastern and Continental ticket counters, apparently causing Eastern to cease its flights from New York to Bermuda (*ITF News*, Jan. 1990, 23).

8. Under the Railway Labor Act, the president can appoint an emergency board to engage in fact-finding regarding a dispute over contract terms. Appointment of an emergency board requires that the status quo be maintained (i.e., employees would go back to work) while the board studies the case (for up to thirty days) and then for an additional thirty days after the board releases its findings. Thus, the procedure would have bought time for the unions and have placed the issues more squarely in the political arena.

9. Of course, the very use of the terms "primary" and "secondary" in the context of strikes or boycotts implies that only the workers at a struck firm have a direct stake in the outcome of the struggle. The notion that labor-management conflicts are private, restricted affairs in which the larger labor movement has little legitimate interest is thereby institutionalized.

References

AFL-CIO. 1987. "Report of the AFL-CIO Executive Council—1987." AFL-CIO, Washington, DC.

———. 1988. *Numbers That Count: A Manual on Internal Organizing.* Washington, DC: Department of Organization and Field Services, AFL-CIO.

Air Line Pilots Association (ALPA). 1987. "Concepts for the Future." 1986–87 president's report. Washington, DC: ALPA.

———. 1988a. *Negotiator's Factbook of Selected Economic and Financial Statistics.* Washington, DC: ALPA.

———. 1988b. *Negotiator's Summary of Pilot Agreements.* Washington, DC: ALPA.

Aldrich, Howard E. 1979. *Organizations and Environments.* Englewood Cliffs, NJ: Prentice-Hall.

Aldrich, Howard E., and David A. Whetten. 1981. "Organization-Sets, Action-Sets, and Networks: Making the Most of Simplicity." In Paul C. Nystrom and William H. Starbuck, eds., *Handbook of Organizational Design* 1, 385–408. New York: Oxford University Press.

Aldrich, John H., and Forrest D. Nelson. 1984. *Linear Probability, Logit, and Probit Models.* Beverly Hills, CA: Sage Publications.

Arabie, Phipps, Scott A. Boorman, and Paul R. Levitt. 1978. "Constructing Block-models: How and Why." *Journal of Mathematical Psychology* 15: 21–63.

Astley, W. Graham, and Charles J. Fombrun. 1987. "Organizational Communities: An Ecological Perspective." In Samuel B. Bacharach, ed., *Research in the Sociology of Organizations* 5: 163–85. Greenwich, CT: JAI Press.

Bacharach, Samuel B., and Edward J. Lawler. 1980. *Power and Politics in Organizations.* San Francisco: Jossey-Bass.

Bacharach, Samuel B., Ronald L. Seeber, and David J. Walsh. Forthcoming. *Research in the Sociology of Organizations* (special issue on unions and collective bargaining).

Baicich, Paul. 1990. "What's Happened to the Eastern Airlines Strike?" *Labor Notes* 130: 11.

Baily, Elizabeth E., David R. Graham, and Daniel P. Kaplan. 1985. *Deregulating the Airlines*. Cambridge: MIT Press.

Baitsell, John M. 1966. *Airline Industrial Relations: Pilots and Flight Engineers*. Boston: Division of Research, Graduate School of Business Administration, Harvard University.

Baker, Frank H., and Lawrence J. Hubert. 1981. "The Analysis of Social Interaction Data: A Nonparametric Technique." *Sociological Methods and Research* 9: 339–61.

Barnes, John A. 1979. "Network Analysis: Orienting Notion, Rigorous Technique or Substantive Field of Study?" In Paul Holland and Samuel Leinhardt, eds., *Perspectives on Social Network Research*, 403–23. New York: Academic Press.

Bernstein, Aaron. 1990. *Grounded: Frank Lorenzo and the Destruction of Eastern Airlines*. New York: Simon and Schuster.

Blau, Peter M., and W. Richard Scott. 1962. *Formal Organizations: A Comparative Approach*. San Francisco: Chandler Publishing.

Borgatti, S. P., M. G. Everett, and L. C. Freeman. 1992. UCINET IV, Version 1.00. Columbia, SC: Analytic Technologies.

Breiger, Ronald L., Scott A. Boorman, and Phipps Arabie. 1975. "An Algorithm for Clustering Relational Data with Applications to Social Network Analysis and Comparison with Multidimensional Scaling." *Journal of Mathematical Psychology* 12: 328–83.

Brown, Anthony E. 1987. *The Politics of Airline Deregulation*. Knoxville: University of Tennessee Press.

Cappelli, Peter. 1985. "Competitive Pressures and Labor Relations in the Airline Industry." *Industrial Relations* 24: 316–38.

———. 1987. "Airlines." In David B. Lipsky and Clifford B. Donn, eds., *Collective Bargaining in American Industry*, 135–86. Lexington, MA: Lexington Books.

———. 1988. "An Economist's Perspective." In Jean T. McKelvey, ed., *Cleared for Takeoff: Airline Labor Relations since Deregulation*, 49–64. Ithaca, NY: ILR Press.

Carney, M. G. 1987. "The Strategy and Structure of Collective Action." *Organization Studies* 8: 341–62.

Chaison, Gary N. 1986. *When Unions Merge*. Lexington, MA: Lexington Books.

Chaison, Gary N., and Dileep G. Dhavale. 1990. "The Changing Scope of Union Organizing." *Journal of Labor Research* 11: 307–22.

Chernish, William N. 1969. *Coalition Bargaining*. Philadelphia: University of Pennsylvania Press.

Clark, Paul F., and Lois S. Gray. 1991. "Union Administration." In George Strauss, Daniel Gallagher, and Jack Fiorito, eds., *The State of the Unions*, 175–201. Madison, WI: Industrial Relations Research Association.

Close, Arthur W., Gregory L. Bologna, and Curtis W. McCormick, eds. 1989. *Washington Representatives—1989*. 13th ed. Washington, DC: Columbia Books.

Cohen, Isaac. 1990. "Political Climate and Two Airline Strikes: Century Air in 1932 and Continental Airlines in 1983–1985." *Industrial and Labor Relations Review* 43: 308–23.

Conway, James E. 1988. "Standards Governing Permissible Self-Help." In Jean T. McKelvey, ed., *Cleared for Takeoff: Airline Labor Relations since Deregulation*, 201–20. Ithaca, NY: ILR Press.

Cook, Karen S. 1977. "Exchange and Power in Networks of Interorganizational Relations." In J. Kenneth Benson, ed., *Organizational Analysis: Critique and Innovation*, 46–63. Beverly Hills, CA: Sage Publications.

Cook, Karen S., and Richard M. Emerson. 1984. "Exchange Networks and the Analysis of Complex Organizations." In Samuel B. Bacharach and Edward J. Lawler, eds., *The Sociology of Organizations* 3: 1–30. Greenwich, CT: JAI Press.

Craft, James A. 1991. "Unions, Bureaucracy, and Change: Old Dogs Learn New Tricks Very Slowly." *Journal of Labor Research* 12: 393–405.

Craypo, Charles. 1986. *The Economics of Collective Bargaining*. Washington, DC: Bureau of National Affairs.

Cummings, Thomas G. 1984. "Transorganizational Development." In Barry M. Staw and L. L. Cummings, eds., *Research in Organizational Behavior* 6: 367–422. Greenwich, CT: JAI Press.

Cutcher-Gershenfeld, Joel, Robert B. McKersie, and Kirsten R. Wever. 1987. "The Changing Role of Union Leaders." Working paper. Sloan School of Management, MIT.

DiMaggio, Paul. 1986. "Structural Analysis of Organizational Fields." In Barry M. Staw and L. L. Cummings, eds., *Research in Organizational Behavior* 8: 335–70. Greenwich, CT: JAI Press.

Doreian, Patrick, Klaus Teuter, and Chi-Hsein Wang. 1984. "Network Autocorrelation Models: Some Monte Carlo Results." *Sociological Methods and Research* 13: 155–99.

Dow, Malcolm M., M. L. Burton, and D. R. White. 1982. "Network Autocorrelation: A Simulation Study of a Foundational Problem in Regression and Survey Research." *Social Networks* 4: 169–200.

Dulles, Foster Rhea, and Melvyn Dubofsky. 1984. *Labor in America: A History*. 4th ed. Arlington Heights, IL: Harlen Davidson.

Dunlop, John T. 1972. "Structural Changes in the American Labor Movement and Industrial Relations System." In Richard L. Rowan, ed., *Readings in Labor Economics and Labor Relations*, 160–73. 2d ed. Homewood, IL: Richard D. Irwin.

Estey, Marten S. 1955. "The Strategic Alliance as a Factor in Union Growth." *Industrial and Labor Relations Review* 9: 41–53.

Fantasia, Rick. 1988. *Cultures of Solidarity*. Berkeley: University of California Press.

Freedman, Audrey, and William E. Fulmer. 1982. "Last Rites for Pattern Bargaining." *Harvard Business Review* 60: 30–48.

Freeman, Linton C. 1978–79. "Centrality in Social Networks: Conceptual Clarification." *Social Networks* 1: 215–39.

Galaskiewicz, Joseph. 1985. "Interorganizational Relations." In Ralph H. Turner and James F. Short, Jr., eds., *Annual Review of Sociology* 11: 281–304. Palo Alto, CA: Annual Reviews.

Gifford, Courtney D. *Directory of U.S. Labor Organizations*. Washington, DC: Bureau of National Affairs. Several editions.

Gordon, David M., Richard Edwards, and Michael Reich. 1982. *Segmented Work, Divided Workers*. Cambridge, UK: Cambridge University Press.

Granovetter, Mark S. 1973. "The Strength of Weak Ties." *American Journal of Sociology* 78: 1360–80.

———. 1985. "Economic Action and Social Structure: The Problem of Embeddedness." *American Journal of Sociology* 91: 481–510.

Gricar, Barbara Gray. 1981. "Fostering Collaboration among Organizations." In H. Meltzer and Walter R. Nord, eds., *Making Organizations Humane and Productive: A Handbook for Practitioners*, 403–20. New York: John Wiley & Sons.

Guerrieri, Joseph, Jr. 1988. "Airline Strikes and the Law." In Jean T. McKelvey, ed., *Cleared for Takeoff: Airline Labor Relations since Deregulation*, 247–54. Ithaca, NY: ILR Press.

Guetzkow, Harold. 1966. "Relations among Organizations." In Raymond V. Bowers, ed., *Studies on Behavior in Organizations*, 13–44. Athens: University of Georgia Press.

Gutman, Herbert B. 1977. *Work, Culture and Society in Industrializing America*. New York: Vintage Books.

Hawley, Amos H. 1950. *Human Ecology*. New York: The Ronald Press.

Hechter, Michael. 1987. *Principles of Group Solidarity*. Berkeley: University of California Press.

Hildebrand, George H. 1972. "Cloudy Future for Coalition Bargaining." In Richard L. Rowan, ed., *Readings in Labor Economics and Labor Relations*, 300–17. 2d ed. Homewood, IL: Richard D. Irwin.

Hopkins, George E. 1971. *The Airline Pilots: A Study in Elite Unionization*. Cambridge: Harvard University Press.

———. 1982. *The First Half Century of the Air Line Pilots Association*. Washington, DC: Air Line Pilots Association.

Hubert, Lawrence J., and Frank B. Baker. 1978. "Evaluating the Conformity of Sociometric Measurements." *Psychometrika* 43: 31–41.

International Transport Workers' Federation. 1986. "Report on Activities and Financial Report and Proceedings, 1983–1985." London: ITWF.

Jacoby, Sanford. 1983. "Union-Management Cooperation in the U.S.: Lessons from the 1920's." *Industrial and Labor Relations Review* 37: 18–33.

James, George W. 1985. "Airline Deregulation: Has It Worked?" *Business Economics* 20: 11–14.

Kahn, Mark L. 1950. "Industrial Relations in the Airlines: The Interaction of Unions, Managements, and Subsidized Industry." Ph.D. dissertation, Harvard University.

———. 1952. "The National Airlines Strike: A Case Study." *Journal of Air Law and Commerce* 19: 11–24.

———. 1971. "Collective Bargaining on the Airline Flight Deck." In Harold M. Levinson, Charles M. Rehmus, Joseph P. Goldberg, and Mark L. Kahn, eds., *Collective Bargaining and Technological Change in American Transportation*, 423–610. Evanston, IL: The Transportation Center, Northwestern University.

———. 1977. "Labor-Management Relations in the Airline Industry." In Charles E. Rehmus, ed., *The Railway Labor Act at Fifty*, 97–128. Washington, DC: National Mediation Board.

———. 1980. "Airlines." In Gerald G. Somers, ed., *Collective Bargaining: Contemporary American Experience*, 315–72. Madison, WI: Industrial Relations Research Association.

Klonglan, Gerald E., Richard D. Warren, Judy M. Winkelpleck, and Steven K. Paulson. 1976. "Interorganizational Measurement in the Social Services Sector: Differences by Hierarchical Level." *Administrative Science Quarterly* 21: 675–87.

Knoke, David. 1990. *Organizing for Collective Action*. New York: Aldine de Gruyter.

Knoke, David, and James H. Kuklinski. 1982. *Network Analysis.* Beverly Hills, CA: Sage Publications.

Knoke, David, and David L. Rogers. 1979. "A Blockmodel Analysis Of Interorganizational Networks." *Social Science Research* 64: 28–52.

Kochan, Thomas A. 1979. "How American Workers View Labor Unions." *Monthly Labor Review* 102: 23–31.

———. 1980. *Collective Bargaining and Industrial Relations.* Homewood, IL: Richard D. Irwin.

Krackhardt, David. 1988. "Predicting with Networks: Nonparametric Multiple Regression Analysis of Dyadic Data." *Social Networks* 10: 359–81.

Krislov, Joseph. 1988. "Representation Elections in the Railroad and Airline Industries, 1955–84." *Labor Law Journal* 39: 242–46.

Kruskal, Joseph B., and Myron Wish. 1978. *Multidimensional Scaling.* Beverly Hills, CA: Sage Publications.

Laumann, Edward O., Joseph Galaskiewicz, and Peter V. Marsden. 1978. "Community Structure as Interorganizational Linkages." In Ralph H. Turner, James Coleman, and Renee C. Fox, eds., *Annual Review of Sociology* 4: 455–84. Palo Alto, CA: Annual Reviews.

Laumann, Edward O., and David Knoke. 1989. "Policy Networks of the Organizational State: Collective Action in the National Health and Energy Domains." In Robert Perrucci and Harry R. Potter, eds., *Networks of Power: Organizational Actors at the National, Corporate, and Community Levels,* 17–55. New York: Aldine de Gruyter.

Laumann, Edward O., and Peter V. Marsden. 1982. "Microstructural Analysis in Interorganizational Systems." *Social Networks* 4: 329–48.

Laumann, Edward O., Peter V. Marsden, and David Prensky. 1983. "The Boundary Specification Problem in Network Analysis." In Ronald S. Burt and Michael J. Minor, eds., *Applied Network Analysis,* 18–34. Beverly Hills, CA: Sage Publications.

Lawler, Edward J., and Samuel B. Bacharach. 1983. "Political Action and Alignments in Organizations." In Samuel B. Bacharach, ed., *Research in the Sociology of Organizations* 2: 83–107. Greenwich, CT: JAI Press.

Lefer, Henry. 1987. "How Accelerated Training Met Challenge of Flight Attendant Strike at TWA." *Air Transport World* 24: 64–67.

Levine, Sol, and Paul E. White. 1961. "Exchange as a Conceptual Framework for the Study of Interorganizational Relationships." *Administrative Science Quarterly* 5: 583–601.

Lincoln, James R. 1982. "Intra- and Inter- Organizational Studies." In Samuel B. Bacharach, ed., *Research in the Sociology of Organizations* 1: 1–38. Greenwich, CT: JAI Press.

———. 1984. "Analyzing Relations in Dyads: Problems, Models, and an Application to Interorganizational Research." *Sociological Methods and Research* 13: 45–76.

Litwack, Eugene, and Lydia F. Hylton. 1962. "Interorganizational Analysis: A Hypothesis on Co-ordinating Agencies." *Administrative Science Quarterly* 6: 395–420.

Lukes, Steven. 1974. *Power: A Radical View.* New York: Macmillan.

MacEvoy, Bruce, and Linton Freeman. 1987. UCINET: A Microcomputer Package for Network Analysis. Irvine: University of California.

Marret, Cora Bagley. 1971. "On the Specification of Interorganizational Dimensions." *Sociology and Social Research* 56: 83-99.

Mason, Charles M. 1961. "Collective Bargaining Structure: The Airlines Experience." In Arnold M. Weber, ed. *The Structure of Collective Bargaining*, 217–47. New York: Free Press of Glencoe.

Meyer, John R., et al. 1981. *Airline Deregulation: The Early Experience*. Boston: Auburn House.

———. 1984. *Deregulation and the New Airline Entrepreneurs*. Cambridge: MIT Press.

Mizruchi, Mark S. 1987. "Why Do Corporations Stick Together? An Interorganizational Theory of Class Cohesion." In G. William Domhoff and Thomas R. Dye, eds., *Power Elites and Organizations*, 204–18. Beverly Hills, CA: Sage Publications.

———. 1989. "Similarity of Political Behavior among Large American Corporations." *American Journal of Sociology* 95: 401–24.

———. 1990. "Cohesion, Structural Equivalence, and Similarity of Behavior: An Approach to the Study of Corporate Political Power." *Sociological Theory* 8: 16–32.

Montgomery, David. 1979. *Workers' Control in America*. New York: Cambridge University Press.

Moody, Kim. 1987a. "Flight Attendants at American Airlines Fight Two-Tier System." *Labor Notes* 98: 1, 10–11.

———. 1987b. "Go-It-Alone Mentality Hurts Airline Unions in Era of Deregulation." *Labor Notes* 99: 8–9.

———. 1988. *An Injury to All: The Decline of American Unionism*. New York: Verso.

———. 1989. "Eastern Machinists Draw the Line on Union-Busting." *Labor Notes* 121: 1, 14.

———. 1990. "The Eastern Strike: A Missed Opportunity." *Labor Notes* 131: 10, 13.

Morrissey, Joseph P., Richard H. Hall, and Michael L. Lindsey. 1982. *Interorganizational Relations: A Sourcebook of Measures for Mental Health Programs*. Washington, DC: National Institute of Mental Health.

Muehlenkamp, Robert. 1991. "Organizing Never Stops." *Labor Research Review* 10: 1–5.

Nay, Leslie A. 1991. "The Determinants of Concession Bargaining in the Airline Industry." *Industrial and Labor Relations Review* 44: 307–23.

Nielsen, Georgia Panter. 1982. *From Sky Girl to Flight Attendant*. Ithaca, NY: ILR Press.

Northrup, Herbert K. 1977. "Airline Strike Insurance: A Study in Escalation. Comment." *Industrial and Labor Relations Review* 30: 364–72.

———. 1983. "The New Employee-Relations Climate in Airlines." *Industrial and Labor Relations Review* 36: 167–81.

Olson, Mancur. 1965. *The Logic of Collective Action*. Cambridge, MA: Harvard University Press.

Pennings, Johannes M. 1981. "Strategically Interdependent Organizations." In Paul C. Nystrom and William H. Starbuck, eds., *Handbook of Organizational Design* 1: 433–55. New York: Oxford University Press.

Perlman, Selig. 1928. *A Theory of the Labor Movement*. New York: Macmillan.

Pfeffer, Jeffrey, and Gerald R. Salancik. 1978. *The External Control of Organizations*. New York: Harper & Row.

Powell, Walter W. 1990. "Neither Market Nor Hierarchy: Network Forms of Organization." In Barry M. Staw and L. L. Cummings, eds., *Research in Organizational Behavior* 12: 295–336. Greenwich, CT: JAI Press.

Rachleef, Peter. 1993. "Labor Unity Dissolves at Northwest Airlines." *Labor Notes* 170: 15.

Raybeck, Joseph G. 1966. *A History of American Labor*. New York: Free Press.

Ready, Kathryn. 1990. "Is Pattern Bargaining Dead?" *Industrial and Labor Relations Review* 43: 272–79.

Roethlisberger, F. J., and William J. Dickson. 1943. *Management and the Worker*. Cambridge: Harvard University Press.

Rosen, Seth D. 1988. " A Union Perspective." In Jean T. McKelvey, ed., *Cleared for Takeoff: Airline Labor Relations since Deregulation*, 11–36. Ithaca, NY: ILR Press.

Ross, Arthur. 1956. *Trade Union Wage Policy*. Berkeley: University of California Press.

Sayles, Leonard R., and George Strauss. 1967. *The Local Union*. Rev. ed. New York: Harcourt, Brace.

Schmidt, Stuart M., and Thomas A. Kochan. 1972. "Conflict: Toward Conceptual Clarity." *Administrative Science Quarterly* 17: 359–70.

Schuster, Michael. 1984. *Union-Management Cooperation: Structure-Process-Impact*. Kalamazoo, MI: W. E. Upjohn Institute for Employment Research.

Schwarz, Joshua L., and Karen S. Koziara. 1992. "The Effect of Hospital Bargaining Unit Structure on Industrial Relations." *Industrial and Labor Relations Review* 45: 573–90.

Smaby, Beverly, et al. 1988. *Labor-Management Cooperation at Eastern Air Lines*. Washington, DC: Bureau of Labor-Management Relations and Cooperative Programs.

Staggenborg, Suzanne. 1986. "Coalition Work in the Pro-Choice Movement: Organizational and Environmental Opportunities and Obstacles." *Social Problems* 33: 374–90.

Stevenson, William B., Jane L. Pierce, and Lyman W. Porter. 1985. "The Concept of 'Coalition' in Organization Theory and Research." *Academy of Management Review* 10: 256–68.

Strauss, George. 1977. "Union Government in the U.S.: Research Past and Future." *Industrial Relations* 16: 215–42.

Thompson, James D. 1967. *Organizations in Action*. New York: McGraw-Hill.

Turk, Herman. 1985. "Macrosociology and Interorganizational Relations: On Theory, Strategies, and Bibliography." *Sociology and Social Research* 69: 487–500.

Unterberger, Herbert S., and Edward C. Koziara. 1980. "The Demise of Airline Strike Insurance." *Industrial and Labor Relations Review* 34: 82–89.

U.S. Civil Aeronautics Board. 1984. "Implementation of the Provisions of the Airline Deregulation Act of 1978." Report to Congress. Civil Aeronautics Board, Washington, DC.

U.S. Department of Transportation. *Air Carrier Traffic Statistics Monthly*. Washington, DC: Department of Transportation. Various issues.

U.S. Federal Aviation Administration. 1987. *Airport Activity Statistics of Certificated Route Air Carriers.* Washington, DC: Federal Aviation Administration. Various issues.

U.S. National Mediation Board. *Annual Report of the National Mediation Board.* Washington, DC: National Mediation Board. Various years.

———. *Determinations of the National Mediation Board.* Washington, DC: National Mediation Board. Various years.

Van de Ven, Andrew H. 1976. "On the Nature, Formation, and Maintenance of Relations among Organizations." *Academy of Management Review* 1: 24–36.

Van de Ven, Andrew H., and Gordon Walker. 1984. " The Dynamics of Interorganizational Coordination." *Administrative Science Quarterly* 29: 598–621.

Wallihan, James. 1985. *Union Government and Organization in the United States.* Washington, DC: Bureau of National Affairs.

Walsh, David J. 1988. "Accounting for the Proliferation of Two-Tier Wage Structures in the U.S. Airline Industry." *Industrial and Labor Relations Review* 42: 50–62.

Warren, Roland L., Stephen M. Rose, and Ann F. Bergunder. 1974. *The Structure of Urban Reform.* Lexington, MA: Lexington Books.

Wasserman, Stanley, and Sheila O'Leary Weaver. 1985. "Statistical Analysis of Binary Relational Data: Parameter Estimation." *Journal of Mathematical Psychology* 29: 406–27.

Weber, Arnold R. 1974. "Bargaining without Boundaries: Industrial Relations and the Multinational Firm." In Robert S. Flanagan and Arnold R. Weber, eds. *Bargaining without Boundaries: The Multinational Corporation and International Labor Relations,* 233–49. Chicago: University of Chicago Press.

Weber, Arnold R., ed. 1961. *The Structure of Collective Bargaining.* New York: Free Press of Glencoe.

Weber, Max. 1947. *The Theory of Social and Economic Organization.* New York: Free Press.

Wellman, Barry. 1988. "Structural Analysis: From Metaphor to Substance." In Barry Wellman and S. D. Berkowitz, eds., *Social Structures: A Network Approach,* 19–61. Cambridge: Cambridge University Press.

Wever, Kirsten R. 1988. *Western Airlines and Its Four Major Unions: The Air Line Pilots Association, the Air Transport Employees, the Association of Flight Attendants, and the International Brotherhood of Teamsters.* Washington, DC: Bureau of Labor-Management Relations and Cooperative Programs.

Whetten, David A., and Howard Aldrich. 1979. "Organization Set Size and Diversity: People-Processing Organizations and Their Environments." *Administration and Society* 11: 251–81.

Whetten, David A., and Thomas K. Leong. 1979. "The Instrumental Value of Interorganizational Relations: Antecedents and Consequences of Linkage Formation." *Academy of Management Journal* 22: 325–44.

White, Harrison, Scott A. Boorman, and Ronald L. Breiger. 1976. "Social Structure from Multiple Networks. I. Blockmodels of Roles and Positions." *American Journal of Sociology* 81: 730–80.

Zald, Mayer N., and John D. McCarthy. 1980. "Social Movement Industries: Competition and Cooperation among Movement Organizations." In Louis Kriesberg, ed., *Research in Social Movements, Conflicts, and Change* 3: 1–20. Greenwich, CT: JAI Press.

———. 1987. *Social Movements in an Organizational Society: Collected Essays.* New Brunswick, NJ: Transaction Books.

Zuckerman, Ed. 1988. *Almanac of Federal PACS: 1988.* Washington, DC: Amward Publications.

Index

acquisitions. See carrier mergers

affiliation with national unions: affect of on inter-union ties, 86; See also AFL-CIO; specific unions

AFL-CIO: affiliation with confering legitimacy, 18; Airline Coordinating Committee, functions of, 37; airline union affiliation with, 21, 36–37, 50, 53, 56, 57, 70, 74–75, 78, 86, 87, 109, 114, 162; dispute management by, 12; as hierarchial formal structure, 5, 10; ideological premises of, 15, 16; Industrial Union Department (IUD), functions of, 37; involvement of in Eastern strike, 147–50; See also specific unions

Air Cal Airlines, 40

Air Carriers Communication Employees Association (ACCEA), formation and affiliations of, 48–49

Air Carriers Flight Engineers Association (ACFEA), formation and affiliations of, 48

Air Carriers Mechanics Association (ACMA) formation and affiliations of, 48; See also International Association of Machinists and Aerospace Workers

Air Line Agents Association (ALAA), formation and affiliations of, 48

Airline Industrial Relations Conference (AIRCON), 57, 62, 65

airline industry: as context for inter-union relations, 163–67; importance of to U.S. economy, 5; labor relations in, 38–41; structure of union representation in, 4, 19–20, 28, 29–31; See also carriers; specific airlines

Air Line Pilots Association (ALPA): affiliate unions of, 48–50; affiliation of with AFL-CIO, 36, 37, 38, 50, 56, 57, 146, 147; affiliation of with IFALPA, 38; analysis of, 33–36, 102, 107, 110; disaffiliation of from American Airlines, 50–51; in Eastern Airlines coalition, 135–56; Master Executive Council (MEC) function in, 31, 32, 33–34, 36, 82, 117; in Pan Am coalition, 123–24; strikes by, 55–56, 58, 59, 60; suspension of service (SOS) provisions of, 35; union representation by, 29–32; in United Airlines coalition, 125–29; See also Allied Pilots Association; International Federation of Airline Pilots Associations; TranStar Pilots Association

Air Line Stewards and Stewardesses Association (ALSSA), formation and affiliations of, 48

airline unions, 5, 7, 9–10, 15, 25 AFL-CIO affiliations of, 21, 36–38, 50, 53, 56, 57, 70, 74–75, 78, 86, 87, 109, 114, 147–50, 162; analysis of inter-union ties between, 67–88, 163; coalitions of, 22–24, 64–65, 99–101, 112–29, 135–56, 166; company unions, 18; competition among, 11–12, 17, 25, 27, 37, 52–55, 69, 70, 73, 84, 92, 105, 106, 164; craft-jurisdiction impacts on, 5, 12, 16–17, 25, 28, 43, 49, 69, 70, 73–74, 84–86, 108, 159–60, 164; domain affect on, 17, 28, 69, 73; IFALDA affiliation with, 38; ITF affiliation with, 38; joint actions by, 23, 61–65, 94, 105, 115, 164; in networks, 89–111; non-airline union relations of, 90

Alaska Airlines, 40

About the Author

David Walsh holds a B.A. in social science and a master's degree in social work from the State University of New York at Stony Brook. After several years of social work practice, he entered the New York State School of Industrial and Labor Relations at Cornell University and received a Ph.D. in 1991. He is now on the faculty of Miami University in Oxford, Ohio. His research interests include airline labor relations, labor solidarity and collective action, and the application of sociological and organizational theory to labor relations issues.